THE BRITISH MUSEUM CONCISE INTRODUCTION TO
ANCIENT EGYPT

THE BRITISH MUSEUM CONCISE INTRODUCTION TO
ANCIENT EGYPT

T.G.H. JAMES

THE UNIVERSITY OF MICHIGAN PRESS

ANN ARBOR

Manufactured in China

2008   2007   2006   2005   4   3   2   1

Library of Congress Cataloging-in-Publication Data applied for.
ISBN 0-472-03137-6

Designed and typeset in Minion by Harry Green
Maps by Technical Art Services
Printed in Hong Kong by Paramount Printing

FRONTISPIECE Cartonnage mask for the mummy
of a lady named Satdjehuty. Early Eighteenth Dynasty. H.33 cm.

OPPOSITE Wooden statuette of a local official
named Meryrehashtef. Old Kingdom. H.50.8 cm.

Contents

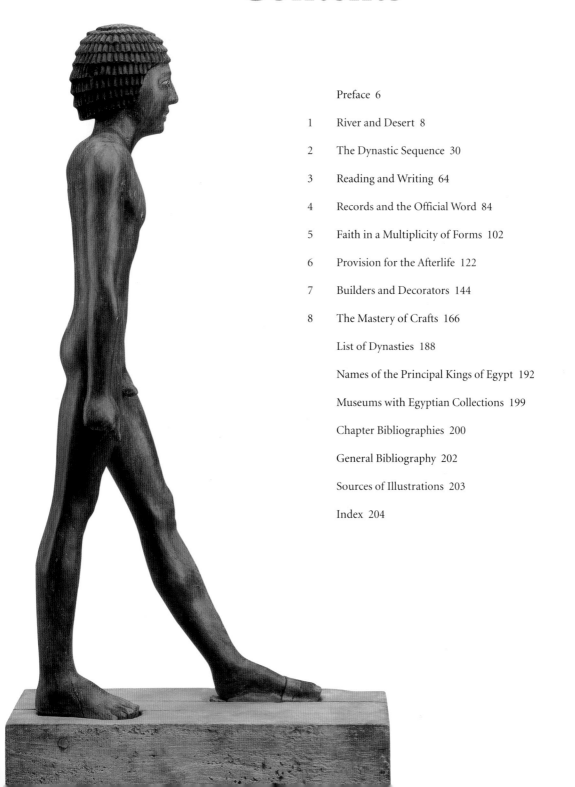

Preface

When I first entered the British Museum as a young Egyptologist in 1951 there were very few books on ancient Egypt which could be recommended to interested members of the public who came or wrote to the Museum with enquiries of a general nature. How things have changed! The past half century has witnessed a remarkable growth in popular interest in the Land of the Pharaohs. The great Tutankhamun exhibitions in the 1960s and 1970s, in London, and in many places in the USA, Canada, Europe and Japan, sparked unexpected enthusiasms: an extraordinary desire to learn about the hieroglyphic script and the ancient language spawned extra-mural classes in universities, correspondence courses, informal groups of enthusiasts, and a demand for books like Gardiner's *Egyptian Grammar*, not exactly a fun book, and too big for bedtime reading; an explosion in overseas travel and the magnetic draw of Nile cruises led travellers to view the wonderful monuments of Egypt, including the temples of Abu Simbel and Philae after their rescue and reconstruction; the proliferation of television programmes, pioneered by the BBC's Chronicle series, stimulated a nascent interest in archaeology. And in addition, there were the books. No year now passes without its new introductions to ancient Egypt. How therefore can one justify yet another volume of generalities about ancient Egypt?

In the case of the volume here presented, may I claim a little originality in that it incorporates many of the ideas that I have formulated but never fully developed in more than fifty years of considering the ancient peoples of Egypt, their history, their monuments and artistic productions, and above all their writings which have survived over many millennia. In dealing with writings, I have regrettably not discussed what might be called Egyptian literature – writings of imagination and thought – which provides keys to the intimate ideas of people who are far distant from us, and yet in their time shared so much that is recognizably part of a cultural continuum extending from Pharaonic times, through the classical civilizations, right up to the present time. Literature deserves a volume on its own, but it is not the only topic which might have found room in this book: the administration of the country, the organization of the legal system, and the practices of trade in a barter economy are other examples. Among the books listed in the general bibliography, the enquiring reader should be able to identify works to fill in the gaps, or to cover more fully the topics which are discussed. In general, however, I have endeavoured in the following eight essays to give a survey of many aspects of Egyptian life and culture, offered from my own particular viewpoint. It is not comprehensive, it is not conventional; some ideas may be thought unusual. It is my own exposition of the richly enigmatic legacy of a fascinating people. It is intended to stimulate, and especially to encourage further exploration of what has been my thrilling field of enquiry throughout a long career.   T. G. H. JAMES   March 2005

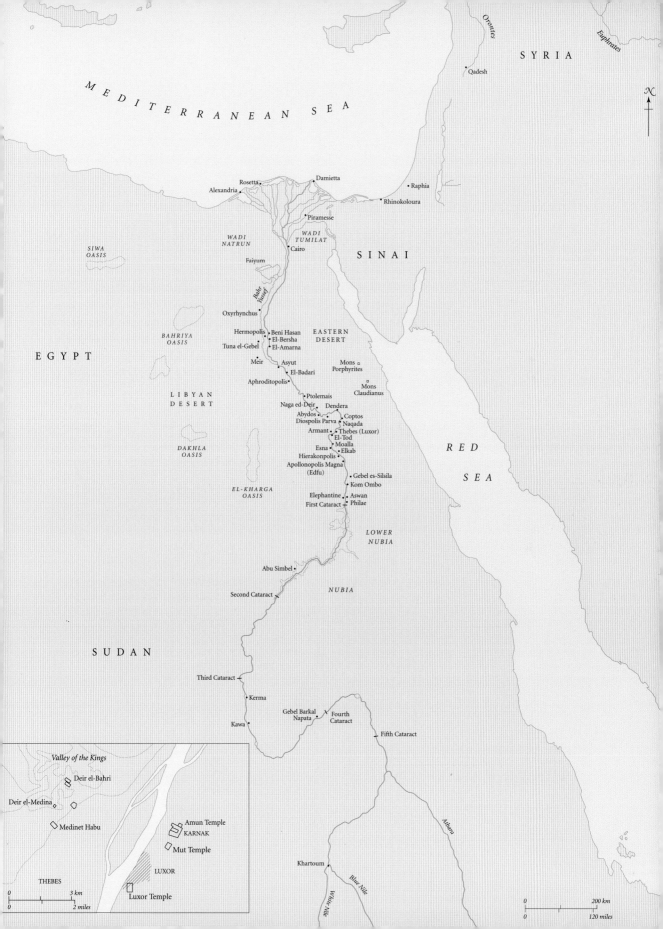

SYRIA

Orontes

Euphrates

Qadesh

MEDITERRANEAN SEA

Rosetta
Alexandria
Damietta
Raphia
Rhinokoloura

Piramesse

WADI
NATRUN
SIWA
OASIS
WADI
TUMILAT
SINAI
Cairo

Faiyum

Bahr
Yusef

Oxyrhynchus

BAHRIYA
OASIS

Hermopolis
Beni Hasan
El-Bersha
El-Amarna
Tuna el-Gebel

EASTERN
DESERT

EGYPT

Meir
Asyut
El-Badari

LIBYAN
DESERT

Aphroditopolis

Mons
Porphyrites

Ptolemais

Mons
Claudianus

Naga ed-Deir
Dendera
Abydos
Coptos
Diospolis Parva
Naqada
Armant
Thebes (Luxor)
El-Tod
Esna
Moalla
Elkab
Hierakonpolis
Apollonopolis Magna
(Edfu)

DAKHLA
OASIS

Gebel es-Silsila
Kom Ombo

EL-KHARGA
OASIS

Elephantine
Aswan
First Cataract
Philae

RED
SEA

LOWER
NUBIA

Abu Simbel

Second Cataract

NUBIA

SUDAN

Third Cataract

Kerma

Gebel Barkal
Napata
Fourth
Cataract

Kawa

Fifth Cataract

Atbara

Khartoum

Blue Nile

White Nile

Valley of the Kings
Deir el-Bahri

Deir el-Medina

Medinet Habu

Amun Temple
KARNAK

Mut Temple

LUXOR

THEBES

0   3 km
0   2 miles

Luxor Temple

0   200 km
0   120 miles

1

River and Desert

Egypt is a country of sharp contrasts. Drive to the edge of the cultivated valley to the west of the Nile in Middle Egypt, perhaps to Abydos where extensive cemeteries and temples are set in the desert, or to Tuna el-Gebel, where the temple-like tomb of Petosiris demonstrates the interaction of ancient Egyptian funerary traditions and Hellenistic Greek artistic representations, and you will clearly observe how the edge of the cultivated area is a sharp edge, a distinct border where the grown crops stop and the desert starts. You may stand with one foot in the 'black land', the true Egypt of ancient times, and one in the 'red land', the tawny barren waste. , Kemet, the Black Land, was the fertile valley of the Nile and the wide expanse of the Delta in the north of the country. This was the area watered by the Nile in inundation and by human ingenuity in-between inundations. 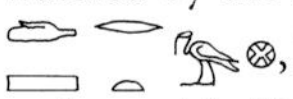, Deshret, the Red Land, was the arid, unfriendly desert, home to wild animals, mythical beasts and unexplained terrors, but also the West, the final resting place of Egyptians who passed the entry examination to eternity.

So it has been in antiquity, and so it is today. The factor of continuity remains the

2 Freight feluccas on the Nile in Middle Egypt, loaded with pottery vessels.

3 Vignette from *The Book of the Dead* papyrus of the royal scribe Nakht, showing the deceased Nakht engaged in agricultural activities in the afterlife. H.35.6 cm.

Nile, or, more precisely, the water of the Nile. A visitor to Egypt today will find it hard to believe that water is a problem. The cultivated valley is green, crops flourish; in towns and cities water is used lavishly, rarely sparingly; it brings life to desert settlements, it irrigates newly developed regions, once barren and inhospitable; it is used as if the tap need never be turned off. Yet, water is not as abundant as may appear. Its provision remains a critical factor in modern Egyptian political life, and will become increasingly urgent as the country's population soars and the expanding requirements for water from other Nilotic countries to the south are met. The High Dam, built in the 1960s to solve Egypt's perennial water problems, may cease to fulfil its expectations as the years progress. The Nile may no longer provide for Egypt the certain insurance against the failure of ways of life which have remained apparently secure from time immemorial.

4 View over the cataract region south of Aswan showing the broken flow of the Nile through granite outcrops.

Water shortages were not unknown in ancient times. They were caused usually by low Niles, occasional phenomena which happened when the river failed to behave in its expected manner. The population of Egypt throughout antiquity remained at a low level, perhaps rarely more than three to four million, a fraction of modern-day Cairo's teeming masses; but it relied for its livelihood and well-being on the Nile and its annual inundation, which fructified the land and secured a successful harvest for the following year. During the First Intermediate Period (*c.* 2150 BC), political difficulties appear to have resulted in a collapse in water management in Upper Egypt, a circumstance made much worse by a series of low Niles which deprived the land of water, with the consequent failure of harvests and widespread misery. The claims made by provincial rulers and other senior officials in the vainglorious inscriptions they placed in their tombs, that they made sure that the peoples of their regions were well looked after while the country in general was in great distress, make it clear that there had been terrible times for some years. Ankhtifi, the nomarch of the third nome, or province, of Upper Egypt, declared in one of several semi-autobiographical texts in his tomb at Moalla, south of Luxor, that 'while the whole of Upper Egypt was dying of hunger, and every man ate his own children, I made sure that no one died of hunger in this nome'. He also took pride in having been able to make loans of grain to other places in Upper Egypt. It was no uncommon boast of nomarchs and other high officials to have been able exceptionally to satisfy the interests of their own local Egyptians, especially the poor and lowly.

To a very great extent the prosperity and future of Egypt and the Egyptians depended in the first instance on the Nile. It was, and is, a remarkable river, recognized as such by the Egyptians themselves, and seen to be so by foreign observers like the Greek historian Herodotus of Halicarnassos. The latter wrote an extensive account of Egypt as part of his History of Greece. He had travelled in Egypt in the mid-fifth century BC and taken a great interest in the monuments, history and physical character of the country. He was fascinated by the Nile, claiming, as he put it, that Egypt was the gift of the river. But he, like everyone else in antiquity, was unable to explain the particular phenomenon of the Nile which characterized it and brought such benefits to Egypt. This was the inundation which happened annually. When things went to plan, the river rose during the summer months, flooding the cultivated area of the Nile Valley up to the desert edge and depositing a layer of fertile silt on the land, before returning to its course in the autumn, when the business of cultivation could start again in earnest.

5 The source of the Nile's flood, as shown in the Temple of Philae; it emerges from the rocky hills of the cataract region. The god of the flood pours water on the fields of Egypt.

Herodotus could provide no satisfactory explanation for the annual inundation; his most plausible reason – the melting of snows in the lands to the south – he rejected because it was inconceivable that there would be snow in such a hot part of the world. The explanation offered him by native Egyptians, that the Nile emerged from bottomless springs south of Elephantine and the First Cataract, was even more implausible and clearly mythical. The Egyptians themselves, not at all averse to providing mythical reasons for divine phenomena, in their own records agreed that the Nile in its flood issued from sources in the First Cataract region, and the event is graphically portrayed in relief in the Graeco-Roman temple of Isis at Philae in the cataract. Whether the Egyptians in antiquity ever seriously investigated the miracle of the annual flood is not known, but cannot be considered as very likely. They do not in their writings or activities display the curiosity which later distinguished the Greeks, for whom a problem identified was a problem to be solved. Egyptians did not like 'abroad', and for the most part penetrated foreign parts only for reasons of security or to obtain exotic products. It is hard to believe, however, that the source of the Nile and its annual inundation were not matters of curiosity as well as of concern to intelligent Egyptians. That nothing was seemingly done to investigate them was undoubtedly due to the absence of ability as well as lack of will to undertake explorations beyond the limits of their own political penetrations up the Nile, perhaps as far as the Fifth Cataract during the New Kingdom. However, the Egyptians should scarcely be reproached for such inability to identify the cause of the inundation. It would be many centuries, even millennia, before the sources of the Nile would be found.

The main stream of the Nile, known as the White Nile, stems from Equatorial Africa, principally from Lakes Victoria, Edward and George in Uganda, and flows with varied channels through the marshy area known as the Sud in southern Sudan. It derives its water from these lakes and many tributaries, which in turn are fed by tropical rains in the mountainous districts of the region. It attains its single main stream as it passes through the Sud, and has become the great river, the lifeline of Sudan and Egypt, by the time it reaches Khartoum. The flow of the White Nile remains generally steady throughout the year, providing the bulk of the stream during the winter and spring months. At Khartoum the main river is joined by the Blue Nile, its major tributary, if such a modest term can be applied to a stream which becomes a raging torrent during the summer months. The Blue Nile and the Atbara, which joins the united Niles about two hundred miles north of Khartoum, both rise in Ethiopia. For most of the year their streams are inconsiderable, but from late May until September they receive the run-off of the torrential summer rains in the mountains in the region of Lake Tana. Their modest trickles become cascades which sweep down the deep gorges of the Ethiopian

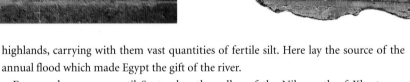

6 Defaulting tax-payers are brought to account; a scene from the Sixth Dynasty mastaba of the vizier Mereruka at Saqqara.

highlands, carrying with them vast quantities of fertile silt. Here lay the source of the annual flood which made Egypt the gift of the river.

From early summer until September the valley of the Nile north of Khartoum, through much of Sudan and the whole of Egypt, was dominated by the flood. In most years the rise in water level was reasonably steady but significant, reaching the southern boundary of Egypt in early June and the district of Memphis/Cairo about two weeks later. The greatest height of the water came in September, and thereafter there was a rapid fall in the flood, which continued at a less dramatic pace throughout the winter months. By the following May the river was at its lowest level, the stream representing the usual flow of the White Nile. In average years the height of the flood was about 8 m (26 ft), confirmed by ancient recordings in so-called Nilometers at Elephantine and elsewhere, which mark levels from the Late Period into medieval times and later. The

7 Scene from the Theban tomb of Nebamun illustrating the inspection of crops for taxation. The elderly official on the left checks a boundary stone. H.11.43 cm.

same rise in the water level also occurred in modern times, up until the construction of the High Dam. When the inundation happened as expected, the waters rose above the banks on either side of the river and flooded the cultivated plain as far as the desert edge. Villages and towns were raised high enough to avoid flooding, and paths were similarly set on what became causeways through the flooded fields. When the waters receded in the autumn, a significant deposit of Ethiopian silt was left, covering and fertilizing the land. One result of the annual flood was the purging of the fields of many significant markers, the delineations of properties and estates, together with the silting up of irrigation and drainage channels. In a year of a high Nile the devastation of the land could be disastrous: villages might be flooded, buildings destroyed, livestock killed, and people also in an exceptional surge of the flood; there might also be significant changes in the main course of the river. Even more disastrous was a low Nile, and

8 The Nile in Nubia before the construction of the High Dam. Most of the area shown is now beneath Lake Nasser.

particularly a sequence of low Niles. Then the flood might rise barely above the river banks, or extend only partially over the cultivated valley, or last for less than the expected several months. Only the prudent intervention of local administrators, like Ankhtifi of Moalla, might be able to relieve the plight of countryfolk and town dwellers. It would always be possible to irrigate, and therefore cultivate, land close to the river; but in the absence of a network of deep canals, fields far from the river would remain parched and barren.

The Egyptian year was in origin lunar, but for practical reasons the civil year was adjusted to allow for the seeming deficiencies of the lunar calendar. The chronological problems arising from the existence of two different years will be discussed in the next chapter. In an ideal year the agricultural cycle began with the retreat of the flood to the main channel of the river. To a great extent the land would reappear from the waters lacking identifying features, and one of the main duties of local officials was to secure the rehabilitation of the land – the clearing of waterways, rebuilding of dykes and establishment of boundary markers; the former to facilitate cultivation and the latter to ensure that proper tax assessments could be made on the expected yields of the next harvest. The manpower for such work was obtained by a form of local state conscription, a corvée, which fell particularly heavily on simple peasants and labourers who were unable to obtain exemption through position, the use of proxies or bribery. Scribes, that is civil servants, and temple officials were exempted, as we shall discover later on, and, no doubt, most people of some status in the community. With the land put back into order, the agricultural cycle of the year could properly begin. According to the ancient calendar the year was divided into three seasons, each of four thirty-day months, its beginning marked by the rising of Sirius, the dog-star, before the sun at dawn; the event is now called the heliacal rising of the star. It occurred roughly at the start of the inundation, and the first season was called *akhet*. During this time no work could be carried out on the land, but great building projects on desert land above the valley could proceed, further advanced by the availability of labour. *Akhet* was followed

by *peret*, the season of coming-forth, when the land re-emerged from the flood. After its prolonged soaking, and having received its annual layer of silt, the land was easily ploughed and sown. The principal crops were barley and emmer-wheat, to be used for bread and the brewing of beer (the common and essential drink for hygienic as well as pleasurable reasons), and flax, for the production of cloth and oil. Planting took place throughout the winter months, and crops ripened in the favourable conditions of wet and warmth during the third season of *shemu*. Harvesting which followed was a time of great activity, including the cutting of crops, threshing, winnowing and storing. It was also a time of great stress for farmers, who were then subjected to official inspections and the exacting of taxes in the form of harvested products, assessed on the promise not the actuality of the yield, during the period of planting and growing. A farmer whose crops may have been destroyed by locusts or damaged by other predators would still be expected to pay his dues. Nevertheless, the ancient Egyptian farmer, in spite of suffering at the hands of unyielding and probably corrupt officials, had a relatively easy existence compared with his counterparts in other Near Eastern countries: his land was rich and well-watered; it was not stony and hard to plough; even in winter the sun shone on most days, hastening growth; rain was not needed – indeed it was more of a nuisance than a help. A devastating thunderstorm in the hills, particularly to the east of the valley in Upper Egypt, might be followed by torrents pouring down from the rocky *wadis*, destroying crops and even villages. Rain in the Delta during the winter and spring, caused by the proximity of the Mediterranean Sea, was more common, but expected and less destructive.

In antiquity Egypt was very much the land of the Nile Valley, the cultivated Black Land. Its limits were established in the earliest dynastic times – no date can be determined for its first defining – and they remained almost precisely the same until the end of the Pharaonic Period. The southern boundary lay at the First Cataract of the Nile, its northern at the Mediterranean Sea; to the east and the west lay mountainous and sandy deserts which hedged in the fertile valley. Why the southern boundary was fixed at the First Cataract is not known. The reasons may have been complex, but principally geographical and ethnic: geographical because the nature of the river changed south of Elephantine where the rocky barrier of the cataract prevented easy access by river to the south; ethnic because to the south the inhabitants of what is known as Nubia were quite distinct from the Egyptians, speaking different languages and considered alien and unfriendly. One of the principal tasks of the nomarchs of the most southern nome was to keep a wary eye on the tribes of Wawat which controlled the southern routes to goldmines and the even more distant lands of Equatorial Africa from which desirable commodities were imported into Egypt. In the Old Kingdom an expedition into Nubia was fraught with uncertainty and danger.

Although Egyptian foreign policy sought to occupy and dominate Nubia increasingly from the time of the Old Kingdom, no move was ever made to incorporate the region south of Elephantine into the land of Egypt. No new nomes were created south of the cataract. From that most southern point as far as the Mediterranean was the ancient, distinct and integral land of Egypt. Today we talk of Upper Egypt and Lower Egypt, the latter being the broad area of the Delta north of Cairo. The division of the land into two parts can be traced back to the earliest recorded times: Upper and Lower Egypt, the Two Lands – *Ta-Shemau*, 'the Southern Land', and *Ta-Mehu*, 'The Northern Land'. One of the five royal names made association with the Two Ladies, the tutelary deities of Upper and Lower Egypt, Nekhbet and Wadjyt; the first of the two royal cartouches was distinguished by the title *ny-su-bit*, 'he who belongs to the sedge and the bee', symbols of the south and the north. Egypt was seen as the union of the two lands, shown heraldically by the representation of the binding together of the plants of the two parts, the papyrus for the Delta and the lily for Upper Egypt; the king was 'Lord of the Two Lands'. When unity in the country failed, as it did, for example, in the First and Second Intermediate Periods, it was perceived as being disastrous, even unnatural; politically and socially things could only be righted by the re-establishment of the union of the Two Lands, as happened at the end of the Eleventh Dynasty and at the beginning of the Eighteenth Dynasty.

The two parts of Egypt were very different in physical character. Upper Egypt lay

9 The Narrowing of the Nile at Gebel es-Silsila. Only a very narrow strip of land is available for cultivation.

south of Cairo and Memphis, the ancient capital established in the First Dynasty. In this southern land the cultivated river valley varied in width from practically nothing at Gebel es-Silsila, where the Nile runs through sandstone hills that march on both banks, to as much as ten miles in areas north of Asyut, where a branch of the Nile, the so-called Bahr Yussef, runs northwards to the west of the main stream, leading in due course to the Faiyum depression, an area of lake and lush cultivation. This Upper Egypt is historically and culturally the better known of the Two Lands. Its cities and great buildings – temples and tombs – have survived above the floodplain for the most part; although much, once inaccessible to the inundation, now lies below the level of the water table and is therefore less yielding to excavation. Upper Egypt was divided into

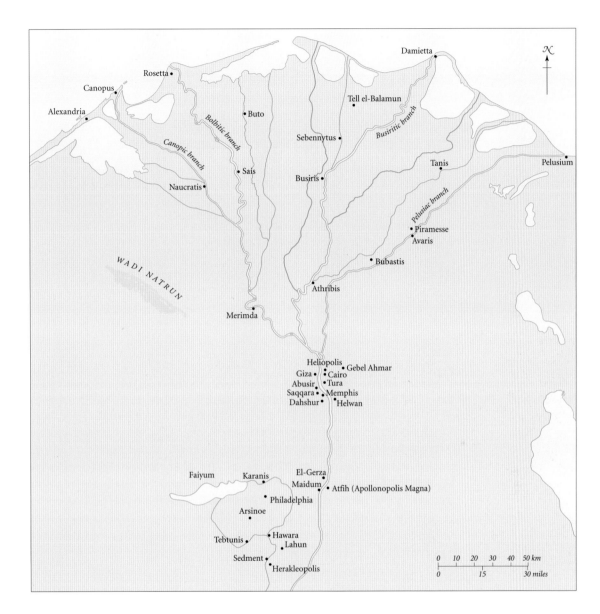

10 Map of Lower Egypt. The Delta and part of Middle Egypt.

twenty-two administrative districts (*sepat* in Egyptian), usually called nomes, a Greek term. The senior official, the governor, in each district was the nomarch, a position which at times became hereditary within strong local families. The nomarch was responsible to the king for the proper stewardship of his nome, and responsible to the inhabitants of his nome for their just and benevolent administration. The capital of the first Upper Egyptian nome was Elephantine, that of the twenty-second was Aphroditopolis (modern Atfih), about fifty miles south of Cairo; Thebes lay in the fourth nome, Abydos in the seventh, and El-Amarna (Akhetaten) in the sixteenth.

Memphis, the first capital of a united Egypt in the First Dynasty, was probably the most important city, politically and administratively, in Egypt right down to Ptolemaic

11 The Rosetta branch of the Nile meets the Mediterranean Sea; the 'clash' of waters is shown by the line of breaking waves.

times. It was the principal city of the first Lower Egyptian nome. Lower Egypt, the Northern Land, was essentially the Delta region of the Nile Valley, a wide alluvial area watered now by two branches of the main river, which reach the Mediterranean Sea at Damietta and Rosetta. In antiquity there was a third branch running into the sea at Pelusium, which silted up in later antiquity. Other minor branches mentioned in classical writers may in some cases have been artificial, cut for irrigation and communication purposes – in effect, canals. During the New Kingdom the three main streams were known as 'the Water of Pre' (Pelusiac branch), 'the Water of Amun' (probably the Busiritic or Damietta branch) and the 'Water of Ptah' (probably the Canopic or Rosetta branch). The Delta remains the lesser-known part of Egypt from the point of view of antiquity. Because of the nature of the land – flat, well-watered and without notable physical features apart from the mounds that represent the remains of ancient cities and settlements – the Delta has never in the past offered such immediate returns from archaeology as Upper Egypt, where the proximity of hills and desert, the easy availability of building stone and the greater general aridity allowed vast structures to be built and elaborate tombs to be cut into hillsides. Yet the Delta may always have been the most productive part of Egypt, and possibly more important than Upper Egypt in the political and religious life of the country. The archaeological exploration of the Delta is only now gathering momentum after very modest beginnings. Work here has to be conducted on a less expansive scale than in Upper Egypt, with the employment of scientific methods of kinds never exploited in Egypt. It will be the case of painstaking recovery of evidence and long-term interpretation before an adequate picture of the ancient Delta may be achieved. At present not even the nome structure of this fascinating region is fully known. In classical times there were twenty nomes, but it is possible that this number was much smaller in Early Dynastic times up to the Middle Kingdom, when the region was slowly developed and vast areas of swampy land drained and cultivated.

ABOVE RIGHT

12 Unexcavated mounds
marking part of the site
of the ancient Delta city
of Sambehdet, modern
Tell el-Balamun.

The character of the Delta was very different from that of Upper Egypt. The region had an expansiveness about it which made communication very difficult, especially in an east-west direction. Even today, with an increasingly developing road system, it is easier to travel from south to north than from east to west. One can feel remote in the Delta in a way that is scarcely possible in Upper Egypt, where the Nile and the hills provide easy points of orientation. Nevertheless, just as the Delta is today the most developed part of Egypt, it was in antiquity no primitive backwater but a land of tradition and primeval history, in which many of the most important divine cults were rooted; it was the land of very ancient places, the names of which resonate in the mythology of the whole of Egypt. The earliest shrines of Horus, Osiris, Isis, Neith and many other important deities were probably situated in the Delta. Sadly, the nature of the land has not favoured preservation of vital evidence like papyri. Furthermore, the absence of building stone has resulted over the centuries in the large-scale destruction and reuse of ancient stone buildings, which has continued up to modern times. Visitors to Egypt in the nineteenth century spent much time ranging across the Delta, where there was certainly more to see than today. The earliest Baedeker handbook to Egypt of 1878 dealt just with Lower Egypt, a second volume on Upper Egypt appearing only in 1892. Many of the earliest excavations of the Egypt Exploration Fund (Society) examined Delta sites, but these were to a great extent prompted by a desire to discover evidence concerning the sojourn of the Children of Israel in Egypt. Archaeological work in the Delta was difficult, labour-intensive and not always very rewarding in terms of exciting and precious finds. The twenty-first-century return to the Delta should, through advances in scientific methods and better excavation techniques, yield results that may throw new and possibly unexpected light on sites of which little is so far known. Lower Egypt may be rehabilitated in the history and culture of Egypt as a whole.

As it now exists, the Delta is entirely the product of the Nile and its annual inundation,

13 Area beside the Second Pyramid at Giza showing traces of ancient quarrying.

the result of regular deposits of Ethiopian silt over many millennia. The same can be said of the cultivated Nile Valley in Upper Egypt, Nubia to the south of Aswan, the part of Sudan lying to the north of the confluence of the White and Blue Niles at Khartoum, and the Atbara with the main stream north of Khartoum. From these points the river is interrupted at six places where the underlying granite bedrock rises above the stream's level, creating rocky hazards which impede the flow and provide difficult passages for river traffic. These are the cataracts, the first being at the southern limit of Upper Egypt and the second to the south of Abu Simbel and the present-day boundary between Egypt and Sudan. They are in a sense the remains of the granite barriers through which the Nile, many millions of years ago, forced its way to the north. The character of Egypt is now determined both by the fertile valley and by the desert lying to the east and west of the river. While the former secured a relatively easy way of life for the inhabitants of the cultivated land, the latter yielded a huge range of materials which enabled the civilization of the valley people to develop in quite distinct and rich ways. The Eastern and Western deserts were by no means the same in character or as sources of raw materials.

Above all, however, the hills immediately edging the valley were made of fine building stones which were exploited from the beginning of the Dynastic Period, when the skills of quarrying and working stone were developed to a remarkably high degree. The principal building stone of the Old Kingdom was limestone. It was easily obtained from the whole length of the Nile Valley from just south of Cairo to about Esna, thirty miles upstream from Luxor. Its texture and quality varied considerably, and its colour ranged from a dirty yellowish grey on the Giza plateau to a brilliant white in parts of

14 Part of the great sandstone quarry at Eastern Silsila where blocks have been cut neatly from the rock faces.

the eastern hills to the west of Luxor. A particularly close-grained hard variety was found in the eastern hills south of Cairo at about the level of Memphis. This limestone, especially from the quarries of Tura, was employed for the outer casings of Old Kingdom pyramids, and in the mastaba tomb chapels of high officials of the period in the so-called Memphite Necropolis. Exposed to the air, Tura limestone took on a slightly pinkish tone and developed a hardness which made it particularly useful for the outer walls of structures; for these reasons, it was in later times very much valued as an easily available, ready-quarried stone, and ultimately very suitable for the building of medieval Cairo. This fine limestone was also the ideal material for the low-relief carvings found in Old Kingdom tombs, and it was a fortunate coincidence that deposits of similarly hard white stone were to be found in parts of the Theban Necropolis, the Valley of the Kings and a few places where private tombs were cut. Exquisite reliefs and inscriptions were in consequence executed in many royal tombs like that of Sety I, and in the tombs of viziers like Ramose and Kheruef. Even so, areas of fine limestone might quickly deteriorate into areas of poor texture, where satisfactory carving could not be attempted.

Limestone was used for general building purposes down to the New Kingdom, but was superseded by sandstone as structures became bigger and wider roof spaces had to be spanned. Sandstone, grainy in texture and of a regular tawny colour, was less receptive of very fine carving, but very well suited for the construction of mighty temples. It was also easily retrievable from quarries close to the Nile. Fine limestone was mostly cut from quarries excavated into the hillside, the work producing vast cathedral-like caverns in which the best stone was often difficult to reach, especially as great mounds

15 Reconstructed
grano-diorite seated statue
of the high official Sirenput,
governor of Lower Nubia in
the Twelfth Dynasty. H.1.52 m.

of chippings filled up the workings. In places like Gebel es-Silsila, south of Edfu, the sandstone hills come right down to the river. The stone was quarried by cutting away the revealed surfaces, and was then loaded directly on barges moored very close to the quarries, making transport over very long distances easy. The stone was cut out very neatly in layers, with a minimum of waste, and in most cases in the sizes which were required for constructing particular buildings. The visible marks of the ancient quarrying show clearly how the work was carried on. Enormous quantities of stone were cut for the building of the great New Kingdom temples at Thebes – Luxor, Karnak, the Ramesseum, Medinet Habu – and all the mighty structures of the Graeco-Roman Period – Dendera, Edfu, Esna, Kom Ombo, Philae. The sandstone was plentiful and the ancient quarrying in no way exhausted the deposits. They have even been used in modern times for important works like the construction of the Esna Barrage across the Nile. The ancient workings are, however, an important part of the heritage of ancient Egypt and consequently under the protection of the archaeological authorities. The great quarry at East Silsila, although not a structure, is one of the most remarkable sights among the many that have survived from antiquity.

Sandstone continued in the hills as far south as Aswan, where some deposits are wonderfully variegated in colour – from pink to deep purple – in the heights to the west of Elephantine in which the tombs of the nomarchs and high officials of the Old and Middle Kingdom are situated. But granite is now the stone of the district, the stone of the cataract region through which the Nile at low water threads its way by many broken channels. From early times granite was possibly the stone of first choice for use in buildings 'for eternity', as the ancient Egyptians characterized their tombs and temples. Granite is, however, very hard, crystalline in texture, and extremely difficult to quarry and even to work at small scale. Drilling, pounding and grinding, using sand as the medium, were the techniques available to the ancient workman and craftsman, while bronze remained their hardest metal for tools. Sculptures and small stelae of granite were made in the earliest dynasties, and the stone was used architecturally in a megalithic manner as early as the Fourth Dynasty in the inner chambers of the Great Pyramid, the Valley Temple of Chephren's pyramid and even as the casing stone of the Mycerinus pyramid – the last an ambitious intention frustrated undoubtedly by the inordinate expenditure of labour needed to shape and dress the stone blocks. It is possibly the case that in early times, and later also when convenient, the granite was acquired not from quarrying but by selecting potentially suitable boulders which littered the desert surface in the cataract region. Because of its extreme hardness, and therefore durability, granite became the stone valued above all for important architectural features – colossal statues, obelisks, even occasionally monolithic columns and architraves. One can only marvel at the courage of the ancient architects who chose such a material for their buildings, and at the skill of the masons who worked the stone so precisely. Even high officials aspired to have granite false-doors in their tombs in the Old Kingdom; but generally had to be contented with limestone painted and textured to resemble the harder stone.

16 The eastern face of the Valley Temple of the pyramid complex of Chephren, constructed of huge blocks of limestone and granite. Giza.

So little is known about the activities carried on in the quarry regions of the Nile Valley, but one can conjecture the presence of large numbers of skilled stone-workers and a great many labourers, the latter employed to shift prepared blocks from the worked quarry faces to the river bank. Once loaded on transport craft, stones could be taken by water with relatively little difficulty to the construction site, whether in Thebes or Memphis. What nothing is known about is the way in which the best sites for working stone were identified, a process of exceptional importance when rock for obelisks or colossal statues was to be cut. The great Ramesses II chose on occasion to claim that he himself had discovered just what was wanted. In an inscription of his Year 8 (*c.* 1271 BC), recording a visit to the quartzite region of the Gebel Ahmar near Heliopolis:

> He discovered a great quartzite rock such as had not been found since the time of Re, and larger even than a granite obelisk … It was His Majesty who uncovered it …
> His Majesty found another quarry beside it, for statues … and he ordered pieces for the temple of Ptah.

No doubt, a perspicacious or ambitious quarry-master had directed his king to the right spot. One should not, however, underestimate the skills of craftsmen and their masters, who spent their lives in the environment of the hills seeking the best places for quarrying. They also found places where other fine and exploitable stones could be quarried: Egyptian calcite – so-called alabaster – in the region of El-Amarna, basalt in the Faiyum, diorite in the Nubian desert to the west of the Nile, and greywacke (a slaty stone) in the Wadi Hammamat in the Eastern Desert. In later periods, and especially in Roman times, purple porphyry and a dense grey granite (gneiss) were worked at Mons Porphyrites and Mons Claudianus in the remote Eastern Desert.

Not all fine and hard stones were found in deposits of workable size, but throughout

23

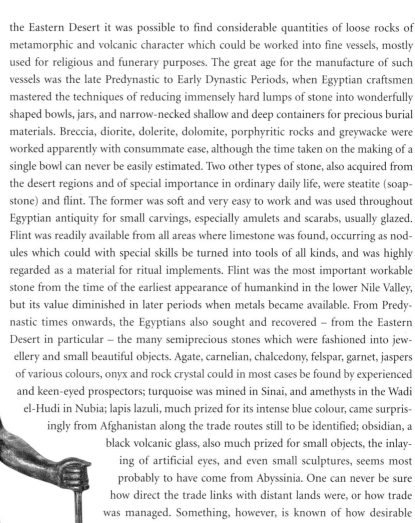

the Eastern Desert it was possible to find considerable quantities of loose rocks of metamorphic and volcanic character which could be worked into fine vessels, mostly used for religious and funerary purposes. The great age for the manufacture of such vessels was the late Predynastic to Early Dynastic Periods, when Egyptian craftsmen mastered the techniques of reducing immensely hard lumps of stone into wonderfully shaped bowls, jars, and narrow-necked shallow and deep containers for precious burial materials. Breccia, diorite, dolerite, dolomite, porphyritic rocks and greywacke were worked apparently with consummate ease, although the time taken on the making of a single bowl can never be easily estimated. Two other types of stone, also acquired from the desert regions and of special importance in ordinary daily life, were steatite (soap-stone) and flint. The former was soft and very easy to work and was used throughout Egyptian antiquity for small carvings, especially amulets and scarabs, usually glazed. Flint was readily available from all areas where limestone was found, occurring as nodules which could with special skills be turned into tools of all kinds, and was highly regarded as a material for ritual implements. Flint was the most important workable stone from the time of the earliest appearance of humankind in the lower Nile Valley, but its value diminished in later periods when metals became available. From Predynastic times onwards, the Egyptians also sought and recovered – from the Eastern Desert in particular – the many semiprecious stones which were fashioned into jewellery and small beautiful objects. Agate, carnelian, chalcedony, felspar, garnet, jaspers of various colours, onyx and rock crystal could in most cases be found by experienced and keen-eyed prospectors; turquoise was mined in Sinai, and amethysts in the Wadi el-Hudi in Nubia; lapis lazuli, much prized for its intense blue colour, came surprisingly from Afghanistan along the trade routes still to be identified; obsidian, a black volcanic glass, also much prized for small objects, the inlaying of artificial eyes, and even small sculptures, seems most probably to have come from Abyssinia. One can never be sure how direct the trade links with distant lands were, or how trade was managed. Something, however, is known of how desirable commodities from Equatorial Africa reached Egypt, as we shall see shortly.

The Eastern Desert was also rich in metal deposits. Egyptians in antiquity were never as accomplished in the working of metals as their Near Eastern neighbours, and it is generally thought that many of the metallurgical techniques employed by Egyptian crafts-

OPPOSITE 17 Colossal granite bust of King Ramesses II, shown wearing the double crown and holding the crook and flail, symbols of kingship. From the Temple of Khnum on Elephantine Island. H.1.42 m.

LEFT 18 Cast silver figure, partly overlaid with gold foil, of the Theban deity Amon-Re. New Kingdom. H.21.3 cm.

19 View of the Wadi Natrun with the early medieval monastery of the Syrians (Deir Suryani).

men were learned from abroad, and possibly even practised in Egypt by foreigners. In one respect, however, the Egyptians seemed to have mastered all the basic skills – the acquisition of gold. From Predynastic times gold was used for jewellery and the embellishment of finely made objects. Its use was developed over the centuries until, by the New Kingdom, the country was considered by its neighbours to have gold in abundance, like the sand of the desert; it was a powerful lever in the exercise of influence in foreign lands, and considered the proper return for diplomatic support and even allegiance. The metal was obtained from alluvial deposits by washing and sieving, and more especially by mining. There were three principal areas rich in gold in antiquity, from which came 'the gold of Coptos' (to the east of Coptos in Upper Egypt), 'the gold of Wawat' (from mines in lower Nubia), and 'the gold of Kush' (from mines in the Eastern Desert south of the Second Cataract). The principal reasons for Egypt's interest in Nubia lay undoubtedly in the desire to acquire gold and control the mining areas. Modern attempts to revive gold-mining in the Eastern Desert in Egypt have met with only partial success because the ancient prospectors and miners were so successful in identifying places where gold might be found and in extracting it almost to its maximum retrievability.

Copper ore was also mined in the Eastern Desert, but there remains some uncertainty about the main areas of exploitation. Sinai, outside Egypt proper, was the site of turquoise mines, and it is clear that copper was extracted there also, undoubtedly a more important material for the everyday life of the ancient Egyptians than turquoise, but invested with fewer religious implications. Copper objects, including tools, were commonly used from the late Predynastic Period, and some use of the metal can be traced back to Badarian times; but without supplements of other materials, it lacked the hardness to make it truly effective for the working of hard materials. From the time of the Old Kingdom, arsenic was commonly added to toughen the metal, but it was not until the

Middle Kingdom, generally speaking, that tin was added to copper to produce an alloy that can properly be called bronze. Neither arsenic nor tin was readily available in Egypt, and they were undoubtedly imported from the Near East along with the appropriate technology which had long been known in the civilizations of Mesopotamia and Anatolia. The great increase in bronze objects from the New Kingdom onwards was largely due to the exploitation of copper deposits at Timna in the Wadi Araba, east of Sinai in what is now Israel. Some copper may also have been imported from Cyprus.

Silver, although present in association with other metals in the Eastern Desert was not easily mined there in antiquity. Its precious qualities were recognized, but it was also seen to be less durable and less versatile in its uses than gold. Nevertheless, until the New Kingdom it was valued more highly than gold. Much, possibly most, of the silver used in Egypt was imported from Asia Minor in the form of small ingots or scrap, the earliest evidence for which is the collection of material, including ingots, jewellery fragments and crushed vessels, known as the El-Tod treasure, of Middle Kingdom date and probably of North Syrian origin. As Egyptian influence spread in the Near East during the New Kingdom, silver in this form became increasingly available, and silver objects became more common among surviving collections of precious materials from the Eighteenth Dynasty onwards. Silver predominates in the royal burials at Tanis in the Delta, most remarkably the solid silver coffins of Psusennes I of the Twenty-first Dynasty, and of Osorkon II of the Twenty-second Dynasty, the later being falcon-headed. It must, however, be presumed that at this period there were difficulties over the acquisition of regular supplies of gold from Nubia.

Although considerable deposits of iron ore were to be found in the Eastern Desert and Sinai, the Egyptians during the Dynastic Period seem not to have exploited them. Indeed, iron technology was not seriously developed in Egypt until Roman times. Small iron objects occur from very early times, but these are almost without exception made of meteoric iron, acquired not from mining but surface finds. In this area of industrial technology Egypt lagged seriously behind Western Asia, and the Hittites in particular. Iron weapons and tools were imported as gifts from Asiatic sources during the New Kingdom, the most notable probably being the blade of one of the daggers in the Tutankhamun burial equipment. It would seem that in spite of the superior usefulness of iron tools and weapons, the technology of production – more laborious than that needed for bronze production – deterred the conservative Egyptians from mastering the necessary techniques for many centuries.

A desert resource which contributed quite distinctly to the character of Egyptian civilization, and particularly to its funerary practices, was natron, a naturally occurring compound of sodium carbonate and sodium bicarbonate, used in antiquity for a variety of purposes including purification, cooking, the making of incense, the production of glass and glazes, and in particular in the process of mummification. Huge deposits occur in the well-named Wadi Natrun, a low-lying, periodically flooded area to the west of the Delta, and in later times and up to the present an important centre of Coptic Christian monasticism. A less important source, also west of the Delta and north of the Wadi Natrun, was Barnugi. In distant Upper Egypt, an area near Elkab was probably the source of the natron used in the south of the country.

The Wadi Natrun may scarcely be graced with the appellation oasis, but there are better designated, well-watered fertile places in the Western Desert which were known to and, to some extent, exploited by the Egyptians in antiquity. The oases of Dakhla, El-Kharga and Bahriya all bear witness, through temple buildings and burial grounds, to the Egyptian occupation during the Dynastic Period. From the New Kingdom at least, they were exploited for the growing of vines and the production of wine; they were also used as places to which criminals might be sent as a kind of banishment. They were not incorporated into the land of Egypt politically, but were administered – in so far as any regular control penetrated so far from the Nile Valley – from Diospolis Parva, the capital city of the seventh Upper Egyptian nome, which lay between the nomes of Dendera and Abydos. The oases were not seen as places of resort to which people travelled except on official or commercial business. However, recent researches have revealed that the desert to the west of the Nile is criss-crossed by tracks, the use of which can be traced far back into antiquity by the great numbers of short inscriptions still visible on exposed rock surfaces. These texts very often consist of little more than names and titles, but by their very number and chronological spread they indicate that the desert was a much busier place than was formerly thought. Apart from the people journeying to the oases on business, there were desert patrols who policed the region, controlling unwelcome visitors, checking on the caravans which used the trade routes, and even intercepting spies, as in one recorded incident during the struggle with the Hyksos during the Seventeenth Dynasty. El-Kharga lay seventy miles to the west of the Nile at the level of Luxor to Hierakonpolis, and Bahriya a similar distance at the level of the twentieth Upper Egyptian nome of Herakleopolis. Dakhla oasis was seventy miles further west from El-Kharga.

20 Scene from the Theban tomb of Sobkhotep, a senior official in the reign of Thutmose IV. African porters bring tribute, the products of Equatorial Africa. H.74 cm.

Traversing the desert has never been the kind of activity that commends itself to the inhabitants of Egypt. It is not difficult to become enamoured of the beauty and solitude of the wilderness, but it is quite another matter to live in the desert and to make it the environment of your way of life. Until modern times the deserts of Egypt formed the domain of the Beduin who were content to make their home there, living a nomadic existence, trading, conducting caravans, herding goats and being generally casual about laws and of personal rights other than their own. It must be supposed that in antiquity there were similar groups who made a living from the wilderness, and in particular made up the companies of the caravans which conducted trade between Egypt and Nubia, and further south into Equatorial Africa. Tomb scenes of the New Kingdom show porters bringing exotic products into the country: they are black and distinctly non-Egyptian or even Nubian; they carry ivory, ostrich feathers, ebony and gold; and lead leopards, giraffes and monkeys. What Egypt could not provide from its own rich resources could be sought elsewhere, and from very early times there is evidence of trading expeditions south of Elephantine; by sea to Punt, a country in East Africa probably and a source in particular of incense; and above all to the Syrian coast.

Boats

Tall trees with substantial trunks for use in large constructions were what Egypt lacked especially. The native woods used commonly for small constructions, wooden sculptures and small coffins were acacia, sycamore fig and tamarisk, none providing substantial timber. So, to acquire suitable supplies of good timber, traders were obliged to travel as far as the Syrian coast to what is present-day Lebanon. From at least the Early Dynastic Period, supplies of cedar were brought to Egypt, probably already in the form of seasoned planks and baulks; examples of the latter have been identified in pyramids of the Fourth Dynasty, and the great boat of Cheops, a full-scale river-worthy craft, was constructed of that wood. So important and well established was the timber trade with Lebanon that any Egyptian sea-going vessel was called *kebnet*, 'Byblos boat', a term taken from *keben, kebny*, the Egyptian name for Byblos, the principal port in Lebanon.

21 The river-going boat found beside the Great Pyramid of Cheops. Giza. Fourth Dynasty.

Its geographical character made Egypt an unusually favoured country, and it was seen to be such in antiquity by neighbouring peoples. You migrated to Egypt when times were tough elsewhere. It was land ripe for plucking by hostile and predatory Asiatics, yet difficult of access because of its situation, protected by deserts and the sea. It was in many ways a self-contained and self-sufficient unit, capable of independent existence without having to maintain contact with the outside world. Egyptians had good reason for thinking that their country, confined within its fixed limits from the First Cataract to the Mediterranean Sea, was special. The Nile was, of course, the crucial feature in its geography, and it even helped exceptionally by actively assisting the obligatory river traffic: for most of the year the prevailing wind blew from the north, allowing ships to travel south under sail; to travel north ships could coast downstream with the flow of the river. The Nile was the highway for the country, and in Upper Egypt few places were far from the riverbank. In the Delta the existence in antiquity of more than two river branches certainly aided communication, and most cities were established on, or within easy reach of, one of the branches. Nevertheless, as already mentioned, to travel from east to west, particularly in the northern extremities of the Delta, was not easy, especially as the principal method of travel was by donkey. The horse was not introduced into Egypt until the Second Intermediate Period, and then was used principally with chariots for military purposes, and by royalty and high officials for local travel. The camel was a very late introduction, probably not before Roman times, and then used chiefly as a beast of burden. There is, however, not much evidence to suggest that the ancient Egyptians travelled much, and when they did they took to the river. For the most part, like country folk elsewhere, they stayed at home, attached to their places of birth, their families and their local gods. For better or worse they travelled only from necessity. It was almost always 'for better' that the Egyptian chose to stay at home; where could be better than such a favoured land as Egypt?

The Dynastic Sequence

Ancient history in the academic world has usually been considered to be the history of Greece and Rome. For these successive cultures there have survived from antiquity excellent accounts, composed by fine early historians who developed an instinct for what they needed to record. Results are deemed generally acceptable even by the austere specialists of the present time. For preclassical cultures there was no Thucydides or Tacitus, or even Herodotus or Livy. For ancient Egypt there was one annalist, a priest named Manetho – possibly from the city of Sebennytus in the Delta – who lived in the early third century BC and wrote an account in Greek of his country, calling it *Aegyptiaca*. It was, as far as one can judge, a general work on Egypt which included an historical narrative in which the royal succession from the time of Menes down to the

THE PERIODS OF EGYPTIAN HISTORY

Predynastic and Dynasty 0 *c.*4500–3100 BC
Dynasties 1–2 *c.*3100–2686 BC Early Dynastic
Dynasties 3–8 *c.*2686–2181 BC Old Kingdom
Dynasties 7–10 *c.*2181–2025 BC First Intermediate Period
Dynasties 11–13 *c.*2125–1750 BC Middle Kingdom
Dynasties 14–17 *c.*1750–1550 BC Second Intermediate Period
Dynasties 18–20 *c.*1550–1069 BC New Kingdom
Dynasties 21–24 *c.*1069–715 BC Late New Kingdom (Third Intermediate Period)
Dynasties 25–30 *c.*747–332 BC Late Period
Macedonians/Ptolemies 332–30 BC Greek administration
Roman emperors 30 BC–642 AD Roman/Byzantine administration

conquest of Egypt by Alexander the Great in 332 BC was arranged in a series of dynasties, numbered First to Thirtieth. Unfortunately no contemporary text of Manetho has survived, and what he wrote is preserved only partially in later writers, Josephus (first century AD), Julius Africanus (third century AD), Eusebius (fourth century AD) and Syncellus (about AD 800). These later summaries (or epitomes, as they are often called) are generally unreliable, inconsistent with each other, and clearly garbled through inaccurate transmission. To what extent they represent the nature of Manetho's original text is now impossible to determine, but in one particular and important respect Manetho has bequeathed to modern historians of ancient Egypt the dynastic framework which is still employed for the order of the kings and the determination of successive periods. In British history, the Tudors, Stuarts and Hanoverians, for example, are more fully identified as the House of Tudor, the House of Stuart and the House of Hanover. In Manetho's ordering of the monarchs of Egypt, the successive dynasties are only in very general respects identifiable as distinct 'houses', although in many cases his changes of dynasty do represent family changes. Nevertheless, Manetho's dynastic sequence has proved to be too useful a basis for the organization of Egyptian history to be rejected. The dynasties of this book are therefore essentially those of Manetho.

In addition to the *Aegyptiaca*, there has survived in very damaged condition a monarchic sequence written on papyrus, of Nineteenth Dynasty date, known as the Royal Canon of Turin. A much valued part of the collection of the Egyptian Museum in Turin, its texts first record the divine predecessors of the dynastic kings of Egypt, and then list, with minimal individual information, the historic rulers of the land, beginning with Menes and continuing, with many gaps, down to the end of Manetho's Seventeenth Dynasty, that is to the threshold of the New Kingdom. The Turin Canon includes, unlike Manetho, what purports to be the full listing of the kings of the Second Intermediate Period (Dynasties Thirteen to Seventeen), many of whom remain unidentified on surviving monuments. The Turin Canon is particularly valuable, in spite of its sadly tattered form, because it was compiled probably in the reign of Ramesses II of the Nineteenth Dynasty, from archival sources better informed than those available to Manetho, writing almost a millennium later.

There are also monumental sources for the bare annalistic record of the sequence of Egyptian history from the foundation of the single state of Upper and Lower Egypt at the beginning of the First Dynasty.

22 The ceremonial Battlefield Palette in siltstone with a carved relief scene of a lion, possibly the king, savaging slain and dying enemies. Late Predynastic Period. H.32.8 cm.

The Palermo Stone, a fragment of a substantial slab of basalt – along with some smaller fragments in Cairo and elsewhere, which may be parts of the same monument – is inscribed with a list of kings from late Predynastic times down to the mid-Fifth Dynasty. Reigns are recorded year by year, each year characterized by significant events mostly of a religious nature. In its damaged condition it provides only modest information on those reigns, the listings of which survive only in parts. There is, however, a reasonable possibility that the monument was not a product of the Fifth Dynasty, but a copy or supposed copy made in the Twenty-fifth Dynasty, a period of reverent attachment to earlier times. Nevertheless, the content of the stone may yet reproduce with some accuracy what was known about the early dynasties and of Old Kingdom history from archival sources preserved in Memphis.

23 Part of the king-list from the temple of Ramesses II at Abydos. The central register contains the cartouches of kings of the Eighteenth and Nineteenth Dynasties with the omission of the Amarna kings. H.1.38 m.

Simple king-lists were also set up in some temples and tombs during the New Kingdom. Of these the best preserved, and most comprehensive, is carved in the Abydos temple of Sety I. In the scene accompanying the list, the young crown prince Ramesses reads out to his father the list of kings written on the papyrus roll he holds. Seventy-six royal names are inscribed: a list, in no way complete, of the predecessors of Sety who were considered proper recipients of honour and offerings. It starts with the first king who traditionally unified Egypt, here named Meni, continues through the First to the Eighth Dynasties, omits the Herakleopolitan kings of the Ninth and Tenth Dynasties (still clearly considered upstarts), resumes with the last kings of the Eleventh Dynasty and those of the Twelfth Dynasty, wholly omits the rulers, real or ephemeral, of the Thirteenth to Seventeenth Dynasties and ends with the successive kings of the Eighteenth Dynasty, and Sety's father Ramesses I. Of particular interest is the omission of the Amarna kings, from Akhenaten to Ay. This list therefore is only partly a good historical record, perhaps more interesting for its omissions than its inclusions.

The cautious approach needed by the historian of ancient Egypt, illustrated by what has been said already about the surviving annalistic records, is an essential part of the exploitation of the wealth of other documentation from antiquity. Egyptian culture, as we shall see in the next chapter, was to a great extent literate. From the earliest dynastic times things were written down, carved in monumental hieroglyphs, recorded officially on papyrus in the hieratic script, and noted casually (as occasion demanded) also in hieratic on papyri and on ostraca – the slivers of limestone and fragments of pottery vessels which served as the scrap paper of ancient Egypt. These written records, official and private, form the bulk of the raw material from which Egyptian history may be written; they may be supplemented by the graphic record preserved in tombs and temples, and increasingly by the results of careful excavation. In the use of these various kinds of text for the writing of Egyptian history, a considerable degree of scepticism needs to be exercised, and the modern historian learns to distinguish between the simple recording of an event and the overblown vaunting of achievement for personal reputation.

Since the time of hieroglyphic decipherment, as more and more texts have been published and studied, the quantity of good historical documentation has steadily increased, and a far richer account of Egyptian history can now be written than in the days when the principal sources were those classical writers who included accounts of

Egypt in their works, and the Old Testament. The classical writers and the Old Testament remain useful sources for the later history of Egypt, especially from the Twenty-sixth Dynasty onwards (after *c.* 650 BC). Similarly, cuneiform texts from Mesopotamia and adjacent Near Eastern countries and Hittite records (in cuneiform and Hittite hieroglyphs) provide invaluable information on relations with Egypt, which may confirm, or supplement, what is known from native Egyptian sources, and even serve to modify the Egypto-centric accounts composed for home consumption.

From the above, it should be evident that the historical record is, to say the least, rather patchy. Many periods remain obscure, and may always remain so. Occasionally a lucky find illuminates a dark corner, like the Kamose stela, discovered by chance in 1954, which provided new information about the rise of Thebes against the Hyksos in the last years of the Seventeenth Dynasty. But in general the rags and tatters of evidence, as one scholar has described what faces the historian of Egypt, will remain a challenge for interpretation. In the historical outline that follows, the failure to produce a seamless story of dynastic progression will be only too evident.

Beginnings: Predynastic Egypt and the Early Dynastic Period

As far as the ancient Egyptians were concerned, their history started with the unification of Upper and Lower Egypt by a king called Menes, which is now dated to about 3100 BC. With Menes began the dynastic sequence of Manetho. The position was the same when the king-lists of Abydos, Saqqara and Karnak were inscribed on monuments of the Nineteenth Dynasty. Where the name can be read, it is Meni, and so too it is in the Turin Royal Canon of about the same date. What happened before unification was clearly either unknown to Manetho and the compilers of the king-lists, or considered to be of no historical importance. In those distant times Egypt could only have been ruled by gods and divine beings. Manetho claimed this to be the case, and the same story is told in the Turin Canon. Egypt did not, however, appear as a sovereign, united state from a divine haze of mythical speculation.

The Nile Valley provided not surprisingly an attractive and benevolent environment for early man, and traces of palaeolithic activity have been found in many places in Egypt, mostly on the desert fringe of the cultivated area; evidence of actual settlements are scanty, largely because of the alluvial nature of the valley itself, where the regular annual rise in the land surface has obliterated what may have been established there in the distant past. Recognizable traces of distinctive Egyptian cultures occur during late neolithic times, a period which in Egypt is commonly called Predynastic. Farming communities dating to the sixth millennium BC have been identified on the western edges of the Delta (Merimda), around the lake in the Faiyum and in Middle Egypt, in the region of Asyut. A sequence of predynastic cultures from which developed the primitive kingdoms immediately preceding the unification has been identified as sites in Middle Egypt. The most important of these cultures, first discovered in El-Badari, revealed a people which practised well-developed farming and stock-rearing, made fine distinctive pottery and had some simple skills in working copper. The sequence of subsequent cultural stages was first developed by the ingenious, innovative (but obsessive)

The human figure

The making of small figurines in ivory, bone and terracotta during predynastic times resulted in small sculptures of very varied skill and quality. The Badarian lady in ivory illustrated here (fig. 24, H. 11.14cm) can scarcely be regarded as a good representation of contemporary womanhood. A terracotta example of the same period, also in the British Museum (EA 59679), sadly headless, displays the plastic skills of a much superior modeller. The fact of survival provides poor grounds for general aesthetic judgement.

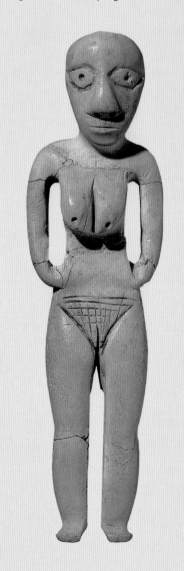

archaeologist Flinders Petrie on the basis of pottery finds at sites excavated by himself at Naqada, about 25 miles north of Luxor (1895) and Diospolis Parva, or Hu, between Dendera and Abydos (1898–9). The system of dating he devised for the predynastic cultures was by no means perfect, and it is not now accepted by scholars who work in this early field, but the designation of Naqada I and Naqada II applied by Petrie to the two main stages of predynastic development continues to be used for practical reasons. Places where the distinctive pottery of the two Naqada periods was found in quantity have also given their names to the successive stages in the development of the predynastic cultures of Egypt. Naqada I is specially identified with El-Amra, south of Abydos (Amratian), and Naqada II with El-Gerza to the south of Cairo and north of Maidum (Gerzean).

Information about these predynastic periods derives almost entirely from the objects found in the extensive cemeteries excavated throughout Egypt, situated as they are mostly above the floodplain. In a few places like Hierakonpolis in Upper Egypt, settlements have increasingly been revealed in excavations, and they should in time enrich the picture of predynastic Egyptian life. The culture throughout was understandably agriculture-based, but with a noticeably increasing mastery of relatively simple manufacturing processes, and the development of mechanical skills in the working of materials, particularly stone. Bricks made from Nile mud were the common building medium for houses, temples, great enclosure walls, and for superior burials. Small sculptures in stone, ivory, bone and terracotta were modelled with ever-increasing skill; stones of every kind, many of great hardness, requiring highly developed techniques for the manufacture of vessels of various types, were found in the mountainous region of the Eastern Desert. Eye-paint palettes, many of which probably served ritual rather than cosmetic purposes, were carved from a dense hard stone usually in the past described as slate or schist but now more properly identified as siltstone or greywacke. The methods of working hard stones developed during the predynastic periods were to expand and flourish in later times when quarrying skills were perfected. On a smaller scale, the working of flints – readily available in the limestone hills of the valley edge – came to its peak in the Naqada II Period. Flint knives and other tools were manufactured to an extraordinary degree of precision and beauty. In many ways the Egyptian mastery in the exploitation of hard stones was one of the greatest achievements of the culture of Pharaonic Egypt, in terms of craftsmanship. Pottery, on the other hand, for the most part was treated as a practical product. So it was in predynastic times, although some very fine decorated wares were made during the Naqada II Period from sedimentary clays found in certain valleys in the Eastern Desert. The resulting light-coloured vessels were much more delicate in texture than those made from Nile mud; in many cases they seem to reproduce the shapes used for stone vessels.

From the restricted evidence derived mostly from burials, it seems clear that a fair degree of homogeneity in predynastic cultures spread throughout the Nile Valley south of the Delta. Evidence from Delta sites like Buto suggests that influence from the Near East led to cultural developments which may have heralded the political moves leading to the unification of the two lands of Upper and Lower Egypt. In general, however, the character of the predynastic culture in the Delta is based on rather modest evidence. But happily, the site of Buto is particularly significant because it was in later times considered to be the political and religious centre in the Delta, the counterpart of Hierakonpolis in Upper Egypt, where, it must be supposed, the process leading to unification developed. From the abundant pottery remains found at Buto in recent years it is clear that the influence on manufacture changed (perhaps in about 3500 BC), coming no longer from Western Asia but Upper Egypt. The fine wares of Naqada II, distinctly superior to the coarse products which previously represented the bulk of ceramic output at Buto, were increasingly copied there, suggesting developing contacts between the North and the South. The much more abundant evidence from Hierakonpolis suggests a better organized polity, controlled by strong, aggressive rulers who were prepared to extend their rule northwards, and over Delta lands.

It must be admitted that the traditional account of the unification of Upper and Lower Egypt is based on rather shaky evidence. The principal source supporting the idea of a military conquest of the north by the south is the Narmer Palette. This large ceremonial palette of siltstone, excavated at Hierakonpolis, shows the king named Narmer in scenes on both sides, in one of which he wears the distinctive white Upper Egyptian crown ⌀, and in the other, the equally distinctive red crown of Lower Egypt ⌀. In the first scene he smites his enemy with a mace, and in the second he advances to view rows of dead enemies. There is much in the detail of the scenes on this palette which remains to be explained, and it must be allowed that on its own it provides probably very uncertain evidence for such an important process as the unification of the Two Lands. It should at this point be stated that the king named Narmer is now generally thought to be Menes, the traditional unifier according to Manetho and the king-lists.

Further evidence of the domination of the North by the South in the period preceding formal unification, the establishment of the First Dynasty and the foundation of the city of Memphis has emerged in recent excavations at Abydos, about 185 miles by river to the north of Hierakonpolis. Throughout Egyptian history Abydos was one of the most sacred places in Egypt. It was thought to be the burial place of Osiris, the divine king of the afterlife, and the entrance to this afterlife was situated in the desert valley in the western hills, at the mouth of which were the burials of the kings of the First and Second Dynasties. But Osiris was not to come on the Abydos scene for several centuries; he was preceded by Khentamentiu ('First of the Westerners'), a necropolis deity, later to be incorporated into the Osiris cult. Recently, the discovery of another royal burial, predating those of the First Dynasty by perhaps as much as 150 years, has provided evidence of substantial links with the North in the form of large numbers of

25 Early Dynastic ivory figurine. The king wears the white crown of Upper Egypt and a short cloak decorated with lozenges, of the kind worn at coronations. From Abydos. H.8.8 cm.

pottery wine vessels of Canaanite manufacture. Do they represent trade or the product of tribute from the North? It is hard to determine the circumstances which led to their presence in the tomb of a king, or at least a chieftain based in the South, and probably at Hierakonpolis. This tomb also contained many small ivory labels originally attached to bundles of commodities, with brief but meaningful legends carved on them, which carry back the emergence of the hieroglyphic script a century or more before its previously accepted beginning.

Why was Abydos so important that it was chosen as the burial ground for the first kings of the united land of Upper and Lower Egypt? It was not the existence of the cult of Osiris, or of his predecessor Khentamentiu; the principal deity at Hierakonpolis was Horus in falcon-form (the name in Greek means 'city of the falcon'), and historically he was never considered a deity of the afterlife. He was essentially the living embodiment of the ruling king, and his image was placed above the formal written name of the king (the *serekh*) from the earliest dynastic times. Abydos may have been chosen as a site for royal burials because it was well within the realm of the Hierakonpolitan rulers, but sufficiently far north to provide a link with the newly established capital at Memphis. And the great tombs of the kings were in a sense counterbalanced by the similarly great tombs built at Saqqara on the desert edge overlooking Memphis. The occupants of the Saqqara tombs remain uncertain, but the balance of evidence suggests that they were the first high officials who were charged with the establishment of the administration for the united country.

The site of Memphis, the new capital of Egypt, was well chosen, a few miles to the south of the apex of the Delta, and strategically placed to command the South and the North. The choice was inspired: the city of Menes remained the most important centre, politically and administratively for most of the Pharaonic Period,

26 Bone or ivory plaque with a scene of Den, fifth king of the First Dynasty, smiting an Asiatic. The signs on the right are an early writing of a statement, 'the first occasion of smiting the East'. H.4.5 cm.

and lost its importance only after the foundation of Alexandria in the fourth century BC. At first its name was, it seems, 'White Walls', after the white-painted mud-brick enclosure containing the original foundation. Very little is known about the activities of the kings of the first two dynasties, but it is evident from an examination of the material remains surviving from the period that many of the enduring characteristics of Egyptian culture were established at this time. An elaborate system of officials was created to administer the country; apart from the important activities of peacemaking and tax-collecting, there was the serious duty to manage the water resources of the country, a matter of continuing concern. The historical tradition credits Menes with constructing dykes to control the annual flood, and the recent examination of a huge dam in the desert to the east of the Nile, near Helwan, opposite Memphis, suggests that this massive structure may have formed part of an elaborate scheme for the management of water pouring in flash floods from the valleys of the Eastern Desert. It is probably to be dated to the early dynasties, although not as early as the reign of Menes.

Unfortunately the dam was never completed, being partly destroyed by the very flash floods it was designed to control.

Furthermore, during the first two dynasties – sometimes called, inappropriately, the Archaic Period – the hieroglyphic script played an important part in the unification of the country and in helping to standardize the writing and the form of the Egyptian language. It remained a method of writing which was tied to the spoken language itself; it was not yet sufficiently developed to be able to express pictorially more than simple ideas and statements. There was, nevertheless, a unity in the progress of the script, which is evidenced in the appearance and use of signs throughout the land. How the dissemination of new graphic ideas, signs, and ways of conveying the spoken word by the written was achieved is hard to explain. One would like to believe that it was part of the evolving bureaucratic system to ensure that writing was standardized throughout the country. One has a feeling, however, that there was an haphazard element in the process. Hieroglyphs were initially mostly used for marking or recording: marking a grave with an inscribed stone or stela, including a name and possibly a title; recording the contents of a container. Written cursively on pots, the script shows its rudimentary changes into hieratic, the form of writing later used primarily on papyrus, a material which seems to have been first made in the First Dynasty, although no written papyrus of the period has yet been found.

In the field of building, the Egyptians were already thinking in big, if not grandiose, terms. Mud-brick remained the principal medium for all structures, but it limited the possibility of massive constructions of the kind usually associated with Egypt in its greatest days. By the end of the Second Dynasty, however, the transition to stone building may be clearly detected. Khasekhemwy, the last monarch of the dynasty demonstrated his desire to build big in the erection of great mud-brick enclosures at Hierakonpolis and Abydos. At the latter site, the Shunet ez-Zebib is the best preserved of the structures; it probably represented, in part at least, the funerary temple and associated buildings devoted to the posthumous cult of the dead king. Khasekhemwy's tomb, the largest of those found at Abydos, lies about a mile to the west; its burial chamber is constructed of stone. Stone was not used in the construction of the Shunet ez-Zebib, but massive quantities of mud-bricks; walls still stand in some places 11 m (36 ft) high and are over 5 m (17 ft) thick. It may seem an extraordinary extravagant use of mud-brick, but such vast structures were built regularly in Egypt to enclose temple areas. They can still be seen at Memphis, Karnak, Medinet Habu, the late temples of Edfu and Dendera, and particularly noteworthy at Tanis in the Delta. It was clearly not just the easy availability of mud-brick which commended its use for great enclosures. Nevertheless, stone was about to enter the building scene in Egypt in a dramatic manner. Traditionally the Step Pyramid of Djoser has been regarded as the first great stone building in Egypt, with nothing earlier worthy of consideration. In recent years, however, a careful survey of the remains of a great enclosure lying to the west of the Step Pyramid complex has revealed substantial remains of walls built of quarried and shaped limestone blocks standing over 4 m (13 ft) in height. Much more work is needed before the history and purpose of this structure are clarified, but its significance in the history of

Egyptian architecture is already abundantly clear; the present view is that it dates to the last years of Khasekhemwy.

It is a pity that the paucity of evidence denies us greater knowledge of Khasekhemwy, during whose reign so much of what would characterize the strong centralized governance of the Old Kingdom rulers began to emerge. For example, the two earliest identifiable stone sculptures of royalty are representations of King Khasekhemwy. Found at Hierakonpolis, they show the king wearing the white crown of Upper Egypt and the tight-fitting cloak associated with the ceremonies of coronation. Inscriptions on the bases refer apparently to victories in the North, giving numbers of slain enemy. It is possible that towards the end of the Second Dynasty, internal problems threatened the Egyptian state. Peribsen, the previous king, had his name written in the usual *serekh*, but surmounted not by the Horus falcon but by the animal of Seth. It seems likely that there may have been some trouble in the Delta needing strong action, which was settled by the king named at that time Khasekhem ('the powerful one, or the power, is risen'), who then signalled the proper reunification of Egypt by modifying his name to Khasekhemwy ('the doubly powerful one, or the two powers, are risen'). His *serekh*-name was written with both the Horus falcon and the Seth animal perched above. The two statues are now generally thought to show Khasekhemwy at a very early stage in his rule. They are stylistically and conceptually the first true royal representations from Egypt and demonstrate the not-unsuccessful skills of early sculptors to translate the royal idea into stone.

What else is known about the development of Egypt during the first two dynasties (*c.* 3100–2686 BC)? The country is thought to have been at relative peace for most of this long period in which great things happened subsequent to the unification under Menes. There is some evidence of expeditions – partly punitive (necessarily so), partly for the acquisition of desirable raw materials – to Nubia (gold), Sinai and the southern Levant (copper) and Syria/Lebanon (cedar wood). The land of Egypt slowly became organized with the administrative framework which would form its local and centralized structure for thousands of years.

The rise and fall of royal power: the Old Kingdom and First Intermediate Period

Three reliefs from the Wadi Maghara in Sinai associate three kings who belong to the Third Dynasty: Sanakht, Djoser and Sekhemkhet. These records show that in this early period the Egyptians were already exploiting the resources of the region – certainly turquoise and almost certainly copper – and were obliged to be traditionally firm in imposing their authority in this eastern borderland. Of these three kings, Djoser is the one who can still be recognized as the monarch in whose reign stone-building in Egypt seriously began.

The credit for the form and construction of Djoser's funerary monument, the Step Pyramid, is traditionally given to his high official Imhotep. Inscriptionally his name is linked to the building, and without evidence to the contrary it would be churlish to deny Imhotep this credit. What cannot be denied is that the posthumous reputation of Imhotep depended initially on his achievement in Djoser's reign. In every respect the

27 The Step Pyramid of King Djoser at Saqqara. In the foreground are reconstructed buildings in the jubilee court. Third Dynasty.

Step Pyramid is remarkable: a structure built entirely of stone. The pyramid itself, although not a true pyramid but a series of mastabas, indicating many changes of plan in the building of it, was an awesome conception, set on the desert escarpment commanding the Nile Valley, and clearly visible from ancient Memphis. It made a powerful statement of royal power, and was the first such monument to be constructed in dynastic Egypt. The dominant building in the whole Step Pyramid complex was Djoser's tomb, set in a limestone enclosure possibly repeating the white walls of the capital city of the Two Lands. Many of the buildings contained within the enclosure were connected with the royal coronation as repeated in the *heb-sed*, the *sed*-festival in which the power of the monarch was revivified, and he renewed his vows to the principal deities of the land.

The Step Pyramid encapsulates the burgeoning of ancient Egyptian culture in many respects. Architecturally and artistically it heralds the wonderful achievements of the Old Kingdom; it provides indirect evidence of a well-ordered state, served by outstanding officials; it demonstrates through its many subsidiary buildings the organization of Egyptian religion, and the requirement of the king to recognize the country's religious diversity. The extraordinary maturing of royal power in the reign of Djoser becomes patently evident during the subsequent Fourth Dynasty. Then, it would seem that all the resources of the state were for a large part of the year devoted to the construction of mighty monuments, which remain to this day as lasting testimonies to what a well-organized state could achieve.

The Pyramid Age, in its strictest and best sense, lasted scarcely one hundred years, if it may be taken to have started with Djoser, and finished somewhat inconclusively with

Mycerinus (Menkaure) in the late Fourth Dynasty. There were, of course, pyramids as royal sepulchres built in the Fifth and Sixth Dynasties and again in the Twelfth Dynasty; but none of these later structures – some of which were of considerable size – began to approach the extravagances of the Fourth Dynasty, or represented the vast expenditure of resources and labour. Pyramids still, for most people, mean the Giza pyramids, but it is not generally appreciated that the greatest pyramid-builder of all was Snofru, the first king of the Fourth Dynasty. Three pyramids at least were begun in his reign, two of which suffered from design weaknesses – that at Maidum about 31 miles south of Memphis and the so-called Bent Pyramid at Dahshur. His third pyramid was also built at Dahshur, less than a mile to the north of the Bent Pyramid. Many lessons had been learned about pyramid construction from the early failures, and the result was in every respect a true precursor of the Great Pyramid built at Giza by Snofru's son Cheops (Khufu).

The architecture of the Fourth Dynasty pyramids is considered more fully in chapter 7. Here these great structures may be treated as the very positive evidence for the supremacy of the king within the state of Egypt. His position vis-à-vis his nobles and officials was probably greater than that of any subsequent king of Egypt, but the concentration of power in the monarchy and the gross expenditure of national resources on the monumental structures of Dahshur and Giza did not make for a well-established regime. The relatively modest pyramid built for Mycerinus at the end of the Fourth

28 The Northern or Red Pyramid at Dahshur; the first true pyramid, built for King Snofru of the Fourth Dynasty. The angle of inclination is less than that of the Great and of subsequent pyramids.

Dynasty suggests that some lessons had been learned from the extravagance of his predecessors' building activities. Furthermore, accommodations seem to have been made with the class of nobles and officials which was gradually building up its influence to become the powerful bureaucracy that in future would run the country along lines of general efficiency, and not just according to the royal whim.

The pyramids of the kings of the Fifth Dynasty were much smaller than those of their predecessors; they were mostly built at Abusir, to the north of Saqqara, and sun-temples devoted to the worship of the sun-god Ra were built at Abu Gurob nearby. The buildings associated with these monuments were splendidly embellished with fine low-relief carvings. Contemporaneously, a wealth of similar decoration was provided in the mastaba chapels of senior officials at Abusir and Saqqara, like those of Ptahshepses, Ti and Ptahhotep. Documentary papyri found at Abusir concern the posthumous administration of the pyramid complexes and demonstrate the development of careful accounting and the spread of bureaucratic involvement in day-to-day activities. The last king of the Fifth Dynasty, Unas, built his pyramid at Saqqara, and in it for the first time were inscribed *Pyramid Texts*, which were composed to assist the king in his journey after death to achieve his destiny in the sky.

In general, the evidence suggests that the administration of the country remained fairly centralized up to the end of the Fifty Dynasty. Changes took place in the subsequent dynasty which had profound effects on the royal power and growth of provincial power. It was during the Sixth Dynasty that the nomarchs, the senior district officials, throughout the land were given the opportunity of acting with some independence in the running not only of local affairs but also of relations with some foreign regions such as Nubia. The tombs of nomarchs and other high officials in the provinces provide for the first time good evidence of how affairs were managed at the local level. Particularly interesting are the rock tombs at Aswan (often rather crudely cut and gauchely decorated) in which inscriptions reveal the extent to which the local nomarch was responsible for organizing contacts with the Nubian tribes to the south, keeping an eye on trading expeditions, and occasionally conducting aggressive forays into what seems still to have been a wild frontier region.

In other directions also, Egypt by intention or necessity expanded its interest externally. Sea expeditions were sent to Punt, a country still to be identified, but probably Somalia in the Horn of Africa. From this region exotic products could be obtained – ivory, incense, ebony – although the sea passage there and back was hazardous; there were possibly local dangers in Punt itself, but evidence unfortunately is scanty. For Sinai, however, there is much more inscriptional evidence of mining activities for turquoise and copper, but safe and regular access to the region required some military action against Asiatics and Beduin tribes, who were ever prepared to make hostile forays into the Eastern Delta.

Within Egypt fundamental changes were taking place in religious thinking, particularly with regard to the posthumous destinies of the king and of non-royal people. Osirian prospects of an afterlife accessible to all, but very different from the sky-focused prospects of the king, greatly enhanced the expectations of the individual, but weakened the overall structure of religious beliefs which previously had offered little to him. The tendency throughout the Sixth Dynasty was towards the diminishing of the supreme authority of the king and the increase in the freedom of powerful nobles along with their greater ability to exercise local governance. Ideas of responsibility and a paternalistic attitude to the exercise of local rule were clearly influenced by the spread of religious beliefs derived from the cult of Osiris, but it is by no means clear that this change in the relationship between king and nobles, nomarchs and other high officials led to the breakdown of central authority towards the end of the dynasty. The long reign of Pepy II marked the end of the autocracy which had distinguished the rule of the kings of the Old Kingdom. The subsequent period, notable for the disintegration of the central authority, is known as the First Intermediate Period.

The lack of good documentary evidence for the decline of the central administration during the Seventh to Tenth Dynasties makes it difficult to chart with any precision how political power passed substantially into the hands of the provincial governors. It was not a long period of semi-anarchy – perhaps not as much as 150 years – but it had a profound effect not only on the image of Egyptian kingship, but also on the attitude of the provinces towards central authority. Nomarchs, who enjoyed a kind of hereditary power, found it necessary to administer their fiefdoms with a degree of independence previously unknown. They developed a real pride in being able to run their local affairs efficiently, and to the distinct advantage of the people who lived within the ambit of the nomarch's regime. Texts like those carved in the tomb of Ankhtifi at Moalla to the south of Luxor – whom we shall meet again later in this book – demonstrate the difficulties faced by such local 'barons', who were feudal in effect, in maintaining a good local administration while at the same time making accommodations with more powerful neighbours.

Very little can be said about the Seventh and Eighth Dynasties. The Ninth and Tenth dynasties represent the leaders of a coalition of northern nomes based on Herakleopolis, who slowly re-established a kind of uniform administration in opposition to southern coalitions which in due course fell under the leadership of Thebes. The process by which the two coalitions, Herakleopolitan and Theban, developed into powerful contending groups seems not to have been simple, but by about 2130 BC the confrontation developed into active warfare between the Khety kings (so proclaimed) of the north and the Intef kings (so aspiring) in Thebes. The struggle was resolved to the advantage of Thebes by Nebhepetre Mentuhotep (II) in about 2040 BC, who could then claim to have reunited Upper and Lower Egypt. His victory marks the end of a difficult period of turmoil, and the start of what is now called the Middle Kingdom – a period of glorious revitalization and splendid achievements.

Rehabilitation and confrontation: the Middle Kingdom and Second Intermediate Period

The foundations of the reunified state under the last kings of the Eleventh Dynasty were consolidated and extended by the powerful and very active rulers of the Twelfth Dynasty. The change of regime seems to have been achieved without serious trouble. Amenemhat I, the founder of the dynasty, may have been the vizier whose name occurs

30 Shrine of King Senusret I
of the Twelfth Dynasty.
Retrieved from the inside of
the third pylon of the Karnak
Temple, it has been
reconstructed in the Open
Air Museum at Karnak.

OPPOSITE 29 Limestone stela
of the treasurer Tjetji. The
semi-autobiographical text at
the top describes his faithful
career under Wahankh, one
of the Intef kings of the early
Eleventh Dynasty. H.1.52 m.

in inscriptions dated to the last Mentuhotep of the Eleventh Dynasty. The new king's name incorporates that of the god Amun, a previously rather insignificant member of the group of eight gods known as the ogdoad of Hermopolis in Middle Egypt. This change in divine patronage from that of Montu, the warlike god of the Theban nome, may have been undertaken consciously for political reasons. It was, however, to have lasting effects: Amun, especially in his form Amon-Re in association with the sun-god of Heliopolis, became the god of the Egyptian state and empire; he would remain supreme throughout the New Kingdom, and, at Thebes, down to Roman times.

A further new stamp was placed on the dynasty by the establishing of a capital free from the provincial associations of Thebes, and the ancient traditions of Memphis, lately used as a capital by the Herakleopolitan kings. The place chosen was to the south of Memphis, near the entrance to the Faiyum; it was called Itj-tawy ('Seizer of the Two Lands'). In the re-establishment of strong administration the Twelfth Dynasty kings worked, probably from necessity, with the nomarchs, whose local powers seem to have been confirmed by the process of reunification. The nomarchs' tombs, especially in Middle Egypt, were large and splendidly decorated, and it is clear that the feudal nature of their local regimes, together with their apparent exercise of considerable local independence, tended to threaten the central royal authority. In due course, steps were taken in the reign of Senusret III to curb the nomarchs' power, although it is not at all certain that the nomarchic system was positively abolished. Wings, however, were clipped, and a new system of administration was introduced based on the three regions of Lower, Middle and Southern Upper Egypt, with high officials royally appointed and answerable to the vizier.

In almost all areas of life, public and private, Egypt flourished under the new regime. Internally steps were taken to overhaul the control of Nile waters. During the First Intermediate Period the breakdown of centralized control combined with a series of disastrously low Niles led to serious water shortages, even famine in parts of the country. Amenemhat III paid particular attention to the Faiyum depression to the west of the Nile, an area watered by a branch of the Nile known as the Bahr Yussef ('Joseph's River'). Its central lake had attracted settlers since remote antiquity, but its potential development for agricultural purposes was never realized until serious efforts were made in the Twelfth Dynasty to control the water supply and its proper drainage during and after the season of inundation. A complex of buildings attached to Amenemhat's pyramid at Hawara probably contained not only his funerary temple, but also a huge administrative centre. It has now almost totally disappeared, but its size and complexity led classical writers to call it the Labyrinth.

A remarkable efflorescence of cultural activity took place at this time. After a period in which the outstanding standards of art achieved in the Fifth and Sixth Dynasties were largely lost, the confidence and vigour of the new dynasty led to a revival of high-quality work, especially in the fields of sculpture, tomb and temple decoration, and additionally in the production of literary and moralistic works. It was a time when scribes came into their own. At last the Egyptian language with its attendant scripts gained a new flexibility and precision, and the exercise of the scribe's *métier* now reached a high point of productivity and achievement. Accounts were kept, letters written, legal documents drawn up; a pattern of power for the written word, which was to characterize Egyptian culture thereafter, became well established.

It seems probable that during the First Intermediate Period, Egypt for the first time experienced significant infiltration of foreigners from Western Asia. A more positive attitude towards such infiltration, and to foreign policy in general, was therefore displayed by the kings of the Twelfth Dynasty. In Nubia in particular, active steps were taken to extend Egyptian influence beyond the Second Cataract. Good trade relations and routes were established, and to this end a series of imposing fortresses were built in the region of the Second Cataract in the reign of Senusret III. Elaborate steps were also taken to control movements and to eliminate the illegal importation of goods to avoid the imposts levied in the Second Cataract area. Under a regime of good stability, the necessary access to gold mines and to quarries for hard stones like diorite and semi-precious stones like amethyst (much used in the jewellery of the Middle Kingdom) was for a time secured. Relations with the Nubian kingdom, centred on Kerma some hundreds of miles to the south, seem to have been mutually satisfactory.

A greater threat, however, came from the north-east, where there existed perennial pressure from the peoples of Western Asia, who could only wonder at, and be jealous of, the settled and cosy life obtaining in the Nile Valley and Delta. Complete isolation from the East was not a solution, because it was essential economically for the Egyptians to maintain good trade relations with the Asiatic lands. Certain vital commodities like silver and tin had to be imported, and there is no doubt that Egyptian life and culture benefited from relatively open contacts with the lively cultures of the Near East. As

31 Head from a colossal grano-diorite seated statue of King Amenemhat III of the Twelfth Dynasty, later usurped by King Osorkon II of the Twenty-second Dynasty. The eyes were originally inlaid. From Bubastis. H.79 cm.

32 Seated granite statue
of King Sobkemsaef, a rare
royal representation of the
Seventeenth Dynasty. H.1.64 m.

early as the reign of Amenemhat I it was felt necessary to impose some controls, and a barrier called 'Walls of the Ruler' was erected in the Wadi Tumilat to cover one of the main routes by which peoples from the East entered Egypt.

The problems arising from excessive immigration from Asia were to become acute in the period following the end of the Twelfth Dynasty. The kings of that dynasty had greatly stabilized the royal succession by using the practice of co-regency whereby the ruling monarch held the throne jointly with his nominated successor for a varying number of years before he died. The system worked well, but in the end seems to have foundered through the lack of an heir for Amenemhat IV. The last recorded ruler of the dynasty was Queen Sobkneferu, of whom next to nothing is known, but her death led to a change of dynasty, which retained Itj-tawy as its capital. It used to be thought that the Thirteenth Dynasty marked the beginning of the Second Intermediate Period, a new time of disintegration. It is, however, becoming increasingly evident that the strong administrative system established in the preceding dynasty continued very positively for many years, with senior officials, especially the vizier and the heads of governmental institutions like the Treasury, maintaining its operation. The kings, on the other hand – numerous in number, although not the sixty mentioned by Manetho – seem to have played modest roles in the running of the country.

An area in which the lack of royal control was particularly felt was foreign policy. Immigration continued both from the south and the east with the apparent relaxing of border controls. Medjay Nubians from Lower Nubia presented a lesser problem, and many were integrated into Egyptian life, some being recruited as soldiers. Asiatics, on the other hand, were potentially much more worrying. They settled in substantial numbers in the Delta and gradually set up power bases which were distinctly threatening to the native Egyptian regime. Their chieftains, referred to as *heqau-khasut* ('princes of desert lands') in Egyptian, are now known as Hyksos, to use Manetho's term. The Hyksos were not, as used to be thought, invaders of Egypt in the positive, aggressive sense, but, as suggested above, immigrants who slowly developed powerful groupings which became capable of taking over parts of the Delta and so threatening Egypt itself. A Hyksos capital was established at Avaris in the Eastern Delta, while Egyptian power retreated to Thebes.

There is much evidence to suggest that the Hyksos were not anti-Egyptian in matters of culture; in many ways they tried to copy or maintain Egyptian traditions. The kings of the Hyksos Dynasty – Manetho's Fifteenth – used Egyptian titles, put their names in cartouches and worshipped Egyptian gods, especially Seth; they usurped the royal statues of their Egyptian predecessors and generally portrayed themselves as representatives of the old tradition. They were not, it seems, the destructive anti-Egyptian enemy described in texts of later times, but they were foreigners ruling parts of Egypt in opposition to the 'legitimate' kings in Thebes, and their ultimate intentions were undoubtedly hostile; they even established friendly relations with Nubian rulers. A clash was inevitable,

but did not occur until about 1650 BC when a new line of kings, the Seventeenth Dynasty, emerged in Thebes and adopted a strikingly aggressive attitude to these foreign upstarts, as they were now regarded. A crisis developed, according to literary sources, in the reign of Seqenenra Taa, who apparently rose to a challenge from the Hyksos king Apepi. No details of campaigns survive, but the skull of the mummy of Seqenenre, discovered in a cache of rewrapped and reburied kings, shows signs of wounds inflicted by an axe, which were possibly the result of a battle engagement. What is certain is that the struggle was seriously joined by his successor Kamose, who took his army to the gates of Avaris. The final expulsion of the Hyksos came under Ahmose, brother of Kamose, and to him is given the credit of initiating a new and glorious era, following the reunification of the Two Lands.

Imperial glory: the New Kingdom

Details of the final campaigns which resulted in the expulsion of the Hyksos by Ahmose are included in the biographical texts carved in the rock tombs of the nobles at Elkab, across the Nile from Hierakonpolis, the site of the ancient city of Nekheb and the cult centre of the vulture-goddess Nekhbet. Ahmose's success with this expulsion and the subsequent reunification led to his being regarded as the founder of a new dynasty, the Eighteenth, which was in succession terms the continuation of the Seventeenth. This marked the beginning in about 1550 BC of the era now called the New Kingdom, an age which continued down to the end of the Twentieth Dynasty in about 1069 BC, a 500-year period which from an imperial point of view witnessed Egypt's years of greatest power internationally, but saw its gradual decline towards a further time of dynastic disunity and internal troubles. Just as the Twelfth Dynasty ushered in a period of national renewal and artistic achievement, so did the Eighteenth infuse a new spirit into the Egyptians, enabling them to rise to exceptional heights in the fields of architecture, sculpture, painting and the minor arts.

National stability, however, was the primary objective of the early kings of the dynasty, who firstly re-established Egyptian authority in Nubia, rebuilding the forts built during the Twelfth Dynasty and subsequently leading expeditions as far south as the Fourth Cataract region; although Egyptian presence there was probably no more than a token show of arms. So too was the extension of Egyptian power in Asia in the early reigns of the Eighteenth Dynasty, with aggressive forays at first, and then a push by Thutmose I as far as the Euphrates. Asia certainly offered a greater threat to Egypt than Nubia, and throughout the New Kingdom one of the chief concerns of the Egyptian king was the suppression of pressures by successive Near Eastern peoples to dominate the Levant – the Syro-Palestine region – and thereby endanger the land of Egypt.

It is not surprising that the city of Thebes now became a centre of special imperial importance. Thebes was the power base of the kings of the Seventeenth Dynasty, and it was in Thebes that the kings of the subsequent dynasties established the religious centre to which they returned for the great festivals organized in honour of the god Amun and his associated deities, Mut and Khonsu; to Thebes they returned for their burials in the Valley of the Kings. Amun, and more specifically in his form Amon-Re,

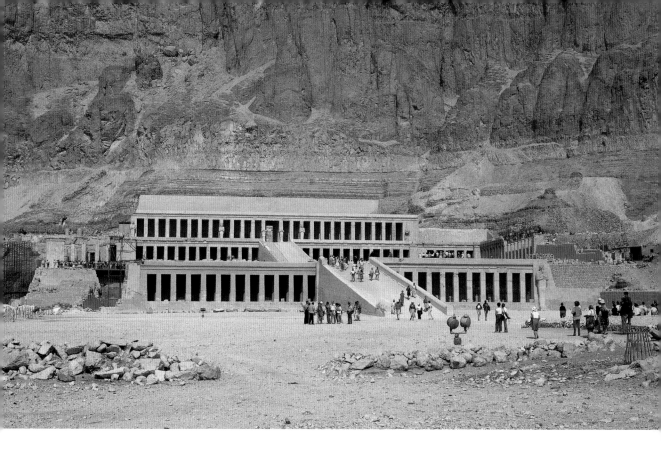

34 The terraced mortuary temple of Queen Hatshepsut, after its reconstruction by Polish archaeologists. To its left are the remains of the earlier temple of Nebhepetre Mentuhotep II of the Eleventh Dynasty.

OPPOSITE 33 Limestone figure of King Amenhotep I shown mummiform in the guise of Osiris. The crossed hands originally held the royal insignia of crook and flail. From Deir el-Bahri. H.2.69 m.

became the god of empire, and much of the tribute derived from foreign conquests was presented to him, enriching the great Theban temples in particular. More or less at the same time Memphis was rehabilitated as the centre of administration in the north, and the weight of this administration moved generally northwards. Thebes was too distant from the serious fields of activity, including trade and external affairs, to remain a seriously functional centre of government. A second, northern, vizier had his base in Memphis, and it is likely that much of Egypt's foreign policy was directed from that city.

Under the early rulers of the Eighteenth Dynasty Egypt flourished as never before. Foreign expeditions and conquests initiated by Thutmose I brought substantial rewards in the form of the tribute mentioned above and of trade with an increasing number of foreign states. In Egypt this prosperity was marked by a notable revival in the building of temples and the production of fine sculpture. A first high point was reached in the reigns of Queen Hatshepsut and of her nephew Thutmose III. Hatshepsut, the daughter of Thutmose I and Queen Ahmose, and wife of Thutmose II, acted initially as regent during the minority of Thutmose III, and then for some years as Pharaoh in her own right. There is still much uncertainty about the sequence of events which led eventually to the sole rule of Thutmose III, and also about the extent of bitterness engendered by the Queen's apparent usurpation of the throne. One outstanding achievement of her reign was the construction of the remarkable mortuary temple at Deir el-Bahri under the supervision of her high steward Senenmut. Set in a bay in the western Theban hills, and adjacent to the earlier temple of Nebhepetre Mentuhotep II of the Eleventh Dynasty, it was designed imaginatively with three rising terraces, the walls of which were carved with wonderful reliefs including scenes of notable events during Hatshepsut's reign, such as an expedition to the land of Punt to obtain incense trees and the transport by river of two great granite obelisks from Aswan to be erected at Karnak.

Although Hatshepsut may not have wholly neglected the new aggressive tradition of Egyptian foreign policy, it is certain that Thutmose III on becoming sole ruler felt it necessary to conduct a vigorous campaign against the forces of Mitanni, at that time the dominant power in Western Asia. At the battle of Megiddo in Syria in about 1458 BC he achieved a great victory, thereby re-establishing Egyptian authority in the region. He then reinforced this authority in a series of annual campaigns which extended Egyptian influence to the borders of the Hittite empire in Anatolia. His successors Amenhotep II and Thutmose IV further consolidated Egyptian power in the Asiatic region, so that when Amenhotep III became king in about 1390 BC things seemed very settled and peace apparently prevailed. In consequence, the fruits of victory and empire could be harvested and enjoyed in a period of unprecedented prosperity. The reign of Amenhotep III has been characterized unfairly as one of peace, luxury and excess. There is plenty of evidence to show that during this reign Egyptian culture flourished, demonstrated by the exceptionally fine building undertaken: the Luxor Temple with its very beautiful open court, work at Karnak including the initiation of the great Hypostyle Hall, and the largest and most splendid mortuary temple for the king in Western Thebes. This last noble complex is now marked only by the two great quartzite statues known as the Colossi of Memnon. The temple was levelled in antiquity, probably during the late Nineteenth Dynasty, but the many fine sculptures discovered in the temple area testify to the high level of artistic achievement during this reign. At the same time, private tombs were finely decorated and the minor arts flourished. It was also a time of progressive religious thinking, possibly encouraged by the royal consort Tiye, and which was to be promoted vigorously by the crown prince Amenhotep, who would rename himself Akhenaten.

The nature and the implications for Egyptian religion of the cult of the Aten are considered more fully later in this book. Its elevation into the main state religion by Akhenaten and his wife Nefertiti had disastrous consequences for Egypt both in domestic and foreign affairs. Coming to the throne as Amenhotep (IV), he espoused openly the worship of the Aten, the sun-disc, and built unusual temples at Karnak, outside the great Amun temple complex but provocatively close to it. He changed his

35 Granite statue of Senenmut, steward of Hatshepsut, responsible for the Deir el-Bahri temple. He is here shown enfolding the queen's daughter Neferure in his cloak. From Karnak. H.72.5 cm.

OPPOSITE ABOVE 36 Façade of the great Luxor Temple, showing the additions made by Ramesses II to the original structure of Amenhotep III.

name to Akhenaten, and then, to escape the overwhelming presence of the worship of Amon-Re in Thebes, established in his sixth year a new capital called Akhetaten in a virgin site on the east bank of the Nile in Middle Egypt. It is now called El-Amarna.

There is still some debate about whether he shared the kingship with his father in a co-regency. The balance of evidence seems to weigh against such a sharing of power; his move to the new capital was most probably an independent decision. At Akhetaten a kind of closed society developed in which the king and the immediate royal family pursued a way of life devoted to the worship of the Aten. There is evidence from surviving diplomatic correspondence in cuneiform that foreign affairs were neglected and Egyptian influence in Western Asia rapidly declined. The position would have been even graver had there not been a strong northern administration based in Memphis.

One area in which Atenism had a profound and lasting effect was art. The emphasis on the natural world and on an apparent greater freedom of expression led to a minor revolution, not only in what might be represented artistically, but particularly in the ways it might be represented. At first certain grotesqueries characterized the work, notably evident in the reliefs in the Aten temples at Karnak and the great sculptures of the king placed there. There has been much argument about whether the distortions of the royal features and the apparent feminizing of his body reflected his own particular physical condition. They were also extended to the representation of Nefertiti

37 Colossal quartzite head of King Amenhotep III, found in the ruins of the king's mortuary temple in Western Thebes. H.1.33 m.

51

38 Granite statue of a king holding before him an offering table weighed down with the produce of Egypt. The inscription names the king as Horemheb, but the features suggest that it was originally carved as a representation of Tutankhamun. H.1.68 m.

and the royal children. But as the reign progressed, the 'distortions' were modified, and a greater, even traditional, elegance marked the sculptures that were made at Akhetaten. The famous head of Nefertiti in Berlin is usually considered the outstanding example of late Amarna art, but some maintain that less gaudily painted sculptures of the queen and other members of the royal family provide far better evidence of the very high capabilities of the artist-craftsmen who worked at Akhetaten.

There is not much evidence that Atenism was recognized throughout the country as an acceptable alternative to the many cults which ordinarily sustained the religious aspirations of people, and its collapse following the deaths of Akhenaten and Nefertiti allowed a fairly rapid return to what may be described as the normalcy of religious life with its varied and multifarious practices. On Akhenaten's death he was succeeded by the co-regent of his last years, Neferneferuaten, who was probably his brother Smenkhkara, but who, some writers claim, was Queen Nefertiti herself. The abandonment of Akhetaten and the return to Thebes and the old religious ways took place under the young successor Tutankhaten, then renamed Tutankhamun; he may have been Akhenaten's son by a subsidiary wife Kia.

The re-establishment of the old, pre-Amarna regime during Tutankhamun's reign occurred seemingly with no difficulties. The Amarna interlude had not lasted sufficiently long to destroy the possibility of a seamless return to the old worship of Amon-Re and of other gods throughout the country. The reigns of Tutankhamun, who died in his late 'teens, and that of his successor Ay were in a sense interludes before the reign of Horemheb, general under Tutankhamun, who had, as one may understand, been instrumental in maintaining some stability in the Egyptian state in its time of inanition. As general of the army, Horemheb took some steps to re-establish Egyptian authority in Syria, and it was almost inevitable that he took over the kingship on the death of Ay. His legitimacy was to some extent established by his marriage to Mutnodjmet, sister of Nefertiti. He was subsequently recognized as the true successor of Amenhotep III, and as such was placed in the king-lists put up in temples of the Nineteenth Dynasty.

Horemheb was clearly a practical, perspicacious ruler, who recognized what had to be done to restore the state of Egypt to a properly functioning great power, confident at home and respected abroad. His reign of about twenty-eight years witnessed a transformation in national life: a revitalizing of trade, a reorganization of the legal system, a renewal of great building projects, especially in the Karnak and Luxor Temples. Respect for Egyptian power began to return in relations with the Near East. With a proper regard for the future, he also groomed his own protégé to succeed him. Appointed northern vizier by Horemheb, Ramesses in due course initiated the Nineteenth Dynasty in about 1295 BC.

The threats from Western Asia, recognized by Horemheb, were to become increasingly troublesome in the early years of the new dynasty. After the brief reign of Ramesses I, his son Sety I took up the challenge presented by the Hittites, who had now moved south from their Anatolian homeland, to bring pressure on the Egyptian presence in Syria. Sety's campaigns were successful up to a point, but not conclusive, and a climax would be reached in the early years of his successor Ramesses II. In the meanwhile Egypt enjoyed a new prosperity in Sety's reign, marked by buildings of exceptional architectural interest and beauty. He continued work at Karnak originally planned in the reign of Amenhotep

A play on signs

This unusual statue of King Ramesses II (fig. 39) shows him as a squatting child with a sun-disc on his head, and holding a plant, the whole under the protection of Horus as a falcon, and here identified with the Asiatic god Hauron. It is made of granite, but the face of the falcon has been replaced with a limestone insert. The royal figure on its own forms a rebus, a playful representation of the king's name: *Re* – the sun-disc, *mes* – the child, and *swt* – the plant, the three elements making Ra-mes-su, i.e. Ramesses. From Tanis. H.2.31 m. (Cairo Museum)

III; a magnificent tomb was prepared for him in the Valley of the Kings, surely the best-decorated sepulchre in that place. At Abydos he began an original and very handsome temple dedicated principally to the cult of Osiris. It was unfinished at the time of his death, and its completion became one of the declared intentions of Ramesses II following his coronation.

In due course Ramesses was to fulfil this intention, and he also built an Osiris temple of his own just to the north of his father's. It was not as grandiose as the earlier foundation, but it was probably the first of the many to be built in Ramesses' reign, and the first to carry on its external walls scenes commemorating the great battle of Qadesh which was fought in his fifth year, about 1275 BC. A brief campaign in his fourth year, a tester of the water, as it were, was followed by the full-scale military expedition which led to the clash at Qadesh on the Orontes river. A bitter, hard-fought battle took place in which neither side could confidently claim victory. The clash was decisive as far as Ramesses was concerned, and it became the principal achievement of his reign, which was to continue until its sixty-seventh year. Victory or not, it did certainly lead to a kind of long-lasting, uneasy peace, which was reinforced in Ramesses' twenty-first year by a treaty with the Hittites, copies of the terms of which are preserved in Egyptian and Hittite records, and then by a marriage between Ramesses and the daughter of the Hittite king. The peace which then prevailed for the rest of his reign was uneasy, as mentioned, not just because the threat from the Hittites remained, but also because of expected trouble with the Libyans, to the west of Egypt, and with the Sea Peoples from the north.

Within Egypt, however, Ramesses' reign saw unprecedented building of temples, many of which carried scenes concerning the 'great' victory at Qadesh; the greatest of these was his mortuary temple, known now as the Ramesseum, supposedly built to emulate that of Amenhotep III nearby. He also developed the vast Delta Residence not far from Avaris. It was named Piramesse ('the House of Ramesses'), and it became the place of the king's principal palace and his forward base; it was richly embellished with statues and obelisks, mostly removed from other places like Memphis and Heliopolis. A divine cult of the king was also promoted which was particularly marked by the construction of many temples in Nubia, including the dramatic rock-cut speos at Abu Simbel.

The threat from Libya and the Sea Peoples materialized in the fifth year of Ramesses' successor Merenptah. The intention of the foreign invaders was to establish colonies in the fertile lands of the Delta. Merenptah successfully repulsed the onslaughts, but the peace that followed was uncertain and clearly temporary. Happily for Egypt it lasted during the final, rather ineffective reigns of the Nineteenth Dynasty, but trouble erupted seriously in the fifth year of Ramesses III, the second king of the Twentieth Dynasty. It was fortunate for Egypt that this Ramesses, who ruled for thirty-two years, saw himself as the true successor of his great namesake Ramesses II, and he was able in some respects to repeat his military successes at crucial times during the reign. Dramatic reliefs on the walls of Ramesses III's mortuary temple at Medinet Habu in Western Thebes commemorate his triumphs, twice against the Libyans, and also against a coalition of Sea Peoples and Asiatics. The pressure from the West was not, however, completely nullified by Ramesses' victories, but it became less organized; subsequently, slow immigration from Libya inevitably led to the development of Libyan enclaves in the Western Delta, just as had happened in the East when Asiatics settled in large numbers during the Second Intermediate Period. Other problems which point to difficulties in maintaining a unified Egypt became apparent in the later years of the Twentieth Dynasty, including an excessive concentration of the nation's wealth in the holdings of the great temples throughout Egypt, and a breakdown in the commercial fabric of the country. Civil disturbances in the Theban area, which had to be suppressed by Medjay (Nubian) police, were a further indication of discontent, and even greater troubles may have erupted elsewhere in the country but are not mentioned in surviving records. By the end of the dynasty Egypt was for all practical purposes a tripartitie land: the pharaonic line continued at Piramesse in the Delta, the vizier Smendes maintained a separate regime at Tanis in the northwest of the Delta, while in Thebes a semi-theocratic state operated under Herihor, high priest of Amon-Ra. Further disintegration followed the death of Ramesses XI in about 1069 BC, and the ending of both the Twentieth Dynasty and the New Kingdom.

Time of turmoil and restoration: the Late New Kingdom and Late Period

The term 'Third Intermediate Period' is now commonly used to describe the period following the Twentieth Dynasty, down to the end, for some, of the Twenty-fourth Dynasty, or, for others,

40 Upper part of a seated statue of King Sety II from Karnak; a sensitive, rare representation of one of the later kings of the Nineteenth Dynasty. Sandstone. H.1.66 m.

OPPOSITE BELOW 42 The towered entrance to the temple precinct of Medinet Habu, mortuary temple of King Ramesses III. In the foreground are the funerary chapels of the God's Wives of Amun of the Twenty-fifth and Twenty-sixth Dynasties.

41 View of part of the great temple area of Tanis in the Delta. Most of the colossal sculptures were brought from Piramesse, and earlier from Memphis and Heliopolis.

the Twenty-fifth Dynasty. No real comparison exists between this era of political division in Egypt and the turbulent times of the two earlier Intermediate Periods. The term preferred here is Late New Kingdom, one that suggests a continuity in cultural and even political terms from the Twentieth Dynasty. After the death of Ramesses XI, a new dynasty – the Twenty-first – was established with Smendes as its first king. Tanis, previously his base as Lower Egyptian vizier, became the new royal capital, and here a great temple was built as well as other fine structures by Smendes' successors, who plundered the old Delta Residence of Piramesse for building stone and embellishments.

There was a degree of isolation in this northern kingdom which was undoubtedly increased by the steady growth of small semi-princely enclaves of Libyan immigrants, whose influence slowly spread southwards as far as Middle Egypt. The Libyan threat was equally recognized by the regime in Thebes, which was now effectively religiously based with the ruling authority resting with the high priest of Amon-Re, and later with the office of God's Wife of Amun, a priestly position usually occupied by a woman of princess status who secured her successor by

43 Kneeling bronze figure of Pimay, a little-known king of the Twenty-second Dynasty. He is shown offering bowls of wine to a deity. H.25.5 cm.

the adoption of her chosen candidate as God's Adorer of Amun. In the future this process of adoption was to become increasingly subject to political pressure. At first the Theban regents, if they may so be termed, were for most practical purposes independent, and able to build up the power of the Theban principality without interference from Tanis. They never, however, adopted royal titles, although some did have their names written in cartouches, indicating a kind of aspiring to royalty. Among the best known activities of the high priests were the investigation of tomb robberies in Western Thebes, the trials of tomb robbers – dramatically recorded in court transcripts, amazingly preserved on papyri – and the rescue and reburial of the bodies of the kings of the New Kingdom. Otherwise Thebes to a great extent became a religious backwater. In the north the Tanite kings have left few records of their activities. They established a new royal cemetery within the great temple precinct in their capital which would be used also by their successors of the Twenty-second Dynasty. The princelings who preceded the kings of this new dynasty were of Libyan origin, and were well established at Bubastis in the Eastern Delta; they had undoubtedly been participants in the local struggles which had engrossed the attentions of the kings of the Twenty-first Dynasty. The transition of power seems to have been without serious difficulties, and the relationship between Tanis and Thebes continued on terms similar to those which existed in the preceding dynasty.

The Tanis regime did not, however, prevail throughout the Delta, and in time the successive Twenty-third and Twenty-fourth Dynasties of Manetho were able to establish themselves briefly, the latter, under Tefnakht, proving to be a serious threat. Tefnakht's power base seems to have been Sais, the ancient cult centre of the goddess Neith in the Western Delta. By this time in the late eighth century BC the only part of Egypt in which some kind of order was maintained was the Theban principality. But things there were about to change in a most dramatic invasion of the country from the south. A Kushite kingdom was long established in Nubia with its capital at Napata in the region of the Fourth Cataract of the Nile. By a tradition inherited from Egypt, the principal cult of these Kushites was that of Amun, the centre of whose worship was at Gebel Barkal, where a great temple was constructed on the site of a foundation going back possibly to Horemheb of the Eighteenth Dynasty, and enlarged by Ramesses II. The first Kushite king actively to involve himself in Egyptian affairs was Kashta, who possibly secured the adoption of his daughter Amenirdis as God's Adorer of Amun by the current God's Wife of Amun, Shepenupet. It seems certain that Kashta actually came to Thebes with a hostile force but withdrew to Napata, leaving it to his son Py (Piankhy) to make a serious invasion in 727 BC. There is great uncertainty about the nature of Napatan involvement up to this point, and it is not unlikely that it was Py rather than Kashta who secured the adoption of Amenirdis some years before his expedition north. The motive for the invasion has also been seriously questioned: not the desire to rescue and revivify the worship of Amun in Thebes, but the seizing of the opportunity of Egyptian political disunity to occupy the land.

Py met minimal opposition in his campaign, and little serious resistance until he encountered the forces of Tefnakht, who was prepared to dispute the control of the Delta with the Kushite king. Although he was in due course defeated, and obliged to submit to Py, Tefnakht was allowed to maintain a kind of subsidiary regime in Lower Egypt, while Py retired south and shortly afterwards withdrew to Napata. He left a powerful regent in Thebes in the person of Amenirdis, who was now God's Wife of Amun. Py's successor Shabako spent more time in Egypt, finally reuniting the whole country after defeating the rulers of the Twenty-fourth Dynasty. He and his successor Taharqo paid much more attention to Egyptian affairs than Py, their actions meeting very little internal opposition, apparently. They respected existing institutions and even helped to rehabilitate some of the cults of the country, like that of Ptah in Memphis. The peaceful conditions now established throughout Egypt led to an unexpected renaissance in cultural matters, notably evident in the revival of ancient sculptural traditions. Striking royal and private statuary was made in quantity, far more than for

44 Granite sphinx with a head representing King Taharqo, one of the Kushite kings of the Twenty-fifth Dynasty, a somewhat brutal, un-Egyptian portrait. The double uraeus is characteristic of royal images of the period. From Kawa in Nubia. H.42 cm.

many generations. Fine hard stones were exploited, and many pieces were sculpted in the styles of previous ages, especially the Middle Kingdom and the Eighteenth Dynasty, a distinct archaizing tendency.

The relatively successful rule of the Kushite kings was not to last. Assaults on Egypt by the Assyrian king Esarhaddon and then by his successor Ashurbanipal between 671 and 667 BC brought about the downfall of the Kushite dynasty. The last of these southerners, Tantamani, withdrew to Napata, leaving Egypt to be ransacked by the Assyrians who carried away much booty to Nineveh. It is not clear what precise plans the Assyrian kings had for Egypt after this conquest. In the event, however, they seemed content to allow the country to be administered through local authorities, like the God's Wife Shepenupet II in Thebes, who was actively supported by the very influential mayor of the city Mentuemhat. In the Delta the tendency to split into small principalities was aided no doubt by the awkward geography of the region, divided as it was from south to north by the branches of the Nile. Necho of Sais for unexplained reasons caught the attention of the Assyrian king, and his son Psammetichus, who ruled his own small realm at Athribis in the southern Delta, slowly built up a power base in the Delta with the help of Greek and Carian mercenaries. He finally reunited the whole of Egypt in 654 BC, his authority in Thebes established by the adoption of his daughter Nitocris as God's Adorer of Amun by the ruling God's Wife Shepenupet II.

The new Twenty-sixth Dynasty, the Saite, ruled Egypt with considerable success. The cultural renaissance started in the preceding dynasty continued and expanded; temples

and cults were revivified, an active foreign policy was pursued. Expeditions were sent into Nubia; a force under Necho II defeated Josiah, King of Judah, at Megiddo in Syria. Foreigners were encouraged to settle in Egypt and special arrangements were made for Greeks to set up a trading station under favourable terms at Naucratis in the Western Delta. Internally the country flourished and foreign trade relations prospered. The adoption of the demotic script as the standard form of writing, superseding hieratic, also led to an increase in the use of documentation. The Egyptians had from early times been devoted to documentation, establishing state archives and even private collections, but this tendency seems to have increased markedly from the time of the Twenty-sixth Dynasty.

The activities of the Saite kings inevitably led to their downfall. In Western Asia the dominant power now was Persia, and in 525 BC the armies of Cambyses invaded Egypt, defeating Egyptian forces at Pelusium in the Eastern Delta. With the end of the Twenty-sixth Dynasty the control of Egypt fell into foreign hands and the effective native rule of the country came to an end. Under the Persian kings of the Twenty-seventh Dynasty Egypt was treated as a satrapy of the Persian Empire. To a great extent the country was left to administer itself as a distant outpost of Persian rule, which seems in general to have been benign. There was, nevertheless, much unrest in the country, details of which are unclear. On the death of the Persian king Darius in 405 BC, a degree of independence returned to Egypt, but the rather

45 Massive siltstone lid of the sarcophagus of the God's Wife of Amun Ankhnesneferibre. In this powerful representation she is shown holding the crook and flail, traditional symbols of Egyptian kingship. From Thebes. H.2.57 m.

ephemeral rule of the kings of the Twenty-eighth and Twenty-ninth Dynasties probably existed under the constant threat of interference from the Persians. During the final Manethonian dynasty, the Thirtieth, a kind of revival took place with considerable temple-building in the Delta and as far south as Philae at the head of the First Cataract just south of Elephantine. But this flicker of a renewal of native rule never ignited properly, and it came to an end with the reoccupation of the country by the Persians in 343 BC. They in turn were to be ousted by the Macedonian forces of Alexander the Great, which reached Egypt in 332 BC.

Ptolemies and Romans

The kings of the Thirtieth Dynasty are commonly regarded as the last native rulers of Egypt. But the Pharaonic Age did not end with the deposing of Nectanebo II in 343 BC. The Ptolemies who ruled Egypt from 305 to 30 BC, although Macedonian Greek in origin, behaved as the true successors of the Pharaohs of the preceding ages. They owed

46 Finely carved head in greywacke of a king, probably Nectanebo I of the Thirtieth Dynasty. The head of the uraeus, now missing, may have been an insert in gold. H.38.5 cm.

OPPOSITE 47 Striding figure of a king in grey granite, a traditional pose, here presenting one of the Ptolemies. It is unfinished, never having received its final polish and inscription. H.92.5 cm.

no allegiance to an outside power; their base and their regime were entirely Egyptian. Unlike the Romans who followed, whose emperors also superficially behaved as Pharaohs within Egypt but who were wholly Roman, the Ptolemies seem to have done their best, at least at first, to accommodate their rule to Egyptian ways. They administered in Greek: through Greek officials at the top level, but locally through Egyptians who were not obliged to learn Greek, although it would probably have been to their advantage to be able to communicate in the language which had become the lingua franca of the Mediterranean world.

After Alexander invaded Egypt and founded the city of Alexandria, his campaigns took him as far as India, and he died prematurely in 323 BC. His great empire was then divided into three satrapies, with Ptolemy Lagus, one of his bodyguards, administering the Egyptian division, firstly for Alexander's brother Philip Arrhidaeus and then for his son Alexander. In 305 after the death of young Alexander, Ptolemy declared himself Pharaoh of Egypt, instituting thereby the Ptolemaic Dynasty. Alexandria became the capital of the country; it was the final resting place of Alexander's body, and its future character was to be that of a Greek city, described as being not 'in Egypt' but 'near Egypt'. It was cosmopolitan, and was to become the intellectual centre of the Greek world, a magnet for philosophers, poets and dramatists, who blossomed in the benevolent regime nurtured by the Ptolemies. The cultural centres in Alexandria – the Museum, an academy for scholars, and the great Library – nourished the Greek intellectual tradition in particular, and its influence spread throughout Egypt wherever settlers established important enclaves of Greek life; such were the towns around the lake in the Faiyum like Karanis, Tebtunis, Philadelphia and Arsinoe, the special foundation of Ptolemais in Middle Egypt and the provincial town of Oxyrhynchus. At these and many other places Greek culture prevailed and was developed, and from their rubbish dumps have been recovered the earliest copies of many of the greatest Greek literary classics written on papyrus.

The Ptolemies equally endeavoured to maintain, if not actively promote, the indigenous culture of Egypt. The religious cults were respected, and the temples in many places added to or even replaced with great new structures. The outstanding monument to this sympathetic encouragement of Egyptian religious traditions is the temple at Edfu, the centre of the cult of Horus as a solar deity. For the Greeks, Horus could be equated with Apollo, and Edfu was called Apollonopolis Magna. The temple there was initiated by Ptolemy III Euergetes in 237 BC, and dedicated in 71 BC by Ptolemy XII Auletes. The structure survives almost complete, apart from the disfigurement of many of the reliefs inflicted in later times when the temple was inhabited by Christians and then Moslems. The temple is huge and completely Egyptian in plan and intention: in the many scenes of rituals and other ceremonies the presiding Pharaoh is Ptolemy, shown as an Egyptian king with his names written in cartouches and provided with the appropriate royal titles and epithets.

When Alexander the Great came to Egypt he gained merit with the Egyptians by visiting the famous oracle at Siwa, and more particularly by making offerings to the Apis cult – the worship of the bull-form of Ptah – in the temple of Ptah in Memphis. Ptolemy I, recognizing the importance of the Apis, invented – the word is scarcely exaggerating the process – a new Egyptian deity and cult, that of Serapis, which incorporated the cult of Osiris-Apis and elements of the Greek gods Zeus, Dionysus and Pluto. The new god was shown as a bearded man, rather more Greek than Egyptian in appearance, his great new temple in Alexandria being called the Serapeum. This last name has also been applied erroneously to the subterranean burial catacombs of the Apis bulls at Saqqara. This divine invention was to prove to be a great success, not only in Egypt but also as an export, one of the exotic deities who were later followed by devoted supporters in many places in the Roman Empire, including London.

The benevolent attitude of the early Ptolemies towards Egyptian cults and temples was so appreciated by the Egyptian priesthoods that in 196 BC a synod of priests meeting in Memphis issued a decree honouring Ptolemy V Epiphanes for his benefactions and services to the indigenous temples and cults. This decree was to be inscribed in hieroglyphs, demotic and Greek on stelae to be set up in temples throughout Egypt. The one surviving example, substantially complete as far as the texts are concerned, is the Rosetta Stone (EA 24), discovered in 1798, and in due course providing the key to the decipherment of the Egyptian scripts.

Egypt flourished agriculturally and economically under the Ptolemies, but the Hellenization of the general fabric of the administration, and thereby of Egyptian daily life, began to cause resentment which eventually led to civic disturbances and even open revolt. As time advanced, Egypt began to attract the attention of the Romans, whose power in the Mediterranean world was growing. As early as the reign of Ptolemy Philadelphus commercial relations with Rome began, with the export of grain being of great importance for both sides. As ever, Egypt incurred the envy of its neighbouring Hellenistic state of Syria, and an invading force from that country was met and defeated in 217 BC by Ptolemy IV Philopator at Raphia to the east of the Delta. In 170 BC, however, Antiochus Epiphanes of Syria succeeded in seizing the Egyptian throne. The Romans did not view this change of regime favourably, and in 168 BC they issued an ultimatum which led to the Syrian withdrawal and the reinstatement of Ptolemy VI Philometor. There was no further serious Roman intervention in Egyptian affairs until

48 Scene on the rear wall of the temple of Dendera. On the left Cleopatra VII is shown in the company of Caesarion, her son by Julius Caesar, making offering to Isis, Horus (as Horsamtawy) and Osiris (as Unnefer).

the reign of Cleopatra VII who, by her wiles – according to the various traditions – ensnared Julius Caesar, by whom she had a son Caesarion, and then Mark Antony. She was clearly a woman of talent; for example, she is said to have been the only Ptolemy to learn Egyptian. But her support for Antony and opposition to the Romans under Octavian fatally ruined her ambitions. In 31 BC at the battle of Actium the Romans triumphed; her suicide and that of Antony followed, and Egypt was absorbed into the Roman Empire.

So ended the existence of Egypt as an independent power. From the time of the first emperor, Augustus (as Octavian now became), Egypt was strictly governed by a prefect specially appointed, and the country was carefully administered by Roman officials. The Roman emperors may have been shown in temple scenes as Pharaohs with their names in hieroglyphs in cartouches, but these were empty gestures which signified little to the Egyptians. Foreigners ruled the land, and foreigners of different kinds would continue to do so until the revolution of 1952, when a new native ruler, Gamal Abdel Nasser, often described in Pharaonic terms, became President.

Reading and Writing

49 The god Thoth, scribe of the gods, here ibis-headed; he holds a scribe's palette in his left hand. In the temple of Ramesses II at Abydos.

Apart from mummies and pyramids, perhaps the most characteristic aspect of ancient Egypt, as far as the generality of people goes, is the hieroglyphic script. It is immediately recognizable; it is very decorative and often therefore mauled and distorted by modern designers who do not understand what they are using, or, rather, misusing; it is known to be a way of writing a language which is equally beyond the comprehension of most people; it is strikingly evocative of many different aspects of the mysterious culture of ancient Egypt, according to the knowledge and interests of the individual.

Hieroglyphic script

It may be supposed that a very large part of the population of Egypt in antiquity was in a state of respectful ignorance as far as the hieroglyphic script was concerned. Literacy, although greatly prized by certain classes of Egyptian society, was not common, and probably not thought to be particularly useful for peasants, labourers, even possibly small tradesmen. The last might just be able to recognize a few signs appropriate to their daily activities, and also to employ the simple signs for numbers necessary in commercial transactions. For most people, hieroglyphs would be known as the formal script used in the scenes on the walls of temples and occasionally elsewhere in texts set up for celebratory or proclamatory purposes in and around towns, and in those places throughout Egypt where such texts needed to be seen, even if they could not be read and understood.

An illiterate but intelligent Egyptian might be able to recognize the cartouche of the reigning king. The cartouche-form would be known as the graphic container of a royal name, and if it were to be seen with signs which as a group could be associated with the monarch, then by enquiry and repetition it could be identified on sight. However, our illiterate but intelligent Egyptian would not be able to 'read' the signs, particularly as names in cartouches had their signs arranged as much for graphic effect as for intelligibility.

A versatile script

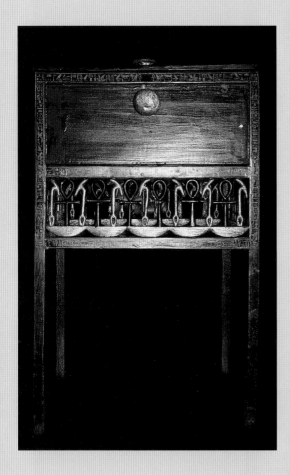

Some individual signs from the great range of hieroglyphics would be quite generally known because, again, they would be met in the general run of life. In particular there were the signs representing amuletic values, such as the eye of Horus 𓂀 , offering 'completeness' and 'protection', the *djed*-pillar 𓊽 , possibly representing the backbone of Osiris, and offering 'stability'. Signs like 𓋹 , the *ankh*, meaning 'life' and 'living', although not strictly amuletic but of powerful force, and 𓌀 , the *was*-sceptre, indicating divine power, were to be seen held in the hands of the great deities shown on temple walls, and also familiarly used, partly decoratively, on small personal objects like scarabs. The scarab-beetle itself 𓆣 , which has its own proper place in the corpus of hieroglyphs with the meanings 'become, come into being', would be very familiar as an object used in jewellery; its meaning as a sign in the hieroglyphic script, and its great religious significance, might not be fully appreciated by most ancient Egyptians.

50 A chest from the funerary equipment of Tutankhamun, demonstrating the decorative use of amuletic signs: the open-work frieze is made up of repeated groups consisting of *ankh*- and *was*-signs on oval baskets, meaning 'All power and life'. H.70 cm. (Cairo Museum)

In the classical periods of Egyptian history – the Old, Middle and New Kingdoms – the corpus of hieroglyphic signs amounted to many hundreds. It is difficult to give a precise figure because many signs were used rarely, or for limited periods of time, or for specific categories of text. A standard list gives over seven hundred and fifty forms, but some of these may be classed as variants of more common signs. The preparer of a hieroglyphic text might modify a form for a particular reason; he might, for example, place in the hand of a man-hieroglyph a weapon or a ritual object in order to clarify or emphasize the sense. The standard god-sign could be modified by the addition of different headdresses. In this respect the script was very flexible; variants would be instantly comprehended by a reader who was fully acquainted with the hieroglyphs. Signs could be varied, or used in combination with others, to produce what may rightly be described as graphic puns – plays on signs rather than on words. Elaborate examples were developed in the Graeco-Roman Period when each great temple, such as Dendera, Esna, Edfu, Kom Ombo and Philae, used ranges of signs quite specific to each place, and incomprehensible at first sight even to visitors from elsewhere who were otherwise competent in reading the texts in their own familiar temples.

These hieroglyphic writings of the monumental texts of the Graeco-Roman Period represent the last and rather desperate stage of the noble script which characterizes the inscriptional writings of the great earlier periods. They appear three thousand years after the beginnings of ancient Egyptian writing, about which much remains to be discovered. It used to be thought that the idea of writing came to Egypt from the east, from Mesopotamia, where the Sumerians developed a semi-pictorial script which in time became cuneiform. Until recently, the earliest Egyptian texts – primitive hieroglyphs used very sparingly – could be dated to about 3100 BC, a few centuries later, perhaps, than the accepted dating of the earliest Sumerian texts. However, during recent years, small bone and ivory 'tickets' or dockets have been found in pre-First Dynasty royal tombs at Abydos, the place of burial of kings of the First and Second Dynasties, and of their predecessors of what is, for convenience, termed Dynasty 0. Signs engraved on these dockets are without a doubt the earliest recognizable hieroglyphs. Not in every case are they identifiable with signs in the later, well-established corpus, but there are enough clear parallels, not only in form but also in the way they are grouped, to demonstrate with considerable certainty that the Egyptians were developing their own script almost two hundred years earlier than previously believed. It is perhaps premature to be able to declare categorically that the Egyptians invented writing, or that they developed writing more or less contemporaneously with the Sumerians. It does not truly matter who came first; it was not a competition. Writing was developed for quite specific reasons, which were undoubtedly common to Mesopotamia and Egypt. And one thing is clear: the scripts that became the elaborate systems of Egypt and Mesopotamia were totally different in form and character, and, it must be admitted, in versatility. Hieroglyphs were totally Egyptian, and could not be used for the writing of any other language. The Mesopotamian script developed into cuneiform, which, on the other hand, could be used for many different languages, and which in due course could become an international script in the Near East. It was, however, never employed for the writing of Egyptian.

The paucity of written material from the earliest periods, and the narrow range of signs used until the middle of the First Dynasty, make it difficult to determine how Egyptian writing began, and who supervised its progress. The process may have been inspired and promoted by official initiative, but it seems more likely that the first steps were taken by individuals involved in trade. In the movement of goods in a country like Egypt, all length and very little breadth south of the Delta, the nature and source of goods brought from distant parts of the country, and even from abroad, required some identification. This could be accomplished by a tag or docket with a sign – some recognizable mark – known to indicate the object or product concerned, also the name of the place of origin. A pot containing beer or wine or fat could have its distinctive sign written on it in black, perhaps in a form which simplified a more exact 'hieroglyphic' sign. This was the beginning of a cursive script, which would develop side by side with the hieroglyphic script. Numerals to indicate quantity were written with simple strokes, based on a decimal system, with special signs for 10, 100 and later 1000, etc.

To trace the full early development of the hieroglyphic script is not at present possible, and perhaps may never be so. It is clear, however, that the convenience and usefulness of writing was gradually but reasonably quickly appreciated, and that in a matter of a few centuries, the number of hieroglyphs grew rapidly, and enabled those who employed them to write names, inscribe royal objects with label texts, prepare simple funerary monuments, and generally to exploit the new medium of communication with confidence and a degree of virtuosity. Very few of the signs found on the earliest inscribed objects are not included in the established corpus of hieroglyphs of the Old Kingdom and later. Furthermore, there is clear evidence that the meanings of particular signs in the South obtained equally in the North. It was a peculiar script, it must be admitted, but it suited the Egyptians for whom its disadvantages were less apparent than its advantages. In its enlargement and development in the centuries that followed the early dynasties, it became a script tailor-made for the writing of the Egyptian language. It was scarcely influenced in any way by the writing systems that developed elsewhere in the Near East and did not, in consequence, become a flexible, universal medium for communication beyond the land of Egypt.

At some point, quite early in the process of hieroglyphic evolution, the state – however one may conceive this at the beginning of the third millennium BC – through its bureaucracy began to coordinate and systematize writing. Signs, which might represent men, women, animals, birds, natural objects, buildings, tools, all the elements of life, were roughly standardized in form and in significance, for meaning and for phonetic value. A small group of signs were, to use an anachronistic term, alphabetic, representing single sounds: so ⊂⊃, a mouth, was used for the letter *r*; 𝄈, the leg and foot, for *b*; 𓅓, the owl, for *m*. These were, in our terms, consonantal; there were no purely vowel hieroglyphs. Some signs represented two consonants, others three; some signs were simply representational, confirming the nature of the words they accompanied. So, words signifying strength or violent action were commonly 'determined' by the sign of an arm striking with a stick, 𓂡; words concerned with some human activity connected with the head,

51 Part of the false door of the priest Iry, who is shown seated with his wife Inet at an offering table. The hieroglyphs are finely formed and carved. Provenance uncertain. Fourth Dynasty. H. 71 cm.

like 'think', 'eat', 'talk', were determined by a seated man with one hand raised to his head, 𓀠. Other signs could represent in writing precisely what they looked like, with or without the support of other, consonantal, signs: ⊙, the sun-sign, for example, could by itself stand for the sun, the sun-god Re, for *hrw* meaning 'day', and also as a determinative for words relating to time. Similarly, the sign representing the simple plan of a building, ⊏⊐, was used by itself for *pr* 'house'; within other words starting with the same phonetic group, such as *pri*, ⊏⊐ ⌂ △, 'go forth', the sign is supplemented by ⊂⊃ (*r*) and determined by walking legs to indicate movement; the same sign ⊏⊐ was also used to determine words meaning buildings of various kinds, in which it had no phonetic force, as in 𓊨 ⌂, *nst* 'seat', in which the 'letters' of the Egyptian word are represented by the pot-stand sign, supplemented by ⌒, the letter *t*, which here indicates the feminine status of the word. It is wholly unknown how the hieroglyphic system developed in this complex way.

It will, I suspect, be evident from the preceding paragraph that hieroglyphic writing is not a simple sign-by-sign method of representing ancient Egyptian. The complexities have only been touched on, to suggest a few basic ideas, and to indicate that even for an educated ancient Egyptian, mastering the script – to read it and to write it – was no easy task. It should also be remembered that to read or write an Egyptian text needed not only knowledge of the hieroglyphs, but also understanding of the language written in that complicated script. The process of modern decipherment is discussed later in this chapter, when the dual nature of the task facing the early decipherers will need to be appreciated.

The language

Undoubtedly the ancient Egyptian language had already become a well-developed instrument of communication on the spoken level substantially earlier than the first faltering steps towards its being written down. It is, in its way, an individual language, with characteristics that associate it with both Western Asiatic (Semitic) languages and sub-Saharan (Hamitic) tongues. In its classic stage, usually considered to be the Egyptian of Middle Kingdom texts, it is a rich medium of communication with varied and elaborate constructions, well developed to allow the expression of complicated ideas through particular grammatical and syntactical procedures. It is a language capable of broad literary use, although possibly less adequate for conveying what might be termed philosophical argument. In the realm of literary composition, there are no works that can easily be considered the equivalent, or even the precursors, of the philosophical works of the Greeks. Whether this absence was due to an inability of the ancient Egyptians to conceive and probe problems of ethics, metaphysics and logic, to the inadequacies of the Egyptian language itself, or to the 'earthy' nature of the hieroglyphic script, remains very much in doubt.

During the centuries when the hieroglyphic script moved from being a practical device, useful for simple trading and accounting, to become a rich confident vehicle for religious, historical and literary texts, progress in the enlargement of the corpus of signs and their adaptation for the written expression of the ancient Egyptian language was undoubtedly taken into the control of schools and offices, supervised by high officials including the priests of the great religious cults. It is evident from the way in which the writing of Egyptian formally developed, in regular hieroglyphic signs, that minds of very considerable ability were at work, belonging presumably to priests and administrators who not only guided the development of the script but also had a remarkable instinct for the formation of the signs and the ways in which they were laid out in an inscription.

The basic forms of all hieroglyphs were relatively simple, but many signs were capable of receiving elaborate and detailed treatment. Similarly, the simple basic forms could be further simplified – a process which existed contemporaneously with the initial development of the script – and this simplification developed into a cursive form of writing which is now called hieratic. This hieratic will be considered shortly. At the top end of the scale of excellence in terms of form, the best hieroglyphs were executed by artists who treated each sign almost as an individual work of art, whether it was on a small ivory label, a wooden panel in a tomb, or a substantial stone stela.

Papyrus

Before discussing scribes, their training, their status and their products, mention must be made of an invention which provided the scribe with a writing material that remained unsurpassed until the invention of paper. Papyrus was the product of a marsh plant, *Cyperus papyrus*, which in antiquity flourished in Egypt in the swampy area of the Delta and along the banks of the Nile where cultivation had not led to the draining of land. It is not clear whether the plant was cultivated or just harvested from naturally flourishing thickets. The plant slowly disappeared from Egypt during the latest periods of antiquity, although as a writing material papyrus was used until medieval times. It was a principal medium for written documents and literary compositions in ancient Greece and Rome. A strange survival of true Egyptian papyrus can be found today in Sicily along the shallow rivers near Syracuse; it had been imported for cultivation and for the manufacture of the writing material in Ptolemaic times. Huge areas of wild papyrus also can be found today in Sudan.

52 Papyrus thickets flourishing along the banks of the Ciane river in Sicily. The plant was introduced to the island in Ptolemaic times.

This writing material is itself called papyrus from the Greek name, which in turn may be derived from the putative Egyptian *pa-per-aa*, 'that of Pharaoh', 'the product of Pharaoh', a term not actually found in Egyptian sources, but possibly used in later times; this would suggest that it was a royal monopoly. The writing material was manufactured from the spongy pith of the flower stems of the papyrus plant, which can grow to a great height. The stems are roughly triangular in section, and the pith is contained within a hard outer skin which can be easily stripped away. It is almost white in colour and full of fibres running the length of the stem; it was cut into lengths, sliced longitudinally into strips which were laid side by side, and overlaid with a further layer of strips at right-angles to the first layer. This 'mat' of strips was then turned into a homogenous sheet of fairly even texture in which the natural juices of the plant acted as the binding agent. The exact procedure followed by the ancient papyrus-maker is not certain, and indeed it is not unlikely that it changed from time to time. Of surviving papyri, some of the thinnest and finest come from the Middle Kingdom; the splendid papyrus used for *Books of the Dead* and for important state documents in the New Kingdom is generally rather thick, but of very even quality; much of the papyrus used in later times was seemingly made with less attention to quality. From all periods there are examples of fine and coarse texture, just as in modern times the quality of papers varies immensely. In their attempts to produce papyrus equal to an average ancient quality, modern makers differ over whether the lattice of strips should be 'welded' by being placed between sheets of cloth, or not, by beating with a wooden implement, or by squeezing under pressure. Other methods are employed by commercial papyrus-makers in the 'factories' and 'papyrus-institutes' which proliferate in modern Egypt wherever the tourist penetrates, but their products

53 Unrolled papyrus. It contained *The Book of the Dead* of the high priest of Amun, Pinodjem II. From Thebes. Twenty-first Dynasty. H.33 cm.

bear little resemblance to the fine papyri of ancient times. On first being made, ancient papyrus was almost white in colour; in time it changed to a pale brown, a dun colour, just as the flesh of a cut apple turns from white to brown on exposure to the air. This change of colour is clearly distinguished in ancient representations: in tomb scenes of daily life showing scribes at work in the offices and on the estates of important officials, the papyri on which they write are painted white, as if the sheets are newly made; in royal tombs of the New Kingdom in which ritual texts are laid out on the walls as if they were written on enlarged papyrus rolls, the colour is pale brown, indicating that the texts are reproduced from mature copies.

Papyrus is a superior material for writing. It is light, flexible, and smooth enough to receive ink from a brush without spluttering. The largest sheets made in antiquity – the size no doubt determined by practical considerations in the process of manufacture – were about 48 cm in height and 43 cm in width (18 × 16 in). Large sheets could be halved or cut into quarters to make smaller sheets. For long continuous texts, sheets were joined together to produce a roll – the term 'scroll' rarely being used in the Egyptian context. The earliest identified papyrus fragments have been found in the tomb of Hemaka, a high official of the First Dynasty, at Saqqara. They are uninscribed, and there is some doubt about their identification as true papyrus. Yet the existence of papyrus rolls at this early period is clinched by the hieroglyphic sign ⟨⟩, found in small texts from Saqqara and Abydos. The sign represents a papyrus roll, fastened and sealed with a lump of clay, more clearly shown in later examples of the sign, ⟨⟩, where the cord tying the roll is indicated, its ends sticking out from the seal.

Papyrus was the primary writing material of the scribe: it was used for major official documents like the Great Harris Papyrus in the British Museum, the longest known text, 41 m (134 ft) in length, consisting of seventy-nine written pages; it was used for religious texts placed in tombs, such as copies of *The Book of the Dead*; in daily life it was used for letters, wills, memoranda, judicial documents, literary texts, so-called scientific works – medical, mathematical – and all kinds of documents which might be needed in a developed society. It was easy to store, and there is good evidence that substantial archives of official documents were filed away at administrative centres throughout Egypt, and also in temple 'libraries'. Personal and family archives and estate documents were also kept and maintained, as rare survivals, especially from the later periods, attest. If required, documents could be produced and used as evidence in court cases many years after they were written. When stored in good dry conditions, papyrus was very durable: some years ago, in the British Museum, a religious text was unrolled for the first time after three thousand years, revealing over 7 m (22 ft) of the roll without the use of any relaxing agent. Unfortunately, damp, fire and termites are all wholly destructive of papyrus; it is therefore surprising that so much has survived from antiquity. Sadly, the bulk of what has survived consists mostly of religious and funerary texts, often in multiple copies. The wonderfully rich official archives that have survived in Western Asia owe their preservation to their consisting of clay tablets, which are even more durable if baked in a building destroyed by fire.

Most of the large papyri which have survived were written for official purposes under the supervision of official bodies in scriptoria manned by specialist scribes.

Generally, papyrus was not available for the use of private persons, although numerous letters and short memoranda have been found which are wholly private and personal in character. Most of these occasional documents were written on reused pieces of papyrus, often quite small – such texts are usually termed palimpsests. It is not unlikely that most of these casual writings were probably prepared informally by trained scribes, taking private commissions outside their official duties, or by trained but 'failed' scribes who had not found places in state or temple offices, or on the estates of

The Great Harris Papyrus

This monster document, once in the collection of Anthony Harris, was acquired by the British Museum in 1872. It contains principally a detailed list of the donations made to the temples throughout Egypt by King Ramesses III. It was compiled in the reign of his successor Ramesses IV, and the document ends with a commendation by the deceased Ramesses on behalf of his son. It is an outstanding example of the documents produced in the state chancellery; it is of full height, of superb quality, and written in the best official script of the New Kingdom.

54 Part of the Great Harris Papyrus. From Thebes. Twentieth Dynasty. H.42.5 cm.

important officials. For such people, with useful contacts, it was probably not difficult to get hold of papyri, decommissioned from archives or otherwise considered disposable. Old texts were easy to expunge, although sufficient traces often remain to allow at least the nature of the erased writing to be determined.

Cursive scripts and documentation

In considering the nature of ancient Egyptian writing, its status in the community and the ability of Egyptians to read and write, it is not surprising that most people today (and indeed since late antiquity) invoke the hieroglyphic script. It is what we see when we go to Egypt or visit museums with displays of reliefs, inscribed stones (stelae) and sculptures. Hieroglyphics, as noted earlier, characterize Egyptian culture; the Egyptians themselves described them as 'god's words'. Even in ancient times, therefore, a kind of sanctity pervaded hieroglyphs, and it is clear that as a formal script it was protected and revered by the small body of scribes who oversaw the writing of texts, religious and secular, which were to be carved or painted on the walls of important buildings. Such hieroglyphic texts had ponderous significance but may not have been readable by many Egyptians outside the scribal field. So little is know about the education of Egyptians that the extent of literacy can only be estimated in the broadest terms. One might expect that the young who might be destined for positions in the bureaucracy of the State would receive training in the preparation of documents as well as in the procedures of administration, but one may question whether such training would have extended to their being taught to read and write in the full scribal sense. It is not known, but it seems unlikely. It is even more unlikely that senior officials would have written out reports, or have read the documents submitted to them. In Egyptian writings it is quite commonly said that a person 'hears' a document, which clearly suggests that it is read out to him. Nevertheless, it is not reasonable to suppose that reading and writing were the exclusive preserves of the scribes, who, as we know from many scribal 'training' texts, had no small opinion of the importance of their calling and the superiority of their abilities. 'Be a scribe' was the call that encouraged the young to put their noses to the grindstone of letters. To be a scribe was to be guaranteed a comfortable, respected existence, as was once the case for civil servants and teachers in our own society.

In the context of ordinary Egyptian life, away from the grandiose, impressive sphere of the temples in which the scenes and texts employed the primary hieroglyphic script, reading and writing were concerned principally with the cursive script, hieratic, and in the latest periods, demotic. It was indicated earlier in this chapter that the cursive use of hieroglyphs emerged almost contemporaneously with the formal script. To write a sign or a group of signs to indicate the contents of, for example, a pottery vessel did not require the painstaking drawing of hieroglyphs in all their precise forms and details. Quickly drawn, slightly abbreviated forms were quite adequate. This process of cursive writing developed side by side with the formal script, and began to acquire its own graphic peculiarities when writings were made on papyrus. From the earliest dynasties, the scribe used a rush as his writing implement, and a palette which held two small blocks of solid colour: one black, carbon-based and prepared probably from the soot deposited on cooking pots; the other red, ochre-based. The end of the rush was turned into a brush, probably by chewing, and trimmed to suit the needs of the scribe. This brush, charged with ink from the palette as in watercolour painting, was then used as if in painting, the individual signs being made rapidly before the ink dried. As time advanced the hieratic forms, by further abbreviation in many cases, became quite distinct from the original hieroglyphic signs. Frequently they were run together to form groups, called ligatures, in the way that in modern handwriting the individual letters are 'joined up'. Modern cursive

55 Record in demotic of a loan transaction of grain. The unsealed, unrolled part of the document contains a summary copy to prevent fraud. From Thebes. Ptolemaic Period. H. as shown 23 cm.

handwriting in general lacks the style and grace of the copper-plate and italic styles which were formerly taught in schools. Similarly, the best hieratic writing is very stylish, distinguished by a bold character with flourishing signs and ligatures, and very elegant forms, all deriving from the essentially cursive nature of the script. In the Old Kingdom, hieratic texts were usually written in vertical columns, the signs being made mostly without ligatures. Middle Kingdom formal texts were more cursive, while private documents, now written in horizontal lines, were much more cursive and much less easy to read. In the New Kingdom, scribal practices became even more idiosyncratic: some scribes of senior position like Qenhikhopshef, a member of the workmen's community in the Theban Necropolis in the Nineteenth Dynasty, wrote in a hand that is so difficult to read that he could never have been used to 'pen' an important and readable official document.

By the New Kingdom, hieratic in fact had become such a separate method of writing Egyptian that the spellings of words in an hieratic text were in many cases very different from what might be found in contemporary monumental inscriptions. The very language used in the compositions of the time, both literary and more especially secular, official texts, was very different in many ways from the language of hieroglyphic texts of the same time. The latter were generally couched in a form of Egyptian which harked back to the classic monumental Egyptian of the Middle Kingdom; and this form of Egyptian, conservative and backward-looking, continued to be the standard form used for inscriptions, and even for established religious texts written in hieroglyphs, right down to the Graeco-Roman Period. The vast quantities of text which have survived in the great temples of that last period preserve a kind of atrophied Middle Egyptian, mostly written in hieroglyphs of almost impenetrable obscurity. By this late time, hieroglyphs as a medium of writing Egyptian had ceased to fulfil a meaningful role in the expressing of Egyptian culture. They could still be used for the writing of significant texts, as in the case of the Rosetta Stone; but to a very great extent they had outlived their usefulness, and were on their way to becoming the esoteric symbols interpreted imaginatively by writers of late antiquity like Horapollo of the fifth century AD, possibly an Egyptian, whose *Hieroglyphica* contains an extraordinary mishmash of wild and speculative interpretations together with some which may be considered reasonable.

56 Part of a wall painting from the tomb of Nebamun showing a scribe presenting his account of the goose census. From Thebes. Eighteenth Dynasty. H.71 cm.

At the beginning of this chapter it was suggested that a very large part of the population of Egypt was in a state of respectful ignorance of the hieroglyphic script. The same was probably the case as far as hieratic was concerned. At this point it should be noted that neither of the terms hieroglyphic and hieratic are particularly apposite to describe the two scripts as they existed in their heyday. They were terms used by the Greeks to describe the scripts as they were seen to be used in their own times. Hieroglyphs were literally 'sacred carved letters', not an unreasonable description of the signs making up the texts found on the walls of the great Graeco-Roman temples; hieratic was the 'priestly' script, probably because in the later periods it was used in a rather regularized form for the writing of religious texts on papyrus. In these later periods the everyday script was what the Greeks called demotic, that is the script 'of the people', not indeed an inappropriate description. In the nineteenth century, at the time of decipherment, the term enchorial, meaning 'of the land' in Greek, was commonly used to describe demotic.

Throughout Egyptian history, inasmuch as can be judged from surviving written material, the scripts used in most areas of Egyptian life were cursive – hieratic in its various stages from the earliest dynasties down to the Twenty-sixth Dynasty, and demotic thereafter until the early centuries AD. Hieratic slowly developed its own graphic characteristics which, over the centuries, distanced it more and more from hieroglyphs. Demotic carried the process further, so that in the reading of a demotic text very little relationship with the ancient pictorial script can be discerned, although the language written in demotic is distinctly a later stage of the Late Egyptian found in the hieratic texts of the New Kingdom.

The knowledge of writing was the preserve of the scribal class, and it is doubtful to what extent ordinary Egyptians, even those highly placed in the country's administration, were capable of handling written documentation. This does not mean that there was little appreciation of the importance of the written word among Egyptians, generally speaking. Few transactions in daily life, beyond the very simplest, could be carried through without documentation, and it may be supposed that those who could write and calculate were at a considerable advantage vis-à-vis their unlettered compatriots. In those rare communities in Egypt where literacy was unusually common, like the workmen's village in the Theban Necropolis, today called Deir el-Medina, even quite simple private transactions were recorded – usually not on papyrus, but on smooth flakes of limestone easily obtained from the excavated material from tombs. Such casual 'notes' are called ostraca, a term also applied to fragments of pottery vessels used for the same purpose, particularly in later periods. The relatively lowly but literate inhabitants of the workmen's village could prepare their own documentation 'in house', either individually or by family members. For most Egyptians, however, this convenience was not available; when legal documents had to be prepared and written, members of the scribal class had to be involved. We use lawyers for similar purposes today, but at least we can read and check that we are not being misled or cheated.

57 Hieratic ostracon with a text concerning the ownership of a tomb granted to the workman Amenemope by the oracle of the deified King Amenhotep I, but subsequently disputed. From Deir el-Medina. H.15 cm.

Documentation clinching agreements could be deposited in official archives and then retrieved for consultation as needed. Such procedures are well attested in recorded cases from antiquity, as in the long-lasting dispute over a piece of land set down in inscriptions in the tomb of Mose at Saqqara. He was a treasury scribe in the great temple of Ptah at Memphis in the reign of Ramesses II, and he challenged a court decision made against Nubnofret and Huy, his parents, over the administration of the land in question. Documents had been called up from archives in Piramesse, the administrative centre of the State at that time, but some did not support the claims of Nubnofret and Huy. Mose was able to prove that the documents had been falsified with the collusion of state officials; he found living witnesses to confirm the truth of his parents' statements; and the court's decision was reversed. Here was a dispute about a grant of land made to his descendants by a ship's captain called Neshi during the reign of King Ahmose at the beginning of the Eighteenth Dynasty, three hundred years before Mose's time; it was possible to summon up documentary evidence from a central depository to support, or disprove, the statements of witnesses; that some of the documents were falsified is beside the point, especially as it was possible to establish the charge of falsification to the satisfaction of the vizier's court in Heliopolis. It is also worth noting that the archive in Piramesse must have been moved there from elsewhere, possibly Memphis, after the foundation of that city and its becoming a royal residence and capital during the Nineteenth Dynasty.

The procedures revealed in Mose's inscriptions show to what extent state archives could be used even for private legal disputes, and demonstrate the reliance ancient Egyptians placed on documents – the written word. It is in a sense both comforting and unnerving to observe at what an early date the value, even the absolute reliability, of written evidence had come to be appreciated and recognized. The confidentiality of documents was also understood, and to some extent protected. In the long text setting out the duties of the vizier, inscribed in a number of viziers' tombs of the Eighteenth and Nineteenth Dynasties, the matter is clearly presented:

Any document for which the vizier may send from any court, provided that they are not confidential, should be taken for him along with the register of their curator on the seal of the judges and scribes attached to them, who were in charge of them. Then he should open it [i.e. the document] and after he has seen it, it should be taken back to its place, sealed with the vizier's seal. Now if he asks for a confidential document, let it not be released by the [archival] curators. But in the case of any agent sent by the vizier about it on behalf of a petitioner, he [i.e. the curator] should let it go to him.

58 Ostracon of an elaborately dressed woman suckling a child. The girl (?) in the lower register holds a mirror. From Deir el-Medina. New Kingdom. H.16.5. cm.

The Scribe

The scribe, undoubtedly a person of importance in Egyptian society, held a position that carried with it valuable privileges, including exemption from military service, from the corvée by which labour was recruited for great national building projects and other similar activities; he was also spared the payment of taxes. As all of these obligations, burdensome to unprivileged Egyptians, were in practical terms controlled and operated by scribes – the only people who could draw up lists and make assessments, and who were in consequence well placed to favour some and penalize others – the possibilities for exploitation and corruption were manifold. These dangers were recognized: best

administrative practice, as outlined in wisdom texts and in the detailed duties of the vizier, stated quite clearly how decent and uncorrupt administration should be carried out. But the Egyptians who operated the governance of the country at the practical level were no better and no worse than similar officials in many countries, ancient and modern, who can exploit the system to their own advantage.

'Scribe' was a very flexible title in respect of the duties involved in individual cases. It was applied to a wide range of officials and also to artists: there were scribes who sustained the administration throughout the land, the clerks who wrote documents and handled communication at the lowest level; some scribes specialized in accounting and the activities of trade and taxation, who among other activities made crop assessments for fiscal purposes before the crops were harvested. Senior officials were happy to bear the title of 'scribe'; some were even categorized as 'king's scribe', the precise significance of which is uncertain. The best practical scribes exercised their talents in those offices where important official documents were prepared. Some with particular graphic abilities may have been identified early in their scribal training and encouraged, or directed, to become artists, the 'outline scribes' who laid out scenes and inscriptions in tombs and temples. Large numbers of scribes were employed on the preparation of religious texts written on papyri, in particular copies of the funerary compilation 'The Book of coming-forth by day', now generally known as *The Book of the Dead* (more will be said on this well-known series of 'chapters' or 'spells' in chapter 6). Here it may be mentioned that many copies of *The Book of the Dead* were illustrated with vignettes of particular ceremonies and activities in the afterlife, and those who executed these small drawings and paintings were also scribes, often highly accomplished artists, and in some cases possibly the same scribes who wrote out the texts.

59 Quartzite figure of the high official Pesishuper who served the God's Wife of Amun in Thebes. He is shown as a scribe, squatting on the ground with an open papyrus on his lap. From Thebes. Twenty-fifth Dynasty. H.52.5 cm.

There are very few indications in surviving records from ancient Egypt of the gradual increase in literacy among the classes of people whose work brought them into close contact with written matter. It is generally thought likely that scribes maintained a kind of monopoly over reading and writing; it was their ability to handle the scripts, whether hieroglyphic or cursive hieratic and, later, demotic that placed them in such an important position in the life of the country. And in this respect the focus must be on the scribe who writes, keeps accounts, maintains records and runs the administration. Things began to change, however, in the last centuries of Pharaonic Egypt, when large numbers of foreign immigrants settled in parts of Egypt, especially the Delta and the environs of Memphis, a city that was always a centre – often the most important centre – of official life in Egypt. The Greeks in particular were literate, used papyrus as their principal medium for writing, and displayed an ability to exploit the written word far beyond what was usual or even possible for the Egyptians. It could not have been overlooked by intelligent Egyptians that the Greeks in Egypt enjoyed a far greater freedom in the use of the written word, not least because the Greek alphabet was far less complicated than the Egyptian cursive scripts. The same was also the case in those foreign communities that used Aramaic and the Hebrew script. The possibility of simplification may have been considered by the Egyptian scribal profession, although there is no evidence that change was seriously contemplated. Scribes were, like most specialists, rather conservative in outlook and very protective of their trade and the content of their trade, namely, writing in Egyptian scripts.

When Egypt fell under Macedonian-Greek control in the late fourth century BC, dramatic changes were experienced by native Egyptians. The new rulers of Egypt spoke Greek and administered the land through Greek-speaking senior officials. The centre of state control became Alexandria, a city founded by Alexander the Great, and from the outset predominantly Greek in character and in its institutions. Egyptians for the most part understandably continued to speak Egyptian, to use the demotic script for writing their documents, personal papers and literary texts; but an increasing necessity to know Greek and to be able to read it rested upon those Egyptians whose duties brought them into contact with Greek-speaking and -writing officials. There seems, however, to have been no official policy to diminish the importance of the native language; on the contrary, there is good evidence that the Ptolemaic rulers wished to do what they could to engage the loyalty of native Egyptians, and as part of this policy actively maintained Egyptian religious cults and supported the construction of great temples dedicated to long-established Egyptian deities. Furthermore, in these temples hieroglyphic texts were carved to an extent never previously found in the temples of earlier periods. As indicated earlier, the bulk of these religious texts, composed in good classical Egyptian, were carved in hieroglyphs which included new and strange forms, differing from temple to temple and scarcely offering a medium of communication except among the few select people – the priests of each temple and their scribal associates – who needed to understand what was carved on their temple's walls.

As a useful, living form of writing, hieroglyphs had in effect become obsolete. It was still possible to produce a text written in hieroglyphs of a reasonably standard classic form, as was the case for one writing of the decree inscribed on the Rosetta Stone of

60 The Temple of Isis at Philae, now reconstructed on the island of Agilkia; an outpost of Egyptian religion in late times and the site of the last known hieroglyphic text.

196 BC (discussed shortly); but the fact that the same decree was inscribed in demotic and in Greek indicates how important it was to 'publish' this decree in forms that could be read and understood more generally than the hieroglyphic version. A parallel could be drawn with the use of Latin for monumental inscriptions on public buildings and memorials up to the present day; but the pretension behind such little-understood texts has lost its force as fewer and fewer people can remember the little Latin which they may have learned in school. So, with hieroglyphs, their use diminished steadily in Roman times, and the last known dated text of AD 394 occurs in the temple of Philae just south of Aswan. This may, however, be considered an eccentric survival, offering no proof that the once great monumental script remained alive and well.

Texts written in Egyptian on papyri continued to use the demotic script for secular purposes until the third century AD; religious texts of the old tradition on papyri were rather atrophied in the ways they were written, both hieratic and hieroglyphic in very stylized forms being used from the late Pharaonic Period until the second century AD at least. The great change came about in the third century coincidentally in time with, and partly also as the result of, the conversion of Egypt to Christianity. There may have been a positive revulsion from the ancient scripts, considered to be pagan, but there were even better practical reasons for the adoption of writing based on the Greek alphabet, with the addition of seven letters derived from demotic to represent sounds particular to spoken Egyptian. The Christian scriptures were translated from Greek into Coptic – the term which is now used for written Egyptian and for the Church in Egypt – and the Coptic script rapidly became the sole medium for the writing of the Egyptian language. The name Coptic derives ultimately from the Greek Aiguptios, 'Egyptian', which became

Qipt in Arabic. After the Arab conquest of Egypt in AD 640, Arabic became the official language of the Egyptian state and was increasingly spoken by native Egyptians, who also converted in increasing numbers to Islam. Yet Copts, i.e. Egyptian Christians, remained a substantial minority in the country, and the Coptic language continued to be spoken in parts of Upper Egypt until the fifteenth century; it continued in use for liturgical purposes in the Coptic Church, where it is still employed, although little understood.

61 Limestone ostracon from the monastery at Deir el-Bahri; a letter written in Coptic complaining of the mistreatment of people by a certain Psate. Seventh century AD. H.12.7 cm.

Decipherment

It is not surprising that knowledge of the hieroglyphs quickly faded. Although Greeks and Romans who wrote about Egypt showed great interest in this strange writing, no serious attempt was made, even by the very inquiring Herodotus who was in the country in the fifth century BC, when the ancient script was still used with understanding, to find out and describe how hieroglyphs functioned as a form of writing. After hieroglyphs ceased to be used, there was little possibility of penetrating their secrets. Hieroglyphs were associated with the strange, mystic cults popular in the Roman Empire and supposedly derived from the practices of ancient Egyptian religion. Nobody knew that hieroglyphs were in origin the original script of the Egyptian language. The way was open for highly speculative interpretations. *Hieroglyphica*, the treatise ascribed to Horapollo, about whom next to nothing is known, became the most commonly cited source of information on the ancient Egyptian script. The explications of individual signs given by Horapollo are mostly fanciful, although in many cases shreds of truth can be detected. Nevertheless, the treatise *Hieroglyphica*, dated to the fifth century AD, seemed close enough in time to the age of the Pharaohs – the prime time of hieroglyphic

62 The Rosetta Stone. The top band of text is written in hieroglyphs, the middle in demotic, and the lowest in Greek. Granite. H.1.14 m.

use – to be considered a reliable source. It was also written in Greek, and during the Renaissance and later into the eighteenth century, works written in the classical languages had the status almost of Holy Writ. Scholars who were interested in the ancient world relied substantially on Herodotus and Diodorus Siculus for the history and culture of Egypt, and on Plutarch for the religion of Egypt. Consequently, most attempts to penetrate the mysteries of hieroglyphs began with Horapollo, and in many cases ended with him. Little progress was made while hieroglyphs were considered to be cryptic, and in need of being decoded. Prospects improved when scholars began to address language as well as script. A few notable advances included the suggested identification of the oval cartouches found in inscriptions as royal names by the Abbé Jean Jacques Barthélemy (1716–95), which was generally correct. Even more significant was the correct belief of Georg Zoëga (1755–1809), a Danish antiquary, that Coptic, the language of the Egyptian Christian Church, was a survival of the ancient tongue. Zoëga devoted much time to the study of Coptic, and his researches on obelisks and on the Coptic texts in the Museo Borgiano, in Rome, were in due course to prove useful to Champollion, the ultimate hero of decipherment.

Interest in ancient Egypt in European countries increased dramatically as the eighteenth century advanced, as books were published on travels in the Near East, and as Egyptian antiquities entered public collections like the Ashmolean Museum in Oxford and the British Museum in London. Exotica like mummies and divine statuary whetted the appetites of the curious, and the need to provide more and better information about the ancient Egyptians offered a distinct challenge to interested scholars. It was very apparent that few real advances could be made until the ancient scripts could be read, and that there was little chance of achieving this goal without the discovery of some form of bilingual text of which one language was known. The opportunity arrived, as usually the case in such impasses, quite fortuitously, and as the result of politics and warfare, not of scholarly effort.

The Rosetta Stone, bearing the required biliteral text, turned up in 1799. In the previous year Napoleon Bonaparte had invaded Egypt with a strong force, with the dual aim of establishing French influence in the Eastern Mediterranean and threatening the British hold on India. His expedition included a Commission of Sciences and Arts, made up of scholars in a wide range of academic disciplines, charged with discovering and publishing all there was to be known about Egypt. A member of this Commission was Lieutenant Pierre François Xavier Bouchard, who in July 1799 was in charge of the strengthening of the defences of a fifteenth-century fort just outside the Delta port of Rashid (Rosetta). In the course of the work, a block of dark stone, 1.14 m (3½ ft) high, was retrieved, part of a large, free-standing monument, which was inscribed with texts in three different scripts. Lieutenant Bouchard could recognize the top band of text as being written in hieroglyphs, and the bottom band in Greek. The central band, as later became established, was in the demotic (enchorial) script. He rapidly realized the potential scholarly value of this stone and he passed it on in due course to the Institut d'Égypte set up by Napoleon in Cairo as the base for the Commission of Sciences and Arts. From a preliminary reading of the Greek text, Bouchard with a colleague, Michel-Ange Lancret, also a member of the Commission, gathered that the inscription

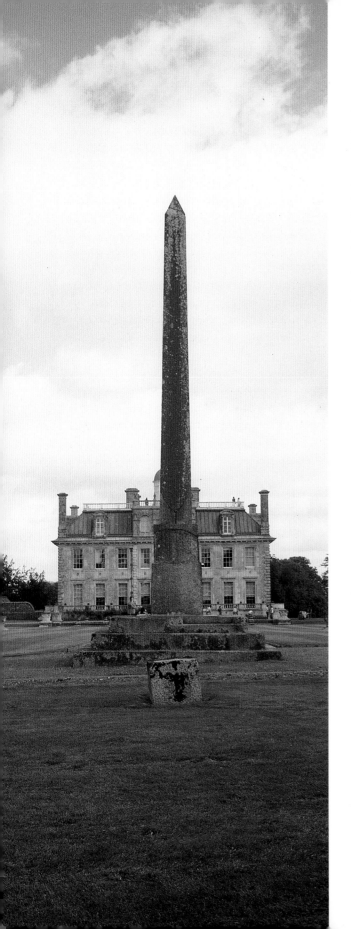

concerned a member of the Ptolemaic Dynasty and also that it was to be carved in hieroglyphs, the documentary script and Greek, and copies set up in all the principal temples of Egypt.

In Cairo the stone, now placed on public exhibition in the Institut, generated a great deal of interest. The Greek was more carefully studied, and it was established that the text recorded a decree of 27 March 196 BC by which a royal cult was set up for Ptolemy V Epiphanes by the principal priests of Egypt meeting in conclave in Memphis, as a mark of gratitude for the king's great generosity towards them. Copies of the three bands of text on the stone were made, and sent in early 1800 to Paris. At last it looked as if a real breakthrough could be achieved in the elucidation of the ancient Egyptian scripts; then could follow the translation and understanding of Egyptian inscriptions, and eventually an unparalleled acquisition of knowledge about ancient Egypt, derived from primary Egyptian sources and not from 'second-hand' classical texts. It would not, however, happen overnight.

After the defeat and capitulation of the French army in 1801, the Rosetta Stone, along with other antiquities collected by members of the Commission, was surrendered to the British army, and in 1802 it arrived in London. By the end of the year it was deposited in the British Museum. Casts of the stone and copies of the texts were made and distributed to universities and interested scholars, and the race towards decipherment began in earnest. It should perhaps be emphasized again that decipherment is a somewhat misleading description of the process by which the hieroglyphic script was penetrated and understood. It was not a code that had

63 Kingston Lacy House in Dorset with, in the foreground, the granite obelisk from the temple of Philae. The Ptolemaic cartouches in the texts were seen by William John Bankes, correctly, as offering useful clues towards decipherment. H.7 m.

to be cracked, but a form of writing with an underlying language, and the scholars best equipped to attempt the task were linguists with some knowledge of the languages of the Near East. Among the first to achieve a little success were Antoine Isaac Silvestre de Sacy, a scholar at the Collège de France in Paris, and Johan David Åkerblad, a Swedish diplomat with considerable knowledge of oriental languages. Their moderate successes, however, were surpassed by those of the young Jean-François Champollion, for a time a pupil of de Sacy, who had from his earliest years been completely devoted to the solving of the mysteries of hieroglyphs. His only serious rival was Dr Thomas Young, a brilliant British physician and natural philosopher, a Fellow of the Royal Society and an accomplished linguist. He and Champollion kept in touch with each other's researches and exchanged information, Young being a little more generous than Champollion. Serious claims have been made on Young's behalf that he should be credited with priority in solving the problems, but it was Champollion without a doubt who was able to present the first reasoned and acceptable elucidation of hieroglyphs. His *Lettre à M. Dacier relative à l'alphabet des hiéroglyphs phonétiques*, presented to the Académie des inscriptions et belles-lettres in Paris in September 1822, is now recognized as the culmination of his researches, and the beginning of the scientific study of the ancient Egyptian scripts and language.

The *Lettre*, however, was but the beginning. Nevertheless, it proved the stimulus for other scholars and a basis of knowledge to be used by them. In retrospect progress seems to have been rapid. At first it was principally a matter of discovering the meaning of words and their 'alphabetic' values; then there was the teasing out of the grammar and syntax of the ancient Egyptian language. The way was led by Champollion himself, but he sadly died in 1832, with his life's work only partly achieved. By then there were many others to take the work forward, particularly in France, Germany and Great Britain. By the time of his death Champollion was able to make reasonable translations of standard texts, and to establish the nature of much that was written on papyrus in hieratic and demotic. His immediate followers made great advances in the reading of Egyptian texts, but it was not until late in the nineteenth century that some proper understanding of the Egyptian language was achieved. It was not the end of the voyage of discovery, and scholars still struggle to elucidate the finer points of Egyptian grammar. Much remains to be done, especially in the field of lexicography. It is rare to find a new text of any length or substance that does not contain a new word or two, or contexts in which apparently established meanings do not apparently apply. Hieroglyphs continue to exercise their own particular fascination, and for many scholars the archaeology of written Egyptian is just as seductive and rewarding as the excavation of ancient sites.

64 Jean-François Champollion (1790–1832). Painted by Léon Cogniet, 1831. (Musée du Louvre)

4

Records and the Official Word

One of the notable features of the civilizations of the ancient Near East, including Egypt, was the rapid acceptance of writing as a method of communication as well as being a way of recording details concerning commodities. There is, however, a great difference between labelling a jar and composing texts which contain all the features of a well-established language. The latter assumes properly constructed sentences, following internal grammatical and syntactical rules, and the existence of both composing writers and comprehending readers. It was no simple process to move from notation to composition, and it did not happen quickly.

Although there is evidence for the existence of papyrus as a writing material as early as the First Dynasty, sadly no examples of written papyrus have survived from the earliest dynasties. The most diverse and significant group of early written texts comes from Abusir in the Memphite Necropolis; they form a true archive, discovered by illicit diggers in 1893. The documents are part of the record of daily activities within the pyramid complex of King Neferirkare Kakai of the mid-Fifth Dynasty (*c.*2470 BC), mostly post-dating the burial of the king. The bulk of the archive is made up of lists, inventories, records of inspections, duty-rotas – the expected documentation concerning the work of the staff employed in the maintenance of the funerary cult of the dead king. Among the most interesting documents are copies of two letters written in the reign of Djedkare Isesi; the texts, unfortunately, are only partly preserved. Both are couched in a framework of epistolary formulae which seems to have been established for use in communications of this kind at an early date, possibly the early Fifth Dynasty.

It is not surprising that the burden of both of these letters is complaint: things have not been done as promised; ration supplies have not been delivered. In neither case is the problem easily understood, but both letters demonstrate quite clearly that the ability to write and grumble was well appreciated at an early date, and that Egyptians took to pen (brush) and paper (papyrus) very readily, as literate people have done throughout history. However, it is no good sending a letter unless you know that the recipient will be able to read it, or have someone available to read it for him. The idea of communicating by writing is by no means an obvious method of sending and receiving information. The Egyptians, however, clearly recognized the many ways in which the written word could be exploited, not just for record purposes, as had been the case during the earliest dynasties – as far as we know. The practice may have started at the highest level, with the king writing approvingly to one of his high officials concerning a task well carried out, or to enquire whether the plans for a project will in fact be completed. These royal communications, although in effect letters, are more precisely considered as formal royal decrees; but they, nevertheless, represent a personal message from the sovereign to his servant. 'Letters' of this nature were understandably greatly cherished by the recipients, and were sometimes inscribed for posterity on the walls of their tombs. Such copies of royal missives were included by the vizier Senedjemib in his mastaba tomb at Giza. They are from Djedkare Isesi of the Fifth Dynasty, who enquires about progress of certain works undertaken by Senedjemib, in particular a lake in the king's jubilee palace. While the general tone of these letters is favourable to the vizier, they also contain a suggestion by the king that perhaps progress is not quite what is claimed: 'Can it be the case that what you say is intended to set Isesi's mind at rest? Let My Majesty know at once how the matter truly stands.' In spite of this questioning of

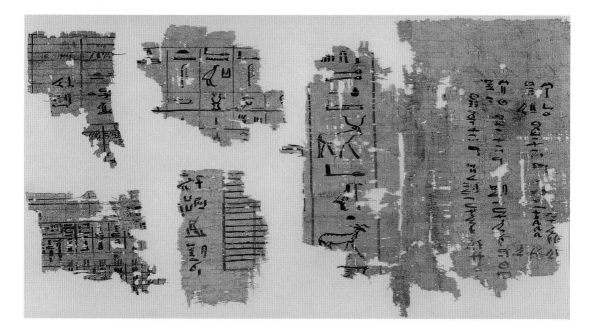

65 Part of the Abusir archive, a group of Fifth Dynasty documents from the pyramid complex of King Neferirkare Kakai. Some of the texts on this fragment are written in careful hieroglyphs, and some in early hieratic. H.20.5 cm.

the veracity of Senedjemib's report, the general tone of the royal decree is so laudatory that the vizier was delighted to have the text included, with other similar decrees, in his mastaba chapel.

Details of 'postal' services in ancient Egypt are scanty, but it appears to have been not too difficult to have letters sent over long distances, even for people in modest circumstances. The Nile was the ideal line of communication, and there would always be boats travelling south and north, with helpful crew-members prepared to carry and perhaps even deliver a letter for a small consideration. The most interesting royal decree of a private nature from the Old Kingdom was sent by King Pepy II, presumably from the region of Memphis in the north, to Harkhuf, a high official based in the first southern nome of Elephantine, some 550 miles to the south of Memphis. Harkhuf had led expeditions into Nubia in the reign of Merenre of the Sixth Dynasty, and then another in the subsequent reign of Pepy II, who became king at a very young age. Harkhuf had sent a dispatch to the king informing him of the success of this last expedition, and telling him of a dwarf (less likely a pygmy) which he was bringing back for his sovereign. Pepy's letter/decree to Harkhuf was so enthusiastic that it was in due course inscribed on the façade of Harkhuf's tomb at Aswan, set high in the cliffs on the west of the Nile, looking out over the river. The text in the tomb is laid out as it would have been in its original form as a papyrus document. After the date and the preliminary acknowledging of Harkhuf's dispatch, Pepy turns to the matter which is of greatest interest to him:

You said in your dispatch that you have brought back a dwarf ... like the dwarf brought back by the God's Treasurer, Bauwerdjed, from Punt in the time of Isesi. And you said to My Majesty, 'Never has his like been brought back by anyone who has reached Yam formerly' ... Come north to the Residence at once. Hurry, and bring with you this dwarf ... If he goes into a boat with you, select trusty men to be beside him on both sides of the boat in case he falls into the water. When he sleeps at night, select trusty men to be beside him in his tent. Make inspection ten times a night. My Majesty longs to see this dwarf more than the spoils of the mining country and of Punt. If you reach the Residence with this dwarf safe and sound with you, My Majesty will do more for you than was done for the God's Treasurer, Bauwerdjed, in the time of Isesi.

66 The façade inscription of the tomb of Harkhuf at Aswan, which includes the copy of the letter sent by King Pepy II to Harkhuf concerning the dwarf he had brought back from Nubia. Sixth Dynasty.

It is not surprising that Harkhuf included a copy of this royal missive in his tomb. Today, presumably, an equivalent laudatory letter from sovereign to private person might be framed and hung in some prominent position where it could be seen and, no doubt, commented on. Communication by letter, however, rapidly achieved an important position in the advancement of business, and in the general broadcasting of information about what might be happening on official and private levels. Sadly, papyrus is not a very durable material, unlike the clay tablets of Western Asia. Unless kept in favourable conditions – when it may survive for thousands of years – papyrus can be destroyed by damp, fire, insect infestation; a letter may be crumpled up and thrown away. In general, however, for private purposes a piece of papyrus could be reused, and there are few, if any, surviving letters written on papyrus that are not palimpsest – that is, written on top of an expunged earlier text. It is, in fact, remarkable that any private letters have survived from ancient times, even though the survivors must represent but a tiny fraction of what must have been written. Matters of grave concern could be addressed in letters. Among fragments of papyri found illicitly on Elephantine Island is a particularly complete letter, dating probably from the First Intermediate Period. The writer is a very high official with the titles, conventionally translated, of Count, Treasurer of the King of Lower Egypt, sole companion and God's Treasurer, Iruremtju; the recipient, the sole companion, lector priest and general, Merrenakht. It seems that Iruremtju has received information from Merrenakht concerning some robbery against him, and a caution not to do anything rash in connection with troubles in Nubia between the troops of Medja and Wawat. As is so often the case, the background is not clear, but Iruremtju is not at all prepared to compromise principle over convenience: 'It is better to approve of what is just than continual crookedness; it is a proper moment to deal with all the shortcomings of this Count [in this case named as Sabni], who is not one who is living on his own resources.' How one would wish to understand fully what lay behind this letter and the disreputable behaviour of Sabni!

Single letters intrigue because they refer to matters unexplained, and there is always the temptation to fill in the background by means of supposition. When more than one letter of an archive survives, then there is a better chance of understanding what is the concern of the letter-writer. Even so, the usual absence of the other side of the correspondence leads inevitably to speculation. Exceptionally, something may be discerned through the fog of uncertainty. A group of letters written by one person may provide unusual and enlightening information about individuals, places, activities, even thoughts, placed in a narrow set of circumstances at a particular time. Such information can be found in a small archive of letters and accounts dating to the Eleventh/Twelfth Dynasty, discovered in excavations in the hills above Deir el-Bahri in Western Thebes. The various documents, written in palimpsest on fairly well-preserved papyri, concern a small landowner called Hekanakhte who writes to members of his family concerning matters of agricultural business, and affairs causing difficulties within his household. It seems clear that Hekanakhte regards the tenure of his land as very secure, although one may suspect that political changes might well lead to his dispossession. He writes confidently:

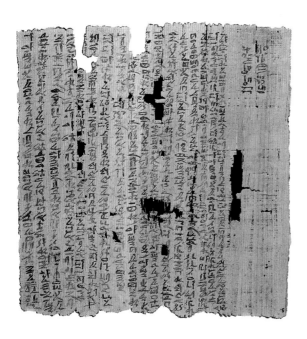

67 The verso of the first letter of Hekanakhte to his household. The address is written at the top right-hand corner, to be visible when the letter is folded as a sealed package. From Thebes. Eleventh–Twelfth Dynasty. H.28.4 cm. (Metropolitan Museum of Art)

Get Heti's son Nakht to go to Perha'a with Sinebnut to cultivate for us 5 measures of land on rent. And they shall take its rent from the cloth woven where you are. Now, if they have collected the value in exchange for the emmer-wheat that is in Perha'a, they shall use it there also. Then you will have no more concern with the cloth about which I said: 'Weave it, and they shall take it when it has been valued in Nebeseyet, and rent land against its value.'

In a second long letter Hekanakhte returns to this matter of renting:

See now, I have sent you by Sihathor 24 copper *debens* (a measure of weight) for the renting of land. Now let 5 measures of land be cultivated for us in Perha'a besides (the land of) Hau the Younger, with copper or with cloth or with barley, or with anything else; but only after you have collected the value there of oil or of anything else.

A matter of considerable concern for Hekanakhte, who was at the time living some distance from his main household, was the provision of adequate rations for his various family and staff members. It is known from independent evidence that there had been a succession of low Niles in the First Intermediate Period and early Middle Kingdom, and that some parts of Egypt had suffered from virtual famine. It seems that Hekanakhte had received complaints from his household that things were tough. He retorts:

> See, the whole land is perished, while you are not hungry. When I came hither southwards I had fixed your rations properly … See, our rations are fixed for us according to the state of the inundation. Be patient, you people! See, up to today I have gone out of my way to feed you.

This matter of rations in difficult times was something that concerned Hekanakhte deeply, and he does not let the matter drop without further comment. He lists in detail the rations apportioned by him for each member of his household, and then chides them for complaining when they are clearly so much better off than others around them, or indeed than the people where he is:

> See, one says 'hunger' about hunger. See, they are beginning to eat men here! See, there are no people who have received such rations as you anywhere else.

Already by this early period, about 2000 BC, a letter has become far more than a vehicle for conveying a piece of information or an instruction: it is a means by which anger can be ventilated, or suspicions levelled by the writer at the recipient. There was trouble over a lady in Hekanakhte's main household, possibly a second or replacement wife – today we might use the term 'partner' – or even concubine. Hekanakhte has heard that she is not being decently treated by some family members while he is away. That is not how things should happen. In his first letter he is evidently upset:

> Sack the housemaid Senen from my house – be sure of this – on the very day when Sihathor (probably the bearer of the letter) arrives. See, if she spends a single night more in my house – look out! It is you who let her do evil to my partner.

The position does not improve, for in the second letter Hekanakhte in some fury writes:

> Anyone who acts against my partner is against me and I am against him. See, we are talking about my partner, and it is known what should be done for a man's partner … Would anyone of you be patient if his wife had been denounced to him? Then should I be patient? How can I exist in the same household with you? You will not, it seems, respect my partner for my sake.

We shall never know how things turned out in this matter. No doubt the position was considerably more complicated than these passing references suggest – emotionally charged though they were – and it is not impossible that there may have been some recourse to law. The tantalizing snippets of information contained in letters provide wonderful opportunities for scholars with imagination to 'interpret' background, current events and outcome. The truth, sadly, is that what we find in such isolated documents can rarely be interpreted beyond a simple level; but what is preserved provides a flavour – sometimes a very strong and rich flavour – of how life was lived in such distant times.

We must be thankful that the ancient Egyptians learned so quickly how to use the noble means of communication through writing, and equally how to exploit the

68 View of the hill of Sheikh Abd el-Qurna, part of the Theban Necropolis. The entrances to a number of private tombs can be seen.

written word for the recording not only of great events, but also the trivialities of daily life. A boring series of instructions can be enlivened by a human comment or two. This is seen in an Eighteenth Dynasty letter written by the mayor of Thebes, Sennefer, to a farmer Baki who has failed to achieve his quota. After pointing out in detail what Baki has not produced, Sennefer suggests ways in which the deficiencies can be made up, and he adds:

> Instruct the herdsman of cattle to get fresh milk in jars for me in advance of my coming. Watch it! You should not be lazy, for I am well aware that you are rather idle, and like eating in bed.

Here we have a mayor of Thebes, a person of no small importance in the administration of the great religious capital, writing on seemingly very casual terms to a simple farmer. That Sennefer should write apparently personally to someone who has failed to fulfil his quota is in itself surprising. That he could end his letter so informally is perhaps even more unexpected. It is not common for people to include in private letters things they might otherwise not wish to make public; things can be said in a letter without formality and with a lightness of touch. It is unlikely that Sennefer in his time would have expected the contents of a private letter to be 'leaked' – not that it would have been seen as a damaging act. He would, however, have been very surprised to know that his casual note to Baki would survive for about 3500 years, and be available for all to read in a museum in Berlin.

Ancient letters are fascinating, but represent a relatively insignificant part of the totality of documentary usage and survival from ancient Egypt. The importance of the scribe in Egyptian life has already been emphasized. The development of their own skills and the tendency to write everything down and then to preserve it in archives led undoubtedly to the establishment of state record offices in which written documents of all kinds could be deposited, to be consulted when necessary, and produced as evidence when matters under legal dispute had to be settled. The procedures are well illustrated by the case of Mose and land tenure cited in the last chapter. We must regret the loss of so much valuable documentation through the disappearance of ancient archives, but be grateful that, by chance usually, some examples of letters, accounts, inventories, wills, conveyances and personal settlements have survived.

The survival of some substantial official reports demonstrates the care with which matters of state interest were recorded, not just for current reference but for future usage. In the late Twentieth Dynasty there was much official worry about the security of tombs, both royal and private, in Western Thebes. Tales of robbery and desecration were circulating, and a commission was set up in the reign of Ramesses IX (c. 1110 BC) to make a physical inspection of parts of the Theban Necropolis, although not including the Valley of the Kings. The report of the commission is written in stylish official hieratic on a roll of fine new papyrus, 218 cm long and 42.5 cm (85 × 16¾ in) in height, which has survived almost complete. It is known as the Abbott Papyrus and is now in the British Museum (EA 10221). The members of the commission included senior officials from East and West Thebes, and it is quite clear that there were tensions between the representatives of the two sides of Thebes. The report is almost an official whitewash of the charges of robbery and desecration; it was almost certainly deposited in the record office of Western Thebes, which at that time was situated in the complex of Medinet Habu, the mortuary temple of Ramesses III.

69 Part of the Abbott Papyrus which contains the official report of the inspection of tombs in Western Thebes in the reign of Ramesses IX. The document is full-size, and beautifully written in the official hieratic of the New Kingdom. H.43 cm.

By an extraordinary sequence of events the contents of a second magnificently written report provide specific evidence of the robbery of one royal tomb of the Seventeenth Dynasty, which is scarcely noted in the Abbott Papyrus. The Amherst-Leopold II Papyrus, half in New York and half in Brussels, seems to have been written by the Abbott scribe and at the same time. It is 245 cm long and 43 cm in height (96 × 17 in). It contains a transcript of the examination of a number of workmen who were accused of robbing the tombs, but whose testimony is strangely neglected in the official (Abbott) report. The examination was instituted by the Mayor of Thebes who was determined to discover the truth behind the allegations of robbery. The document includes, in particular, an account of the robbery of the tomb of the Seventeenth Dynasty king Sobkemsaef II. It is quite remarkable.

The accused was a stonemason, Amenpanefer. Under examination he explained that he, with a group of fellow stonemasons, got into the habit of robbing tombs, and he named his associates. Four years previously, with seven others, not all masons but all craftsmen/labourers of various skills:

We set off to rob the tombs as was our usual practice, and we found the pyramid of King Sekhemre-Shedtawy, the son of Re Sobkemsaef, which was not at all like the tombs of the nobles which we usually went to rob. Using our copper tools we broke into the pyramid [the royal tombs of the Seventeenth Dynasty were regularly marked by small pyramids] … We took lights, went down and broke through into his burial space. We also found the burial space of his queen, Nubkha'as, placed beside his.

Amenpanefer then described how they plundered the two royal coffins and removed all the gold, jewellery and amulets, and then set fire to the coffins. They also took other

70 Part of the Theban Necropolis known as Dra Abu'l Naga, the site of royal tombs of the Seventeenth Dynasty.

pieces of tomb equipment in gold, silver and bronze. In all, they collected treasure measured at 160 *debens* of gold, a *deben* being approximately 90 g (3 oz). Each of the robbers received a share of 20 *debens*-worth of gold. But Amenpanefer was unlucky: news of the robbery became known to the authorities in Thebes, and he was taken and imprisoned in the office of the mayor of Thebes. However, he had with him his share of the 'takings' and he bribed the official scribe, Khaemope, who let him go. Amenpanefer rejoined his associates who compensated him for the loss of his share of the plunder – honour among thieves! He concluded his evidence: 'And so, along with the other robbers who are with me, we have continued up to now in robbing the tombs of the nobles and the inhabitants of the land who are at rest in Western Thebes. Also, a great many people of the land rob them, and are in effect our partners.' Amenpanefer's evidence was then corroborated by his fellow thieves under torture, and they later returned to Western Thebes to identify the tomb of Sobkemsaef. The ultimate fate of the robbers is

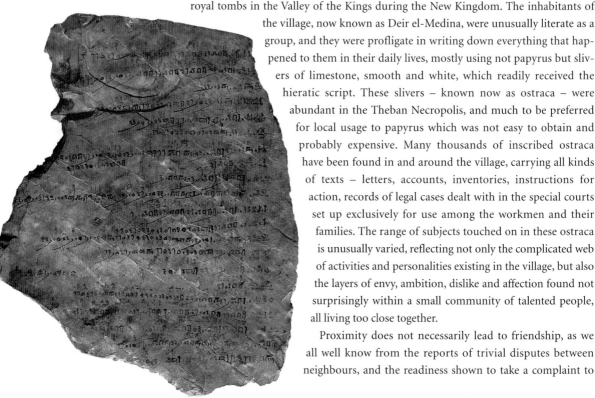

71 Human-headed jasper scarab set in a gold mount, the heart scarab of King Sekhemre-Shedtawy Sobkemsaef II. L.3.6 cm.

not included in the document, but we cannot doubt that it was severe, although not necessarily involving execution.

The coincidence of the survival of these two great documents is made even more remarkable by the existence in the British Museum of a jasper scarab set in gold and inscribed as a heart scarab for King Sobkemsaef. It must have been retrieved from the royal body during the robbery, but subsequently lost, presumably by the thief to whose portion of loot it had fallen. No information exists on how this piece was discovered in the mid-nineteenth century and in due course entered the British Museum's collection (EA 7876, fig. 71). Its certain association with King Sobkemsaef, and therefore with the events of the robbery of his tomb, is provided by the text inscribed on the gold mount of the scarab, which quite explicitly identifies it as the king's heart scarab that would have been placed in the wrappings covering the royal mummy.

Information about Egyptian life, legal practices, personal rivalries, the camaraderie of thieves and the corruption of officials provided by Papyrus Amherst-Leopold II in the context of the somewhat less dramatic narrative of the Abbott Papyrus lies well beyond what might be expected to be found in formal official reports. But how grateful we should be that the ancient Egyptians were so relaxed in their recording of matters that the flavour and colour of life in such distant times can be experienced vividly – one may even say 'convincingly'. The extent to which writing as a daily means of communication could be exploited is in no place more evident than in the small community of workmen whose professional lives were devoted to the making of the royal tombs in the Valley of the Kings during the New Kingdom. The inhabitants of the village, now known as Deir el-Medina, were unusually literate as a group, and they were profligate in writing down everything that happened to them in their daily lives, mostly using not papyrus but slivers of limestone, smooth and white, which readily received the hieratic script. These slivers – known now as ostraca – were abundant in the Theban Necropolis, and much to be preferred for local usage to papyrus which was not easy to obtain and probably expensive. Many thousands of inscribed ostraca have been found in and around the village, carrying all kinds of texts – letters, accounts, inventories, instructions for action, records of legal cases dealt with in the special courts set up exclusively for use among the workmen and their families. The range of subjects touched on in these ostraca is unusually varied, reflecting not only the complicated web of activities and personalities existing in the village, but also the layers of envy, ambition, dislike and affection found not surprisingly within a small community of talented people, all living too close together.

Proximity does not necessarily lead to friendship, as we all well know from the reports of trivial disputes between neighbours, and the readiness shown to take a complaint to

73 Deir el-Medina. In the foreground is the walled workmen's village. Additional houses and tombs are situated in the hillside.

OPPOSITE 72 Reverse of the large ostracon containing a register of attendances at work of the workmen of the royal tomb during the reign of Ramesses II. The reasons for absence are given, e.g. 'brewing'. From Deir el-Medina. H.38.5 cm.

the courts. A text written on a Deir el-Medina ostracon in the reign of King Sety II of the Nineteenth Dynasty, now in the British Museum (EA 65930), preserves an account – probably to be used as an aide-memoire for later formal recording – of a dispute brought to the village court by a workman, Nebnefer. It concerned the theft of a tool by a woman, Herya. She had been observed stealing the tool by another woman. The court put it to Herya: 'Are you the one who stole Nebnefer's tool? True or false!' Herya answers: 'False! It was not I who stole it.' She was then asked by the court to swear the great oath of the Lord, declaring, 'It was not I who stole it.' Herya then swore by Amun and the Pharaoh: 'If it is found that it was I who stole the tool …'; the consequence is not written down. She was then sent to her house along with a court attendant Pashed, and she brought back not only the tool but also a ritual vessel of Amun. Yet she still swore the great oath, declaring, 'It was not I who stole this tool.' Herya was then pronounced guilty by the village court; but sentencing was left for later when the vizier could review the matter, taking into account a similar case of the theft of a vessel in the time of an earlier vizier of the Nineteenth Dynasty. As is usually the case, no other document has been preserved recording the final outcome of this trial. It seems unlikely, however, in view of the theft of the ritual vessel and the desecration resulting from it that Herya would have got off lightly, unless the vizier had decided to probe the evidence a little more rigorously. The village court indeed had conducted the case rather arbitrarily, shocked, it seems, that such acts could have been committed in their close community.

The rich and extensive documentation surviving from the workmen's village has proved to be a very productive source for the study of many aspects of Egyptian life at the modest level of fairly ordinary people. But the inhabitants of Deir el-Medina were not very ordinary, and conclusions about matters occurring within the close community should not necessarily be applied to contemporary inhabitants of small communities elsewhere in Egypt. The fact that literacy was not rare among the workmen made them truly exceptional. Generally speaking, communication by the written word, as we have seen, was common in ancient Egypt, although no doubt confined to a relatively small proportion of the population – those who could read and write hieratic (and in later periods, demotic), or had easy access to someone who could act as a writer or reader.

74 Scene on a pillar in the burial chamber of Amenhotep II in the Valley of the Kings. Anubis embraces the king and offers him life; an example of a preliminary drawing which was never carved, wonderfully executed in black paint.

Now, you may well ask, what about hieroglyphs? The pictorial script which provided the essential form of signs, early adapted for the informal writing we now call hieratic, was throughout the Pharaonic Period the quintessential Egyptian form of writing. Hieroglyphs were *medu-netjer*, 'the words of the god', the god in question possibly being Thoth, the scribe of the gods. Hieroglyphs were special; hieratic was everyday and ordinary. Anything of real substance should be written in hieroglyphs, so that the weight and dignity of the forms themselves could provide extra potency to the subject. The forms were of the first importance: they could be carved in low relief or sunk relief; they could be painted; they could be sketched out – drafted – in paint or ink; and they could be small or monumental. For the most satisfactory effect, however, they should be carefully executed with as much internal detail as the medium allows. It is particularly useful, for example, to look at unfinished texts in royal tombs where it was more important to have the prescribed funerary texts laid out on the walls of corridors and halls in paint than that as much as possible should be carved and painted – which would have been ideal. In the tomb of Sety I in the Valley of the Kings many of the texts designed to facilitate the royal progress through the underworld are drafted in black paint. But what drafting! What clarity of line, what exquisite detailing! It can only be hoped that Sety himself, when he came to make use of these texts, appreciated the care with which the individual signs had been executed.

Hieratic might have been thought to be ephemeral; hieroglyphs, on the other hand, were for ever. The latter therefore were used for all important writings, texts in private tombs, and the inscriptions set up in out-of-the-way places to commemorate an expedition or to mark an achievement in foreign parts; but in particular they were used wherever important statements had to be made, religious rites set out, and royal successes declared in as public a way as possible. The ultimate use of hieroglyphs may be seen in the great temples of Egypt, especially those of the New Kingdom, on the walls of which the achievements or supposed achievements of the great monarchs could be presented along with the graphic representations of expeditions and conquests. The

75 Quartzite block, part of the 'Red Chapel' of Queen Hatshepsut, retrieved from the third pylon at Karnak. The elements of the scene and the texts are notably well set out. The queen as king offers incense before the shrine of the barque of Amon-Re.

religious and ritual texts, equally important in the overall concept of the temple, were mostly carved together with suitable divine representations within the halls of temples where they would not be seen by Egyptians in the normal course of events.

Although the hieroglyphs took precedence among the scripts of ancient Egypt, it is demonstrably clear that texts were always produced to what may have appeared to be the highest standard. What was the highest standard? Who legislated on quality? Did anyone in fact worry too much about quality? When modern experts in hieroglyphs examine the evidence of what has survived from antiquity, it seems not too difficult to distinguish the good from the bad. But are the criteria used for judgement today ones that would have been recognized by the ancient Egyptians? What is good and what is bad may often be decided outside the relevant context according to standards derived from what may be thought to be the very best. The modern scholar recognizes excellence in the fine, stylish texts of the Old Kingdom, particularly those of the Fifth Dynasty, or the exquisitely laid out scenes and texts of the Twelfth Dynasty exemplified by those on the shrine of Senusret I in Karnak. The mid-Eighteenth Dynasty inscriptions, especially of Hatshepsut at Deir el-Bahri and on the recently reconstructed red shrine in Karnak, and of Thutmose III also at Karnak, are models of careful composition and fine detail. The low-relief texts in Theban tombs of the reign of Amenhotep III, of Kheruef and Ramose, almost take away one's breath, so aesthetically satisfying are they in their perfection. But these are reactions of someone who is well-acquainted with the hieroglyphic styles and methods of execution over three thousand years of Egyptian history. It is why most people, even those who may not be connoisseurs of hieroglyphs, find the inscriptions in Graeco-Roman temples rather rebarbative. The signs may be laid out carefully, but individually they exhibit strange forms and variants and conceal 'perverse' values which seem to defy the relatively simple principles that governed the use of the script in what we now consider to be the 'best' periods.

It may not be unfair to maintain a somewhat dismissive attitude towards Graeco-

95

Roman temple texts. Undoubtedly what was carved on these late temple walls was fully acceptable to those who were responsible for the inscribing of the texts. For them, no doubt, it was not the forms of the signs that mattered but the underlying texts which, in fact, consisted mostly of well-established ritual hymns and recitations couched in good classical Egyptian. The consistency of the epigraphic (i.e. inscriptional) presentation of the texts – rather different in each of the late temples, but all for us not very attractive – indicates clearly that what was carved as hieroglyphs was not seen to be unacceptable to those who used the temples and conducted the rituals on a daily basis.

What then did the high officials and dignitaries of provincial places in Egypt think of their inscriptions during those periods when communication with the principal centres of power were poor? Funerary stelae and tomb inscriptions of the late Old Kingdom and First Intermediate Period in places like Moalla, Naga ed-Deir and Dendera are often well-executed but in rather indifferent styles, with strange forms for certain hieroglyphs, apparently locally developed and therefore locally acceptable. So much must have depended on the availability of craftsmen who were capable of producing work that would be acceptable in metropolitan terms. For the most part, the local demand for properly carved monuments, including funerary sculpture, could not be satisfied according to the best standards. The officials who required the work to be made presumably were content with products which we now consider to be hopelessly provincial. For them the important concern was that what was carved by their local, poorly trained craftsmen fulfilled its purpose: that the carved inscriptions could be read, and could properly convey the information they were designed to express.

Consider, for example, the rock-cut tomb of Ankhtifi at Moalla in Upper Egypt, to the east of the Nile and about twenty-five miles south of Thebes. The situation here was strange during the First Intermediate Period. Ankhtifi was nomarch of a group of nomes (provinces) south of Thebes including Edfu and Hierakonpolis. His allegiance during this very chaotic time lay with the Herakleopolitan rulers of the Ninth–Tenth Dynasties whose centre of power was Memphis far to the north. Almost within a stone's throw of Moalla was Thebes, where the local rulers were directly opposed to the Herakleopolitans, and would in due course overcome their northern rivals and establish themselves as kings of a newly united Upper and Lower Egypt in what is now known as the Eleventh Dynasty. Ankhtifi could have sailed downstream to Thebes in a few hours, but politics prevented any ordinary contacts. At Thebes a tradition of good craftsmanship and style persisted to a limited extent, although the metropolitan traditions of Memphis were scarcely to be noticed there during the Old Kingdom. Although Ankhtifi pledged allegiance to the northern kings, there is little evidence in his tomb that the fine Old Kingdom artistic traditions of Memphis were in any way known by or available to influence the craftsmen of the southern nomarch. Nevertheless, when the time came for Ankhtifi to have his tomb prepared, it was his local craftsmen who carried out the work, and it cannot be claimed that his mural scenes and texts were executed in the best tradition. Yet they are now admired for their *naïveté* and simple charm, which is surely not what Ankhtifi was aiming at. He needed the scenes to perform the ritual functions necessary for his posthumous existence, and his texts to express precisely what he wanted them to say. In this latter matter his craftsmen did not let him down. The hieroglyphs may be gauche and even careless, but they can be read, to tell, among other things, of the nomarch's great deeds.

In his semi-autobiographical texts Ankhtifi claims for himself those virtues which are regularly expected of nomarchs and high officials: 'I was as much concerned for the poor man as for the rich. I always found the solution to a problem when it was lacking in the land because of bad deliberations … I am an honest man with no rival, who can state his views openly when others have to remain silent.' Such statements were commonplace in early biographical texts; they tell us no more than what Ankhtifi thought about himself. But then he tells of a summons from the general of Armant, a Herakleopolitan stronghold apparently, between Moalla and Thebes. There was, it seems, a flaring-up in the continuing conflict with Thebes: 'I went downstream to the region west of Armant and discovered that all the forces of Thebes and Coptos had stormed the fortress of Armant … Then my picked forces ranged to the west and to the east of the Theban nome, seeking a straight battle, but no one dared to emerge from Thebes because they were afraid of my forces.' Having in this rather peremptory manner dealt with what for the modern Egyptologist stands out as the most significant historical episode in the nomarch's career, Ankhtifi then calmly proceeds to mention other, domestic matters which at the time had seemed of special importance to him:

76 The nomarch Ankhtifi leans on his staff, accompanied by attendants. From his tomb at Moalla in Upper Egypt. First Intermediate Period.

> All of Upper Egypt perished of famine, and every person became so hungry that he ate his own children. But I did not let anyone die of hunger in this nome. I organized loans of grain to Upper Egypt, and provided grain of Upper Egypt for the North. I do not believe that anything like this was done by any nomarch who preceded me.

Faced with a text of this kind, the historian of ancient Egypt is placed in a strangely ambivalent position. On the one hand, he would wish to regard some statements made by Ankhtifi as worthy of serious historical importance; on the other, he knows from experience and studying similar texts that the 'author' will have put the best interpretation on the events described. It would be fair to accept that Ankhtifi was at some point involved in a foray to the north, which then confirms a state of internome hostility in Upper Egypt during the First Intermediate Period. It would also be fair to conclude that the nomarch put the best gloss on what happened; he would not have reported a failure or a fiasco as such. As for his actions to relieve the famine, not only in his own nomes but also in more distant places, there is a strong similarity between what he says and some of the remarks of Hekanakhte writing perhaps only one hundred years later, not in a carved inscription. It seems as if anyone in a position to do so could claim to have provided relief for others: Ankhtifi publicly in his autobiographical text, Hekanakhte privately in a letter, but probably repeating clichés which were in circulation throughout the times of low Niles and shortages.

The historian of ancient Egypt is constantly faced with the problem of interpreting what may be stated positively in inscriptions. The position is well exemplified by the texts concerning the Battle of Qadesh and the heroic deeds of King Ramesses II. The great temples of the New Kingdom provided huge expanses of space in halls and on pylons, and on the external surfaces of the walls enclosing the sacred precincts – large blank canvases to be filled with scenes and inscriptions, mostly of an historical nature, celebrating the expeditions and martial exploits of the ruling monarch. By the nature of the sacred function of the temples, much of the wall area available for exploitation would not be seen by the majority of Egyptians. Nevertheless it was important that proper records of royal activities should be made in suitable grandeur, and scenes supported and explained by good hieroglyphic texts. The record was being made, just as an inscription in a private tomb was put up even though it might not be seen by many people. The act of inscribing, of recording, was in itself important. In the case of the great temples there were, happily, areas of external walls, and especially of pylons, where the record could be seen by more than the select few. And even if the viewers in most cases were not able to read the texts, they could see the noble representations and know that they celebrated the triumphs of royalty, even possibly of the ruling king.

In the fifth year of his long reign of sixty-seven years (*c.* 1275 BC) Ramesses II conducted a campaign against the Hittites of Anatolia, which culminated in the Battle of Qadesh. It was in many ways the most important event of his reign, and, occurring early in that reign, there was plenty of time available for his memorialists – artists and writers – to compile an exceptional body of commemorative material, adulatory and bombastic. The main places where Qadesh was celebrated were the additions Ramesses made to the Luxor Temple of Amenhotep III, his own mortuary temple in Western Thebes – the Ramesseum – and the great rock-cut temple of Abu Simbel in Nubia. What had been probably one of the best-executed sequence of Qadesh scenes and inscriptions embellished the outer walls of his temple at Abydos, most of which is now sadly lost. A reduced series was carved on the outer walls of the great Hypostyle Hall at Karnak. Not all the sites present the same material, but scenes and texts from all demonstrate that a scheme for celebratory decoration must have been drawn up at an early stage to ensure a high degree of consistency in what should be included. There are three distinct parts in the overall scheme: two long texts and the series of representations of the battle, including many vignettes of significant incidents with accompanying short texts. The main description of the battle, a separate, floridly composed account designed to eulogize the king and exaggerate his prowess, is known as the Literary Record. It is commonly carved apart

77 Part of the great depiction of the Battle of Qadesh on the Second Pylon of the Ramesseum. The mêlée of battle, with the vivid tumble of men and horses, is shown as never previously in Egyptian temple scenes.

from the reliefs, but is not found at Abu Simbel, where space for Qadesh was rather limited. It did, however, circulate as an independent composition, and two papyrus copies are to be found in the British Museum (EA 10181, 10683); it is sometimes called the Poem of Pentawer, the name being that of the scribe, not the author of the composition. The second part, another long text, was designed to be taken closely with the pictorial representations; it is considered to be the Official Report, a less flamboyant and more factual account of the campaign, providing the bald sequence of events. It is almost as if the compilers of the Qadesh memorial recognized that the Literary Record would be seen to be hyperbole rather than truth. It may be difficult for us to conceive what lay behind the thinking of those who designed the ensemble of Qadesh commemoration, other than the need to produce an overwhelmingly praise-filled presentation to glorify the success of the king.

78 Part of the surviving scenes of Qadesh from Ramesses' temple at Abydos. Carved in fine limestone, the representations of horse and men, including a Sherden, are more precise than those in the Ramesseum, but lack the latter's effective disorderliness.

It happened in Year 5 of Ramesses II. Could the compilers have had any kind of premonition that nothing as great would ever happen again in the royal reign, which as far as they could discern might last twenty or thirty years, but scarcely a further sixty-two? And so, early in his reign Ramesses II reached the highpoint, the apogee, of his military career, and his senior advisers chose, rightly as it turned out, to make it the one great event which would characterize his reign and the royal achievement. There would then be not much room left on temple walls for any later major success, if it happened. The graphic result, set out for many to see, and some to understand, was formidable. It established Ramesses' reputation as a great conqueror and saviour of the Egyptian people, in his lifetime and for many subsequent generations. It has also coloured the royal reputation once the texts could be read and the protagonist of the Qadesh battle identified. But, ironically, the success and reputation are hollow, the constructs of Ramesses' propagandists; they provide object lessons for us of how carefully we need to scrutinize what the written word can achieve through extravagance, overstatement,

79 The Literary Record of the Qadesh battle, written on papyrus, a copy made by the famous scribe Qenhikhopshef, who worked during the last years of Ramesses II and in subsequent reigns. His writing is very cursive and difficult to read. From Thebes. H.35 cm.

misrepresentation and invention. 'Lying' is a word that leaps to mind, but we should hesitate to apply it to the contents of the Qadesh compositions because it is not at all how the Egyptian compilers would have viewed their excesses in describing the exploits of the king. All Egyptian kings were divine, and the divine person can behave well beyond the possible capabilities of the ordinary human. The proper order of events, therefore, need not necessarily apply when it comes to composing an account of royal, that is to say divine, achievements. This approach was traditionally Egyptian, and not invented for Ramesses II. Nevertheless it does render the task of the historian of ancient Egypt somewhat difficult when the attempt is made to tease out the facts from the fantasy.

It is known from independent historical sources, especially Hittite records, that Qadesh was scarcely the victory claimed by Ramesses' memorialists. At the best it was a drawn contest, and indeed it is almost accepted as such in the Literary Record. After the serious engagements which made up the battle, in the course of which the two brothers of the Hittite King Muwattalis had been killed – a loss that threatened the future of the Hittite kingship – a message was sent by Muwattalis to Ramesses offering an end to hostilities. Ramesses clearly felt that it was a proposal worthy of consideration, and he put it to his military advisers that the fighting should stop. The advisers heartily agreed:

'Peace is exceedingly good, O Sovereign, Our Lord! There is no blame in coming to terms when you make it, for who can oppose you in the day of your fury?' And so the battle ended, and in due course the Egyptian army withdrew peacefully back to Egypt. The Hittites, on the other hand, as is well established from other records, remained in control in the field in Syria, having retaken territories previously owing allegiance to Egypt.

In this cessation of strife the best possible interpretation is put on Ramesses' decision to stop and withdraw his forces; but is this the same king whom Muwattalis characterized as 'Seth, as Ba'al in person', who in the heat of the fighting described himself as 'like Montu. I discharged arrows to the right and took captives to my left. In their eyes I was like Seth in his time. I found the 2,500 chariots, in the middle of which I was, tumbling before my horse. None found his hand to fight, their hearts disconcerted in their bodies because of fear of me; their arms were unable to shoot.' Thus a king should behave, and if his soldiers declare that he is not talking boastfully, they are not being disingenuous but just accepting the reality of the myth of royal omnipotence. And for us, in reading the words and viewing the scenes displayed so confidently on the walls of great temples, we need to consider them initially as the ancient compilers intended. They proclaim the greatness of the monarch in terms which surely were known to be extreme, but which were not expected to be believed in detail. How then can we be sure that we interpret the intentions of those important Egyptians in a way, or ways, that they would find acceptable? In reading the Qadesh texts we understand that much of the content is extravagant and fantastical; we can also see that threading their ways through the hyperbole are strands of narrative which present an outline of the battle and its preliminaries close to what actually happened. Truth and fantasy, as we have said, are intermingled, and it must be concluded that the monumental accounts of Qadesh, particularly the Literary Record, were composed with the intention of putting the best possible gloss on the campaign and Ramesses' part in it; and to do this, truth and fantasy were essential ingredients.

In this 'suspicious' mingling of fact and fiction may be discerned the power of hieroglyphs for the ancient Egyptians. Qadesh had happened, and its outcome was probably appreciated for its lack of real success; but failure could not be acknowledged, and by the carving of extravagant texts and scenes on great temple walls the reality of events could be significantly modified, and turned into something more appropriate for a royal and divine reputation. Herein lay much of the strength of hieroglyphs as a monumental script. It is written, it is inscribed, it perpetuates a myth; the signs, the *medu-netjer* ('words of the god'), have triumphed.

Faith in a Multiplicity of Forms

80 King Ramesses II is symbolically purified by two gods, ibis-headed Thoth and falcon-headed Horus. In the Hypostyle Hall, Karnak Temple.

Since ancient times a strong element of puzzlement has regularly accompanied the contemplation of Egyptian religion by non-Egyptians, and it has persisted down to the modern world with scarcely any variation in the nature and degree of puzzlement. Early classical visitors to Egypt, although coming from societies in which divinity was diverse and multi-formed, were baffled by the seemingly infinite plurality of the Egyptian pantheon, not only in numbers of deities but also in the forms in which the gods manifested themselves. Herodotus, who travelled to Egypt in the early fifth century BC, tried to find true parallels between the principal Egyptian deities and the Greek gods. He even maintained that the names of the Greek gods came originally from Egypt, although his comparisons and juxtapositions of Egyptian and Greek gods were not very persuasive. He wrote as if he were determined to make Egyptian religion more comprehensible than his impressions allowed him to believe. He also saw in many practices and institutions characteristic of Egyptian religion, like oracles and festivals, the origins of similar proceedings in Greek religion. Centuries after Herodotus' visit certain practices involving Egyptian cults and particular deities acquired their own strong following outside Egypt in the Roman Empire to its furthest borders. Isis worship, for example, became central to the devotions of certain sections of society, although the nature of the activities associated with the cult were far removed from their Egyptian origins.

For most visitors to the Nile Valley, Egyptian religion as manifested in the scenes on the walls of the temples and tombs remains remote from simple understanding: a conglomeration of images which can only be marvelled at or puzzled over. Their wondering is not greatly relieved by the explanations offered by their guides. But any thoughtful person, contemplating the dense undergrowth of representation and imagery, will also consider what Egyptian religion really meant to the ancient Egyptians and the ways in which it influenced belief and behaviour. A system which lasted apparently for three millennia could scarcely have survived so long as a meaningful focus for the undoubted religiosity of a people whose spirituality was clearly demonstrated in its writings and its burial practices. There must indeed be more to Egyptian religion than a system of arcane mysteries peopled by strange, fanciful gods.

One thoughtful visitor to Egypt in the winter of 1873–4 who considered the possibility

Identity is in the name

Any visitor to Egypt who passes observantly through the halls of Egyptian temples is struck by the peculiarities in the depiction of the Egyptian gods: they may be entirely in human form; they may be shown with the heads of animals or birds; they may take animal forms completely. When the hieroglyphic script had been forgotten, the identifying labels – the texts accompanying the divine representations – were meaningless, and the only way of distinguishing particular deities was by equating what was shown with descriptions provided by classical writers. So, an ibis-headed god was Thoth, and a cow-headed goddess was Hathor. But uncertainty could not always be so easily resolved. When hieroglyphs began to be understood again it soon became apparent that the identification of a deity was not just a matter of assigning a name on the basis of iconography. Thus, a goddess shown as a simple female figure with unspecific godly accoutrements might be Isis, Hathor or Nephthys, or some other divine lady. A god in one temple might appear to be quite different from the same god in another temple. Nothing turned out to be simple, nothing certain.

81 The Gayer-Anderson cat, animal manifestation of the goddess Bastet: a bronze almost life-size figure embellished with gold jewellery. Late Period. H.38 cm.

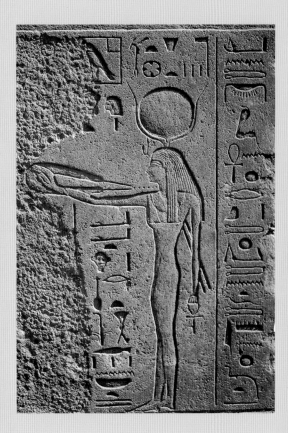

82 A goddess carved on a quartzite block from the Red Chapel of Hatshepsut at Karnak. The text above the figure identifies her as Hathor.

of there being more to Egyptian religion than imagery and inconsistent myths was Amelia Blandford Edwards. She was a successful novelist and travel writer, who took a positive interest in whatever activity she engaged in; she became a strong influence in the birth of popular Egyptology in Britain and America. At the end of her remarkable *A Thousand Miles up the Nile* she adds a short Appendix, 'The Religious beliefs of the Egyptians', in which she very perspicaciously asks: 'Did the Egyptians believe in one Eternal God, whose attributes were merely symbolised by their numerous deities; or must the whole structure of their faith be resolved into a solar myth with its various and inevitable ramifications?' She then quotes mostly in translation the opinions of English and French Egyptologists who, not surprisingly, view the question of divinity in Egyptian religion in differing ways; some, like Maspero, inclining towards the idea of a god 'unique, perfect, and so far incomprehensible that one can scarcely say in what respects he is incomprehensible'. The impression is given of a certain floundering among concepts that are indefinable. Miss Edwards sensibly does not adjudicate between the experts, but sees the matter as 'the great problem of Egyptology … a problem that has not yet been solved'.

Religious questions are notoriously difficult to answer, and in the case of ancient Egypt are compounded in their difficulties by the variety and mass of evidence in texts available for study and analysis. Almost any idea can be supported by an appropriate prayer or invocation; equally, there may always be a contrary text to invalidate any idea. No attempt seems ever to have been made in ancient times to organize Egyptian religion into a coherent system. Over the years, the lumber room of theological ideas became a repository of beliefs and statements about beliefs which were stacked away unsystematically; nothing was discarded, anomalous ideas were not reconciled. New movements of thought developed from time to time, as in the case of Atenism in the Eighteenth Dynasty, and were accommodated within the mass of ideas already existing. In the case of Atenism, as we shall see, the radical nature of some of its ideas were so abhorrent to traditionally minded Egyptians, especially the priestly cadres of the great Theban cults, that a deliberate process of eradication was pursued after the death of Akhenaten; but the fury of rejection was aimed more at people, in particular the Amarna royal family, than at the ideas of Atenism.

It is not easy to trace the development of the cults and associated iconographies from the scanty traces surviving from predynastic times; it is tempting to offer religious interpretations of objects found in burials and settlement sites at places like Badari and Naqada. It does, however, seem clear that there were very many local cults throughout Egypt, identified in neolithic times by totemic or symbolic images, some of which by the late Predynastic Period and earliest dynasties can be found as standards, and other objects which appear to have ritual significance, usually connected with ceremonies involving the king. One totemic standard which survived into historic times was the hieroglyphic sign ⌐; it became the sign for 'god', and is thought in origin to have represented a pole wrapped around with a cloth, the end of which was loose, flapping like a flag. The earliest standards seem mostly to have been of inanimate objects, but by the end of the Predynastic Period standards with emblems representing living creatures, like falcons, can be found in the scenes carved on the great ceremonial palettes, such as the

83 Siltstone ceremonial palette bearing a symbol later associated with the god Min. Predynastic Period. H.29.5 cm.

35501

so-called Battlefield Palette, part of which is in the British Museum (EA 20791, fig. 22), and part in the Ashmolean Museum, Oxford. It cannot be claimed with certainty that a falcon standard at this early period provides evidence for a cult of a god named Horus. There seem to have been several individual falcon cults in late Predynastic Egypt, but without clear inscriptional evidence it cannot be asserted that one in particular was of Horus. What is certain, however, is that from the beginning of the Dynastic Period the principal name of each king was written in a frame, representing a formal palace façade surmounted by a falcon (*serekh*). It is called the Horus name, and in historic times undoubtedly had reference to that god, Horus, the living king. Indeed it is most probable that from at least this early time the king was identified with Horus when he was alive. A second living creature which can be identified historically as a god in the Egyptian pantheon is Seth, mythically later to be known as the brother of Osiris and a malevolent deity. He was shown as an animal with tall ears, forked tail and pointed snout, not yet satisfactorily identified zoologically. Seth may not have developed his evil characteristic at this early time, when he replaces the falcon in the name of Peribsen of the Second Dynasty, and is paired with the falcon in the name of Khasekhemwy, Peribsen's successor.

The general belief nowadays is that throughout Egypt in late predynastic times cults proliferated locally, each with its distinctive cult object, which might be an inanimate object or a living creature – an animal or a bird. Many of these cults persisted into historic times, their sacred elements becoming nome deities, the gods of the individual provinces of Egypt. For political reasons certain cults achieved greater prominence over the majority, the prime example being that of the falcon-god Horus of the city of Nekhen in southern Upper Egypt, which is usually known as Hierakonpolis ('City of

84 Granite tomb stela of King Peribsen of the Second Dynasty. It bears the royal *serekh* containing the king's name; here surmounted not by the Horus falcon but the animal of Seth, partly erased. From Abydos. H.1.13 m.

85 The Hunters' Palette. Men engage in assaults on lions; some carry standards with district or nome signs. The significance of the scene is uncertain. Siltstone. Predynastic Period. L.66.5 cm.

the Falcon'), its Greek name. One of the abiding myths of Egyptian religion concerned the unending struggle for divine royal dominion between Horus and Seth, at first seemingly a direct conflict between the forces of good (Horus) and evil (Seth), and involving in particular the eye of Horus which had been torn out by Seth. It was broken into pieces and was made whole again through the benign agency of the god Thoth. Thus it became 'the whole one' (in Egyptian *udjat* or *wedjat*), and as an object a most powerful protective amulet, used in life and in death.

The Contendings of Horus and Seth, a literary composition of New Kingdom date, describes a much later development in the relationship between the two deities. Here the struggle concerns the succession to the throne of Osiris – the divine dead king, the ruler of the underworld, and the god with whom Egyptians sought identification after death. The origins of Osiris are not clear; he was not specifically a local deity of primeval nature, but was always shown as a dead, mummified human king. He did, however obtain local associations both in Upper Egypt at Abydos, and in Lower Egypt at Busiris (the Greek form of the ancient name Per-Usir, 'House of Osiris'), both places established as the destinations of pilgrimages for the dead – pilgrimages to be accomplished symbolically, if not actually, in mummiform after death. Abydos was the principal centre of the cult of Osiris, the god having been associated with the much earlier jackal deity Khentamentiu, 'First of the Westerners' (i.e. the sacred dead). How the association began cannot be determined, but it is not surprising in view of the necropolis element in the natures of both deities. Abydos was furthermore a place of special veneration for the Egyptians in housing the burials of the kings of the first two dynasties, and a centre of pilgrimage on that account without doubt. Over the centuries one of the early sepulchres, that of King Djer, was identified as the grave of Osiris and a focus of particular devotion. Abydos became one of the holiest places in Egypt, where cemeteries and cenotaphs were established, and great royal temples constructed. Even today it remains a place where visitors may experience strangely the numinous power of ancient gods.

86 One of a series of scenes in the Edfu Temple showing the contest between Horus and Seth. Here, Horus, falcon-headed (face defaced), in a boat spears a tiny hippopotamus, a form of Seth. Ptolemaic Period.

The legend of Osiris, with those of Horus and Seth, is not explicitly related in any surviving ancient Egyptian text. It was not in the nature of Egyptian religious texts to set out clearly the order of events in the 'histories' of the various deities. The general myths were subsumed into religious thinking and tradition, and references would be made to various details or episodes in the texts found in temples and in the words of prayers and invocations on private stelae and other occasional writings. For Osiris, his brother Seth and his son Horus we need to turn to the writings of classical authors, particularly the Greek Plutarch, who lived in the first century AD. His account of the Osiris legend, although neatly simplified for a Graeco-Roman audience, appears to present a narrative which does not materially contradict the ancient sources. It is a sad but heroic tale of sacrifice and martyrdom, of violent action and magical survival.

In the genealogy of Egyptian gods, the first and greatest was Re, the sun-god, whose cult base was Heliopolis (Greek for 'City of the Sun'), to whom we shall return later in this chapter. Re had two children, Shu (Air) and Tefnut (Moisture), who in turn produced Geb (Earth) and Nut (Sky); they had four children, Isis, Nephthys, Osiris and Seth. In line of descent Osiris assumed the divine kingship of the world, but in so doing he provoked the lasting enmity of his brother Seth, who determined to secure the throne for himself. He therefore laid on a great banquet to which Osiris was invited, and he prepared a wonderful coffin which he offered as a gift to whomever it fitted best. It was tailor-made for Osiris, who got into it, fitting it perfectly. Seth quickly fastened the lid and had the coffin thrown into the river. Isis, sister and wife of Osiris, went off in search of her husband's body and eventually found it in the Valley of the Cedar enclosed in a tree. Isis, a mistress of magic, recov-

87 The colonnade in front of the First Hypostyle Hall of the Osiris Temple at Abydos. Conceived and mostly built in the reign of Sety I, the temple was completed as an act of piety by his son Ramesses II.

ered and revived her husband and returned to Egypt, where Seth killed him, cutting up his body into pieces which again he threw into the river. The pieces were distributed by water throughout Egypt, resulting in the development of myths about Osiris' burials and tombs in many parts of the country. Isis, however, did not give up; with the help of her sister Nephthys, who also happened to be the wife of Seth, she scoured the country, collecting the pieces and reassembling Osiris' body; most importantly she recovered his penis which had been swallowed by the oxyrhynchus fish. With everything at last in order, Isis by magic succeeded in revivifying her husband successfully to father a child. In due course Horus was born, and Osiris descended to the underworld where he ruled over the dead in the form of a mummy with the royal regalia of crook and flail. Isis fled to the Delta where she raised Horus,

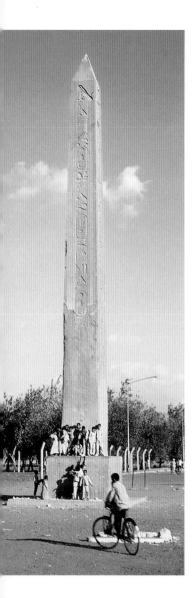

88 The obelisk of Heliopolis, the surviving monument of the great temple of the sun-god. This is the earliest surviving obelisk, erected in the reign of Senusret I of the Twelfth Dynasty. Granite. H.20.4 m.

protecting him by her magic from the natural terrors of the place. Horus was determined to assume Osiris' place as the living king, with whom each successive Egyptian king would be identified, and from whom each would derive his sovereignty. This Horus is essentially the same Horus as the falcon deity of the early dynasties, and eventually the god of the great cult centre at Edfu, not far from Hierakonpolis in Upper Egypt. But he is also the Horus who warred with Seth, and whose battle with Seth – shown as a hippopotamus – is depicted graphically on the inner face of the girdle wall of the Edfu temple. The Egyptians certainly did not worry about contradictions in these different versions of the Osiris-Horus-Seth myth; they represented different approaches to a rich and tangled set of traditions.

The Osirian strain in Egyptian religion, with its attendant legends, was a relatively late development in the sacred tradition of the country. It offered a form of devotion which was in many senses opposed, but not inimical, to the much older solar tradition of which the principal deity was the sun-god Re. Osiris was earth-bound, essentially a god of death and burial, occupying a sphere of belief and activity which will form the theme of the next chapter. Osiris was a regal god, king of the underworld, but yet in every sense was more 'down-to-earth' than Re, and in consequence was more accessible for the worship of ordinary Egyptians. But it was the sun-god of Heliopolis who provided the basis and *raison d'être* for the first and greatest form of Egyptian religion, that is the state religion of the king, attended by the paraphernalia of temple structure and worship, evident in the great temples of the land, and their decorations of ritual scenes and texts.

Heliopolis, known to the Egyptians as Iunu (the biblical On), developed in earliest times as the cult centre for the solar deity known locally as Atum ('the completed one'). It was a place some distance from the Nile, but not too far from the first capital city of the united Egypt – the White Walls of Memphis. As a solar cult Re/Atum was very appropriately adopted as the principal deity of the Egyptian pantheon by the kings of the first dynasties whose domestic deity from the south was Horus, himself a sky-god. As things were eventually ordered in the genealogy of the gods, Horus was not one of the company of nine, the ennead of Heliopolis. He was, however, separately seen as the son of Osiris and Isis, who were members of the ennead as it came to be constituted, along with their divine siblings Seth and Nephthys, their forbears Geb and Nut, Shu and Tefnut, and Atum himself. Subsequently Horus would be more closely associated with Re in the form of Re-Herakhty, 'Re-Horus-of-the-horizon'. The king, the living Horus, would in due course, from the Fifth Dynasty, be named also 'Son of Re'. As a divine person himself he would find his ultimate place in the sky, to traverse the heavens in the company of the great sun-god.

Another important company of gods developed at Hermopolis in Middle Egypt, the ogdoad (the eight), made up of eight deities in four pairs, male and female, representing the characteristics of the chaos from which the earth was created: Nun and Naunet for the primordial water; Heh and Hehet, infinite space; Kek and Keket, darkness of eternity; Amun and Amaunet, invisibility. At Hermopolis emerged the primeval mound on which was laid the egg that produced the sun-god, the actual creator of the world. This tradition was at variance with the Heliopolitan tradition, according to which Atum created the world by self-generation or masturbation. The texts which provide the detail of the creation are, as might be expected, not consistent with each other, and no attempt seemingly was made to produce an account free from contradictions.

A third important tradition of divine creation developed in Memphis itself, concerning the god Ptah, who has been sometimes considered the most intellectual of the Egyptian deities. In historic times he was seen to be the patron of arts and crafts, and was recognized as the great creator, who by assigning names to things and differentiating between aspects of the universe – such as sky and earth, water and land –

89 Bronze group of an unidentified king making an offering (missing) to the Apis bull, manifestation of the god Ptah of Memphis. On death the animal was embalmed and interred in the so-called Serapeum at Saqqara. Late Period. H. of bull 12.3 cm.

created the world as it was known. As the great god of Memphis, Egypt's foremost city throughout the Dynastic Period – the seat of administration, a base for trade and a centre for entrepreneurial foreigners – Ptah had an independent importance which gave him special significance within the Egyptian pantheon. He possessed a quiet authority among the gods. From the New Kingdom his cult developed through the existence of the Apis bull, an animal identified by special markings, which was raised and tended in the precinct of the god's temple and after death was buried with great ceremony in the impressive bull catacomb at Saqqara, known erroneously as the Serapeum. The theology of the Ptah cult is set out in dramatic form in an inscription – said to be very ancient – copied from a tattered papyrus during the Twenty-fifth Dynasty on a slab now known as the Shabako Stone and in the British Museum (EA 498).

In Memphis, Ptah was supported by two other deities who with him formed a sacred family. His 'wife' was Sakhmet ('the powerful one'), usually depicted as a lioness-headed woman. She was a fierce and formidable goddess who wreaked havoc on humankind, especially in years of distress, and had on occasion to be appeased by Re;

90 Two seated and two
standing granite statues
of the leonine goddess
Sakhmet, from temples
at Thebes. The benign
appearance of the goddess
belies her fierce character.
Eighteenth Dynasty.
H. of figure on left 2.26 m.

once by being made drunk, according to legend, when Re coloured huge quantities of beer red, which Sakhmet mistook for blood and drank inordinately. The child of the family was Nefertum, associated with the lotus and its divine fragrance, which appeared at the time of creation. Trios of gods of this kind are now generally called triads, and most great cult centres accommodated triads from the New Kingdom. So, at Elephantine in the cataract district the principal god was Khnum, the ram-headed divine potter who fashioned man and particularly the king out of clay on a potter's wheel. The triad was completed by two goddesses, Satis and Anukis, the former specially linked with the frontier region and the island of Siheil, and the latter with the

cataract region generally. The two most influential triads were Osiris, Isis and Horus, the divine family par excellence, and Amun, Mut and Khonsu, whose cult developed at Thebes. The Osirian triad had no specific cult centre except Abydos in so far as it was the mythical burial place of Osiris and a major focus for pilgrimage. It was, however, included among the number of seven deities with individual chapels in the great Abydos temple of Sety I, along with Amon-Re, Re-Herakhty, Ptah and the king himself. Osiris was undoubtedly the prime subject of worship in this temple and his chapel complex was by far the largest.

The Theban triad was the most majestic of the divine families, especially during the New Kingdom when Thebes was the southern capital of Egypt, the site of Egypt's greatest temples, with the burial places of the Egyptian kings across the river to the West. At this time Amon-Re, 'King of the Gods', was pre-eminent, having superseded but not entirely ousted Montu, the original god of the Theban nome. Amun, a member of the Hermopolitan ogdoad, migrated to Thebes in the Middle Kingdom in mysterious circumstances, which suited his name, 'the hidden one'. He was mostly worshipped in conjunction with Re as Amon-Re and he became the imperial deity, the recipient of booty and the abundant produce of the vast temple estates. The conjoining of Amun and Re was no doubt partly inspired by political motives, but there were other more suitable reasons based on the nature of religious authority and the practicalities of temple worship. The linking of two gods is known as syncretism, and it was a device much used in Egypt to enhance the authority of well-established, but locally focused, deities. So you find Montu-Re and Sobk-Re, but above all the great Re-Herakhty, who under this name was the head of the Heliopolitan ennead in the New Kingdom, and even survived the religious revolution under Akhenaten, being included in the first version of the names given to the Aten, that upstart deity. There is little doubt that the rituals and temple procedures developed at Heliopolis for the worship of Re provided the pattern for the practices employed in all the principal shrines of Egypt, over which the king in theory presided.

91 A scene in which King Ramesses II is shown offering flowers to Amun and Mut, the principal deities of Karnak. Hypostyle Hall, Karnak.

The official formal religion of ancient Egypt, as practised in the great temples, was essentially a private act of worship between the god and the king. The god, in his identification with Re, was responsible for the establishment of order in creation, and the king was responsible for the maintenance of that order on earth, by ensuring that proper services were carried out and proper festivals celebrated. Egyptian temples were not churches or mosques, places where people could congregate and take part in the rituals of worship. The temple was a private enclave, the abode of the deity, whose cult figure was kept in a dark chamber situated in the heart of the main building. In a typical temple of the New Kingdom and later it was approached through a series of courtyards, pillared halls and anterooms, in which the floor levels rose gradually and the

92 View along the axis of
the Temple of Horus at Edfu,
from the Hypostyle Hall
through to the Holy of Holies
and the shrine of the god.
Ptolemaic Period.

93 Granite shrine from
the Temple of Isis at
Philae. The inscriptions
name Ptolemy II Euergetes
and his wife Cleopatra II.
Second century BC. H.2.52 m.

ceilings were lowered similarly. The effect was mysterious and forbidding, and only priests were allowed to penetrate the innermost parts, and only the king or his priestly representative could enter the room containing the cult statue – the Holy of Holies. Limited access to the initial courts was allowed for specially favoured Egyptians, and the whole sacred area was probably teeming with temple staff, priestly and menial, who were not confined in the exercise of their duties, sacred and profane.

The regular daily service in the temple was performed ideally by the king, but commonly by his representative – the high priest of the temple's priestly college, or again no doubt more commonly a deputizing priest. There was a certain domestic aspect to the acts accompanying the morning service: the god was to be prepared for the day ahead, and thereby the continuance and the stability of the god's creation reassured; it was a proper duty for the king to perform. It was the divine reveille. At the break of day the celebrant purified himself carefully before approaching the sanctuary, unbolting the doors and entering the room housing the cult statue. The successive rites were accompanied by appropriate hymns and invocations, and much burning of incense. The image was unveiled and undressed, purified, given breakfast, adorned with clean clothes, anointed with sacred oils, and then returned to its shrine. The celebrant then withdrew from the sanctuary, walking backwards and sweeping away his footprints as he went; finally the sanctuary doors were closed and bolted and sealed.

Some idea of the impressiveness of this daily service can be sensed in the sanctuaries

94 The great pylons of the Edfu Temple. On the bridge between them, above the doorway, the living falcon, Horus, was presented to the populace on festival days. Ptolemaic Period.

of the great late temples at Dendera and Edfu, where the almost total survival of the architectural ensemble allows the receptive mind to contemplate the mystical setting as it might have been two millennia ago. Imagine how much more dramatically the rites would have been enacted in the national temples in Thebes and Memphis during the New Kingdom. The daily service was a very private ceremony, witnessed by very few people. There were, however, other occasions when the general populace was able to see the divine image, and also take part in processions and festivities which in sum may be compared with the religious festivals – processions and fairs – of Christian communities, and the *moulids* celebrating holy men in the Islamic world, which are common even today in Egypt.

95 The mound of Bubastis in 1962, gravely denuded by soil- and stone-removers; site of the Twenty-second Dynasty temple of Bastet, embellished with sculptures brought from Memphis and Heliopolis.

In the great days of Thebes during the New Kingdom, the most important annual festival celebrated on the east side of the Nile was called Opet. It took place during the inundation season, and had strong tones of fertility and renewal in its character. The main event in the month-long festival was the procession of the Theban deities Amun, Mut and Khonsu in their shrines, taken by boat on the Nile from their main sanctuaries in the Karnak complex of temples to the smaller Luxor Temple, largely the construction of King Amenhotep III of the Eighteenth Dynasty, enlarged, and some would say vulgarized, by Ramesses II. The procession accompanying the god's boats was conducted on water and on land, the distance between Karnak and Luxor being about two miles. There were priestly attendants, musicians, dancers and singers, detachments of soldiers, and the crowds. Some idea of the excitement and confusion of the occasion is captured in a series of wonderful low-relief carvings on the inner side walls of the Processional Colonnade in Luxor, through which the gods would pass on their way to the innermost parts of the temple in which the sacred marriage ceremonies of Amun and Mut would be celebrated. It is not known in detail what function would have been carried out by the king in this festival, but it was certainly one that he would expect to fulfil from time to time during his reign. What appears to be a modern survival of the ancient Opet Festival is the *moulid* of Yussef Abu'l Haggag, celebrated in Luxor in the month before the fast-month of Ramadan. A *moulid* may be compared closely with a procession and celebration in honour of a saint, especially in countries like Spain and Italy. In Luxor the local 'saint' is Yussef Abu'l Haggag, whose mosque survives within the walls of the Luxor Temple, occupying part of the great court of Ramesses II; but replaced, though not surplanted, by a modern mosque built adjacent to the temple. In the procession, or *zeffa*, boats are paraded through the streets of Luxor, and Egyptologists, and indeed anthropologists, see in them vestiges of the divine boats of Amun, Mut and Khonsu.

An annual celebration of more ancient date than Opet was the Festival of the Valley, which may be traced back to the Eleventh Dynasty, with divine visitations by the cult statue of Amun to the Deir el-Bahri mortuary temple of King Nebhepetre Mentuhotep.

In its heyday during the New Kingdom, when the Theban Necropolis seethed with activity, the progress of the image of Amun, brought across the Nile to the west, became an occasion for holidays for the workmen of the royal tombs, and for others no doubt. The procession wound its way from royal mortuary temple to royal mortuary temple, the image spending the night in appropriately appointed quarters attached to certain temples like the Ramesseum. It was attended by huge crowds, and provided an excuse for great popular indulgence which might be interpreted as an outward show of devotion to the god.

The most explicit description in Egyptian sources of the excesses which accompanied the great religious festivals occurs in an inscription in the Ptolemaic temple of Horus at Edfu. The festival celebrated annually the sacred marriage between Horus and the goddess Hathor of Dendera. The goddess travelled the distance – over one hundred miles – between Dendera and Edfu by river, and the arrival of her entourage was marked by an appearance of Horus as a living falcon on the platform between the two wings of the temple pylon. Here was the opportunity for a display of enthusiasm and homage by the people en masse. The subsequent procession to greet the visiting deity and the fun and games which followed provided a great opportunity for indulgence in the name of devotion. The text is clear: 'The priests and the divine fathers are decked in fine linen, the royal company accoutred in its insignia, its young men are drunk, its people are happy, its young girls beautiful to behold, festivity is all around, celebration is in all its districts, no one sleeps until dawn.' It would probably be a mistake to see in these great festivals indications of deep-seated religious emotions on the part of the ordinary people of Egypt; but they should not be dismissed entirely as occasions just to let off steam, to have a holiday and a good time at official expense. At the very least they served as reminders of the great cults; and the appearances of the gods – whether in living form like the falcon of Horus, or as a cult statue as in the case of the Theban triad – with refreshments provided, surely acted as moments to be remembered after the event, and to be looked forward to with expectation. At Bubastis in the Delta the annual festival of the local deity, Bastet – shown as a lady with a cat head (called Diana by Herodotus) – was notable for the facts that visitors by river were inclined to behave in a rude and vulgar manner, and that more wine was drunk there then than in the whole of the rest of the year.

The tradition of unbridled licence may have been one that developed during the New Kingdom. A somewhat more reverent picture is provided by an account of an annual festival celebrating the passion and death of Osiris at Abydos. The high official Ikhernofret was sent by King Senusret III of the Twelfth Dynasty to make all the arrangements for the performance of the Osiris mysteries in the sacred necropolis of Abydos. The text describing his activities is carved on a stela which came from Ikhernofret's cenotaph in the necropolis; it is now in Berlin. It describes the elaborate arrangements he made for the beautification of the god's shrine, the shrines of attendant deities and the boat in which the image of Osiris would travel. Above all, 'I embellished the body of the Lord of Abydos with lapis lazuli, turquoise, electrum and all

96 Egyptian alabaster (calcite) head of a cow; part of a cult statue of Hathor in Deir el-Bahri. The eyes were inlaid with rock crystal and lapis lazuli. Reign of Hatshepsut. H.35.5 cm.

the precious stones fit to be the decoration of a god's body. I dressed the god with his accoutrements according to my priestly position. I was pure of hand in embellishing the god, a priest with clean fingers.' Ikhernofret then describes a number of activities involving the god's image and the progress from the cult temple to Poqer, the part of the necropolis where the god's tomb was traditionally situated. There was the 'Going-forth' of Wepwawet, a jackal deity of the Necropolis associated with Osiris as Chief of the Westerners; it was a sally against the enemies of Osiris by the god who acts as his defender. In an attack on the divine barque Ikhernofret repelled the attackers, slaying the foes of Osiris. He managed the great progress to Poqer and the course of the divine boat, presumably on a canal, not the Nile itself. This and other incidents were all successfully organized and carried through by Ikhernofret, who in the end brought the god back to his palace where he was purified. The order of events is not made absolutely clear; but what is clear is that there was a procession to and from the burial place of the god, there was some sort of progress on water, and the death of Osiris was enacted. Although no mention is made in the text of the participation of the people, the various incidents demanded participation. The whole festival was undoubtedly a great act of penitence, the kind of re-enactment of a divine martyrdom, not uncommon in other religious traditions. It cannot be doubted that there would have been some forms of officially supported entertainments and unofficially organized revelry, if only to deflate the emotions inspired by the sufferings of Osiris. But such activities were not to be mentioned in Ikhernofret's self-glorifying inscription.

In the highest levels of Egyptian society, at the summit of which was the king with the royal family and members of the Court, the impressive paraphernalia of official religion presumably represented the formal state of worship and belief. 'Presumably' is used here because very little is known about what went on in the private devotions of

97 Wand of hippopotamus ivory; an amuletic object with magical powers to invoke, and to ward off, the fantastical creatures of Egyptian imagination. Middle Kingdom. L.36 cm.

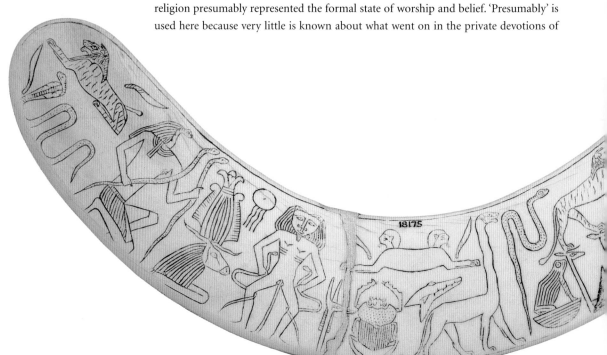

the king and his close family and courtiers. Here an exception should certainly be made for the royal family of the Amarna Period, when Akhenaten and Nefertiti made their devotional preferences very clear in the hymns to the Aten, the worship of whom apparently dominated their public and private lives. Such fanatical adherence to one deity and one form of worship was not common in Egypt. The formality of state religion, for most people involved in the ceremonies of the great temples, could be put to one side once duty had been fulfilled.

It might be expected that in daily life rather more simple forms of worship would have been practised at small family shrines, and even in the royal residences and houses of the great. Official religion was of the greatest importance for the stability and continuance of the Egyptian state, but not for personal devotions. One may again presume that most families, including the royal family, and even individuals would have found spiritual satisfaction in the offering of prayers and gifts to particular deities, who might have been members of the great divine colleges – the Heliopolitan ennead or the Hermopolitan ogdoad. There were also a great many lesser deities, who by their humble status would perhaps be more sympathetic to the pious requests of private persons. For the great majority of ancient Egyptians, the great temples and the gods which inhabited them were altogether too remote to be more than objects of awe; and yet the attraction of the great temples in itself led to the development of local cults, centred in a sense on the temple, but focused on a part of the structure. In Memphis, for example, there was a cult of Horus 'on the corner of the southern door'. It was as if a part, or a taste of a part, could serve as the whole. More commonly, religious attachments were local, and beliefs seem often to have been dominated by magic and those gods who were believed to be capable of offering protection from terrors seen and unseen. Forms of Isis – the great magician – were especially venerated, particularly in her form as mother of Horus, whom she had protected from the terrors of the Delta marshes by her special powers. In daily life there was much to fear in the form of snakes, scorpions, certain animals like the gazelle (for uncertain reasons endowed with evil power), and the unspecific terrors of the night and the threatening spaces of the desert. Amuletic objects could help. In the Middle Kingdom objects made from ivory, known as magical wands, were carved with strange and demonic creatures of uncertain identity, but clearly not considered to be well disposed to evil influences. In later times small freestanding stelae called *cippi* were popular, carrying figures of a mixed deity incorporating characteristics of Horus-the-Child (Harpocrates in Greek) and Shed. The god is shown grasping malevolent creatures in his hands, and trampling on crocodiles; personalized texts contain suitable spells.

Certain deities were popular for specific reasons. The goddess Thoeris (*Ta-urt*, 'the Big One' in Egyptian) – shown usually as an upright-standing pregnant hippopotamus, holding amuletic signs representing 'protection' – was considered specially efficacious for the safe delivery of newborn children. The terrifyingly attractive little god Bes, a dwarfish being with leonine features, was distinctly a domestic deity, and could be used to cheer the home and to protect people at night. His figure might be carved on headrests and beds, and he would terrify away malevolent things by shaking his tambourine. Amulets, reproducing in miniature a wide variety of magical signs, formed

98 Painting from the tomb of Kynebu showing Amenhotep I who was specially revered by the workmen of the royal tomb. Thebes. Late Twentieth Dynasty. H.44 cm.

essential elements in jewellery, worn by men and women. They played a vital part in the equipment of the dead, but were equally potent for the living. Among the most common were the *djed* 𓊽 for 'stability, endurance', the *wadj* 𓇅 for 'freshness, flourishing', and the *udjat*-eye, the eye of Horus 𓂀, for 'completeness, protection'. One sign which is today often worn amuletically is the *ankh* 𓋹, but this was never an amuletic sign in ancient Egypt; as a symbol meaning 'life' it was commonly carried by gods to be offered to the king and other appropriate persons. During the late New Kingdom it was possible to have prepared for you personally a magical amuletic text written on a long narrow strip of papyrus, which could be rolled up, placed in a small cylindrical container and carried on you. In such a text a great variety of terrors and other lifetime hazards could be addressed and, it was hoped, nullified.

The best picture of private devotions in ancient Egypt is to be found in the practices of the inhabitants of the workmen's village of Deir el-Medina, during the Nineteenth and Twentieth Dynasties in particular. That community was by no means typical of modest groupings of people in Egypt. It was a close society made up of highly trained scribes and artisans, who were mostly literate and very conscious of the levels of royal religion in both temple and tomb. Nevertheless in their own expressions of devotion they displayed a wide variety of attachments to deities, the evidence for which is provided by a great many small stelae with prayers and dedications. Some of these stelae were found in association with simple shrines in the neighbourhood of the village, and even on the paths in the hills leading towards the Valley of the Kings; others have been found in the houses in which the workmen lived.

A more formal focus of worship was provided by a chapel built just to the north of the village during the reign of Sety I. It was dedicated to Hathor, a goddess of many characteristics, including love and fertility. She was especially worshipped in the great mortuary temple of Queen Hatshepsut at Deir el-Bahri, and her cult was very popular among the workmen. The great Theban triad was not neglected, or the cult of Ptah of Memphis, very appropriately in his aspect of god of craftsmen. Other members of the national pantheon were subjects of devotion at Deir el-Medina: the Cataract triad of Khnum, Satis and Anukis; the scribe of the gods, Thoth; the great Re-Herakhty himself. The gods of domestic protection, Thoeris and Bes, were prominent subjects of worship on stelae and in the houses of the village, and another goddess, Merseger (serpent-formed), was particularly venerated in an environment where snakes abounded. She was associated with the pyramidal-shaped peak, the Qurn, which dominated the Valley of the Kings, and was in some way linked with

Hathor. Apart from small stelae devoted to her, there are several less formal ostraca drawings of her with short invocatory prayers.

The existence of stelae with texts invoking the help of certain foreign gods suggests the presence of Asiatic workmen in the village, perhaps craftsmen in metals; but the stelae in question are not distinguished by stylistic features different from those devoted to native Egyptian gods. Among the deities represented are the war-god Reshep and the female gods Astarte, Anat and Qudshu. It is not unreasonable to think that some Egyptians found it easier to direct their prayers to a deity free from the Egyptian associations of the great national gods. The same instinct may in origin have prompted the growth of a very popular cult involving the king Amenhotep I and his mother Queen Ahmose-Nefertari. It seems that this cult may have originated in the mistaken belief that this king was the founder of the workmen's village, but some other less obvious reason should be found. The village was actually founded by Thutmose I, son of Amenhotep I. The confusion may have had its origin in another probably erroneous belief that Amenhotep I was the first king to be buried in the Valley of the Kings, the place on which the duties of the villagers were centred.

99 Limestone fragment carved with a royal head, probably of Akhenaten. The unusual features of Amarna royal imagery are here sensitively portrayed. From El-Amarna. H.17 cm.

Temples, shrines and stelae invoking deities, great and small, all represent the outward show of religious belief and devotion at different levels. But what did ancient Egyptians really believe in? The religious instinct among men and women is strong; it need not be directed at specific deities or involve formal practices except in that such activities provide a kind of practical satisfaction for the personal feelings of the individual. Thoughts other than those focused on the cults needed consideration and expression. Some of the literary compositions very popular in all periods are kinds of meditations on spiritual matters. During the Middle Kingdom ideas concerning personal responsibility, involving behaviour in life and preparation for the life in the hereafter in the realm of Osiris, developed in the minds of thoughtful Egyptians, and over time among the upper ranges of society generally. This funerary aspect of Egyptian religion will be treated more fully in the next chapter, but here it needs some consideration because it began to influence the ways people felt about 'god'. It was a development which undoubtedly contributed to Atenism, the sole worship of the sun, promoted by King Akhenaten and imposed on the country, with the exclusion of most other cults.

Atenism evolved during the middle Eighteenth Dynasty in rather unspecific ways. The word *aten* itself was not a new coinage. It was a word used to describe the disc of the sun, and had no special currency until it was used, for example, in the name of the boat used by Queen Tiye, principal wife of Amenhotep III and mother of Akhenaten; the boat was 'The Aten gleams'. Some of the elevated phraseology used in the great hymns to the Aten can be found in texts predating the Amarna revolution. The inscription of two architects, Suty and Hor, contains a passionate invocation of god in the form of Amun and Re-Herakhty, which includes many phrases and sentiments to be found in Akhenaten's great Aten hymn. Again the word *aten* occurs in this inscription but without the strong emphasis employed by Akhenaten. It is not at all clear how the revolution in religious belief and practice was effected. On becoming king, the son of Amenhotep III and Tiye bore the name Amenhotep, 'Amun is content', but by Year 5 of his reign he had become Akhenaten, 'One who is useful to the Aten'. The adoption of Atenism and its tendency towards a monotheistic form of religion may well have started before his accession, and may have been influenced by his mother Queen Tiye and his royal wife Nefertiti. Belief may also have been buttressed by religio-political considerations demonstrated by the desire to break with Amun and with the political establishment in Thebes. A major provocative act taken early in his reign was the construction at Karnak of temples in honour of the Aten. It was a distinctly hostile move. In his Year 6 a complete break was made with Thebes, and a new capital and cult centre were established in Middle Egypt at a virgin site on the east side of the Nile almost opposite Hermopolis. Known today as El-Amarna, the new city of Akhetaten ('the Horizon of the Aten') was a place of great spaciousness with a major temple for the worship of the Aten. It provided a complete antithesis to the mysterious structures of the traditional cults with their dark sanctuaries. All the worship took place in full sunlight, and the king was the principal officiant and the sole mediator between god and the population of Egypt.

Apart from the political aspects of the change from polytheism to a kind of monotheism, what in fact distinguished Atenism from earlier Egyptian beliefs in divinity in whatever forms it might have been expressed? It was above all an ecstatic glorification of the sun-god, made apparent in his disc, and in the wonderful nature of his creation. The flavour can be found in the words of the great hymn to the Aten, inscribed in the tomb of Ay at El-Amarna, and claimed to be the work of Akhenaten himself:

> When you rise in the morning and shine forth as the Aten, in daytime you disperse darkness and give out your rays. The Two Lands rejoice and wake up and stand upright, for you have woken them … All cattle rejoice in their fields; trees and plants become green … all goats frolic on their feet, all that flies, takes off … Creator of children in women, producer of seed in men, who gives life to the son in his mother's womb, calming him that he does not cry, nurse in the womb, who provides breath to put life into all he creates … How many are your works! They are hidden. O single god unlike any other! You created earth as you wished when you were alone, men and cattle, all goats, all that is on earth and goes on its feet, all that is in the sky and flies with its wings …

At the end the king establishes his position vis-à-vis the deity:

> No one else knows you except your son Akhenaten. You allowed him to comprehend your thoughts and your power when the earth came into being by your hand, just as you made them … As for all men who run on earth ever since you established the earth, you raised them for your son who came forth from yourself, Akhenaten.

The concentration of worship on the one god, the Aten, almost always visible in the Egyptian sky, led to the active hostility towards most other gods, especially Amun whose name was destroyed wherever it could be found in accessible inscriptions, even when it was a component in the name of Akhenaten's father Amenhotep. But one divine being that was incorporated into Atenism was *ma'at*, considered in Atenism not as a deity but as a vital concept in the world as the creation of the sun-god. The deity Ma'at was an important participant in traditional Egyptian religion; as a concept in Atenism, *ma'at* is never shown as a deity, but regularly written with the so-called feather of truth. In Atenism *ma'at* provided rightness and order in the creation of the Aten; she was not presented as a spiritual or moral element, but more as the 'glue' that held things together and balanced the universe.

In the long history of polytheistic religion in ancient Egypt Atenism was an anomaly, a phenomenon that did not really fit into the pattern of belief and worship at any level. It was in effect a monotheistic cult, not entirely new in its prime faith in a sun-god, creator of the universe. It was royally promoted, and conceived in its final form as a kind of divine compact between the Aten and the king together with the members of the royal family. It was not a set of beliefs with much moral content. As long as the world worked, balanced by *ma'at*, all was well, and Egyptians had more or less to accept the king's word in the matter. There was not much in it to inspire individual devotion in people outside the highest ranks of society in Akhetaten. Evidence is not abundant to show what effects the change had in other, distant parts of Egypt, like Memphis, for example, which remained a very important administrative centre throughout the Amarna Period. It is unlikely that ordinary Egyptians felt any special devotion to the Aten, but were probably distinctly hostile to it in that it diminished the importance of the multiplicity of deities who formed the subject of the simple religious practices of the people. It is not surprising that Atenism did not survive the deaths of Akhenaten and Nefertiti, and that the return to Thebes and to Amun, re-establishing the old order of things, brought a kind of contentment to Egyptians generally.

100 View over the palace area of El-Amarna (Akhetaten), the new foundation of Akhenaten. Much remains to be explored. The mud-brick walls of the main structure have been completely denuded of any stonework.

This chapter began with a consideration of what the Egyptians truly believed – in many gods, in diversity as exemplified in many forms. Questions posed by Miss Amelia B. Edwards remain to be answered. There are surely no simple answers, and it may be concluded that simple answers are not really needed. The divine in ancient Egypt could appear, or be discerned, in many ways, in many forms; what individuals accepted as worthy of worship was perhaps simple on the individual level. When someone believes, questions do not have to be asked; rationality does not necessarily form part of the matter. Perhaps we should not try to simplify the complicated, to tease out one universal belief from a tangle of diverse and often inconsistent beliefs. The ways in which the Egyptians saw the world and identified their gods suited them for thousands of years, and for the most part they were not troubled by complexity.

6

Provision for the Afterlife

The idea that after death the existence of the deceased would continue in some other realm was not confined to the ancient Egyptians; but the practical steps taken by the Egyptians to ensure that the transition from the world of the living to the world of the dead was effected smoothly and comfortably were exceptional. They had been well developed over the many centuries when the life and culture of Egypt continued without serious interruptions from external forces. There were, of course, periods when things did not go well for the country, when the cohesion of administration faltered, as during the First Intermediate Period. At such a time new ideas gained currency, which over the years influenced Egyptian thinking about the human condition and the future of the individual after death. Even the time when the Hyksos dominated part of Egypt during the Second Intermediate Period did not seriously disturb the general culture of the land; continuity of funerary beliefs and practices may be tracked from the Middle Kingdom to the New Kingdom without much noticeable difference between the two periods. Stability was in fact something which the Hyksos seemed to want to maintain. Although of an alien race and culture, the rulers of the Fifteenth and Sixteenth Dynasties apparently endeavoured to be as 'Egyptian' as possible; the relatively short period of foreign domination in the north of the country left little mark on Egyptian thinking and behaviour.

The tomb and the grave are the sources of much of what we now know about ancient Egypt, and the objects that make up the bulk of the antiquities to be seen in museums and other collections throughout the world have come from tombs. The climatic conditions of many parts of Egypt have ensured that perishable materials like wood, cloth and papyrus have survived in greater abundance than from any other ancient culture. Consequently, a characteristic, good collection of Egyptian antiquities will contain spectacular material mostly of a funerary nature – mummies, coffins, wooden furniture, pottery, basketry, tools and weapons in stone and metal, copies of religious texts like *The Book of the Dead*, inscriptions on wood and stone – in fact, examples of almost every kind of object that might be needed, not just for the survival of the body and for the safe passage of the soul to its destination in the afterlife, but also for the continuation of a comfortable existence in that afterlife. And so, a visit to a collection of Egyptian antiquities leaves a firm impression that nothing much else was of importance to the ancient Egyptian than death and burial, and that in life Egyptian thoughts were firmly fixed on the tomb. It is, of course, a distorted view. There is overwhelming evidence that the inhabitants of the Nile Valley were life-loving people who enjoyed the pleasures of good living, and the comforts of homes well equipped in every respect. Indeed it may well be claimed that such was the Egyptian appreciation of the fortunate circumstances of living in Egypt that there was a determination that this everyday happy experience should be continued in the afterlife, and that proper provision should be made through the materials included in the tomb equipment. The result should be commensurate with the individual's position in life, and with what could be afforded. Nevertheless, although the attitude of the Egyptians in preparing for death might have been pragmatic, and almost unsentimental, yet a degree of personal pride surely inspired the provision of grave goods in some cases to outdo what may have

101 Vignette from *The Book of the Dead* of the scribe Ani, illustrating parts of his funeral: mourning women wail and pour dust on their heads. Early Nineteenth Dynasty. H.12 cm.

been available in life. It has been said that the Egyptian could take his old life with him in death, even if the afterlife turned out to be better than what he had enjoyed in life.

As is the case with almost every aspect of life and culture in ancient Egypt, it is impossible to provide an account of beliefs concerning death and the afterlife, and the equipment needed to secure the proper posthumous solution appropriate for the various levels of society from the king down, and for all periods. Some matters, however, had a universality for most periods and most individuals who, one might say, fell into the category of those who could provide for a good afterlife. In the first place it was thought important that the body should remain as intact as possible; secondly, that food and drink should be provided to nourish the individual. This nourishment was not intended for the body as such, but for the surviving essence of the person, which could for want of a better word precisely representing the ancient conception be called the 'soul'. For the Egyptian this was the *ka*, sometimes described as the 'double'. In some

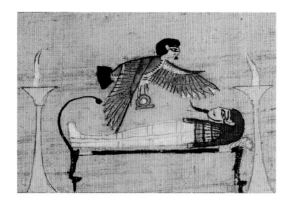

102 Vignette from Ani's *Book of the Dead* showing his mummy on a bier between two torches, with his *ba* hovering above in the form of a human-headed bird. H.12 cm.

respects the *ka* may be more closely considered as the 'self' of a person, wholly associated with the person and yet capable of a kind of independent existence. In earliest times the *ka* was an aspect of the royal being, but during the Old Kingdom it was included as a part of the being of non-royal persons also. Offerings were made to the *ka* of a person, and the *ka* was the recipient of what was provided for the nourishment of the person. The idea of the *ka* is elusive and difficult to identify precisely, but it was a potent element in the nature of being, and its existence could be seen as separate in a way from the individual to which it was attached. In later times it was commonly the case that in temples and royal tombs the *ka* of the king was shown as a separate being standing beside or behind the king, but at a much smaller scale. Such representation of the *ka* was not found for non-royal persons; for them the provision of food and drink was perhaps the most essential part of the process of posthumous existence, and the tomb was above all the 'house of the *ka*'.

Another spiritual entity of the individual which became important after death was the *ba*, sometimes considered in plurality as *bai*. In tomb scenes and the vignettes of illustrated religious papyri of the New Kingdom the *ba* is usually represented as a human-headed bird; it essentially belonged to the body, but could move outside the body and take all kinds of forms which might enable it to travel beyond the tomb, and even undertake activities which otherwise would be impossible for an earthbound or tomb-bound person. The body, however, was the home of the *ba*, to which it returned after its excursions away from the body, and even out of the tomb. The idea of the *ba* did not develop until after the changes in funerary perceptions widened with the spread of beliefs associated with Osiris and his realm in the underworld.

In the period before Osirian ideas about posthumous existence became dominant in the consideration of death and the afterlife, the ultimate fate of the ordinary human being was not specific in detail beyond the idea that there would be a form

103 Limestone stela of the workmen Neferabu and Neferronpe. Above, their mummies and those of their parents are having their 'mouths opened' before burial. In the centre, Neferabu's mummy is prepared by a priest in the guise of the jackal-god Anubis. From Deir el-Medina. Nineteenth Dynasty. H.61.5 cm.

104 Elaborately painted mummiform figure of Osiris from the Theban tomb of Kynebu. Before him stand the four sons of Horus on a lotus flower. Thebes. Late Twentieth Dynasty. H.44.5 cm.

of existence after death, which required the preservation of the body and the provision of what might be necessary to sustain that existence. As for the king, his future lay with the realm of the sun-god; a future not attainable by the mass of humankind. The great corpus of *The Pyramid Texts*, which will be considered later in this chapter, was wholly focused on the king. The development of the Osiris cult during the Old Kingdom introduced completely new ideas concerning the afterlife. Osiris, the martyred living king who through his martyrdom became the ruler of the dead, Khentamentiu, 'Foremost of the Westerners', was in all respects a deity more approachable by, and legitimately accessible to, non-royal people. Identification with this god, who had suffered and triumphed and then ruled over an underworld recognizable in simple terrestrial terms, was clearly attractive to people who needed some comfortable future after death. A dead person could be seen to be an Osiris, and as such the appropriate texts could be addressed to, and on behalf of, the *ka* of the Osiris X. During the First Intermediate Period, when so many stable aspects of Egyptian life crumbled including the authority of the king, the acceptance of Osiris became general. At the same time, parts of *The Pyramid Texts* appropriate to the new Osirian emphasis, together with new prayers and invocations more directly concerned with Osiris, led to a formulation of a new body of religious writings now called *The Coffin Texts*. These texts, often called 'spells', were mostly written on the large wooden coffins of the Middle Kingdom; they contained ideas which distinctly affected the future development of Egyptian funerary thought. So, the ideas concerning the preservation of the body were developed, the processes of mummification improved, the conception of the *shabti*-figure evolved. As time passed, ideas and practices advanced, which in the New Kingdom led to the elaboration of burials and burial equipment and more particularly the compilation of a new corpus of funerary texts which is now quite erroneously called *The Book of the Dead*. Many of these ideas and the concomitant practical results arising from them form the subject matter of the rest of this chapter.

Mummification

For many people the mummy typifies Egyptian culture. Mummies are the things that first draw children to the galleries in museums where Egyptian antiquities are displayed. They continue to fascinate visitors of all ages, if only as visible reminders of the ultimate fate of all human beings. For the ancient Egyptians the mummy represented the attempts made to secure the preservation of the body after death. As far back as one can trace through textual evidence the preservation of the body was important, and long before the time when texts were written there is physical evidence of the measures taken for this preservation. How did it all begin? In predynastic times burials were mostly very simple, with bodies being placed in shallow graves, along with a small collection of grave goods, and possibly wrapped in or simply protected by an animal skin or a woven mat, before finally being covered with sand. Burials were usually made in places above the area inundated by the annual Nile flood, which were also unaffected by ground water or by heavy rain. The dry conditions in much of Egypt, with the heat of the sun beating down on the sand covering the grave, resulted in the natural desiccation of the corpse. On disinterment, by chance or by the activity of scavenging crea-

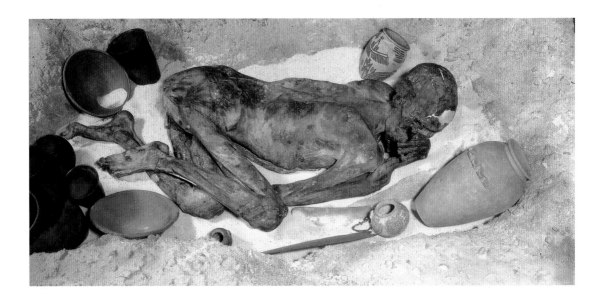

105 Reconstructed burial
of a man including his
naturally desiccated body and
typical grave goods. From
Gebelein. Late Predynastic
Period. L. of body 1.63 m.

OPPOSITE

106 Coffin made for the
incense-bearer in the Temple
of Khonsu in Karnak,
Pasheryenhor, decorated
with ritual scenes, including
the judgement of the deceased.
The finely wrapped mummy
within the coffin is of a
female, and intrusive.
From Thebes. Late New
Kingdom. L. 1.78 m.

tures like hyenas, such dried bodies, showing little sign of decomposition, gave the impression of a well-preserved dead person, although what actually survived was little more than a skeleton covered with skin, but often with quite a lot of body hair.

It is surmised that the condition of a well-dried body was an ideal to be reached. But things changed when in late Predynastic and Early Dynastic times bodies were placed in small chamber tombs and even simple wooden coffins; natural desiccation then did not take place, and the bodies decomposed naturally, leaving only skeletal remains. Was it then the case that consideration was given to developing ways by which the body could be preserved with some semblance of the shape and appearance of the living original? It is thought that it must have been so. In consequence, inefficient first efforts were made to prevent decomposition. The evidence is not ample. In some cases bodies were tightly bandaged, each finger and toe separately treated; the result was not good. Decomposition was hastened by such constriction, together with the warmth engendered by the close conditions within the grave. By the Fourth Dynasty at least, it was appreciated that the body had to receive treatment which included the removal of those parts subject to rapid deterioration after death, in particular the internal organs; and that in other respects the fleshy tissue of the body should be subjected to a process of desiccation which resulted in a dried-out corpse, inert and seemingly imperishable. The evidence still remains sparse and inadequate. However, in the surviving parts of the burial equipment of Queen Hetepheres, mother of Cheops, the builder of the Great Pyramid, there was found an alabaster chest divided internally into four compartments. Each compartment held a package containing part of the internal organs of the queen, still soaking in the remains of a solution of natron. The royal body itself was not, sadly, included among the objects found in what was a kind of secondary burial, so it could not be judged to what extent it had survived whatever treatment it had received.

Mummification was a process that developed very erratically as the centuries passed, and did not achieve anything like a satisfactory result until the late New Kingdom

(*c.* 1000 BC). Certain processes were recognized as being essential by at least the Old Kingdom, but the execution of these processes does not appear to have been followed successfully to the extent that surviving bodies retained a condition adequate to expectation. Middle Kingdom mummies have rarely survived in satisfactory states, and even during the New Kingdom the form provided by the bandaging, often handsomely packaged, may have suggested a well-preserved corpse within, but x-ray examination usually demonstrates how wretched the state of the body itself actually is. Some of the surviving mummies of kings, which can be viewed in the Cairo Museum – the divine cadavers of the great, like Thutmose III, Ramesses II and Ramesses III – are little more than skin and bone. Nevertheless, they still bear some resemblance to living persons, and it may be claimed that the mummification process has achieved a fair degree of success. But it did not always work so well: the mummy of King Tutankhamun, for example, suffered seriously from carelessness or inefficiency, so that very little of humanity can be seen in the pitiful remains which were contained within the elaborate wrappings and the splendour of the nest of coffins which held the royal body.

Egyptian mummification was essentially dehydration. It involved in the first place the removal of the brain and the internal organs as soon as possible after death before decomposition started. The one organ commonly left in the body cavity was the heart, which was regarded by the Egyptians as the seat of understanding, and therefore had to remain in close association with the body. The brain, removed through the nose, was not seen as being of special importance, and was not subjected to any form of preservation. However, the viscera, the internal organs, were rightly thought to be necessary for the overall preservation of the body, and its proper functioning after death. They were therefore treated to a process of dehydration similar to that used for the body itself. Dehydration of the body was effected by the application internally and externally of quantities of natron, a compound of sodium carbonate and sodium bicarbonate found naturally in several parts of Egypt, and particularly in the low-lying area to the west of the Delta, the Wadi Natrun. This natron effectively drew out the bodily fluids, broke down body fats, and generally left the corpse dry but supple. The dehydration process lasted about one half of the seventy days commonly assigned for the preparation of the dead body for burial.

When dehydration was completed, the body was washed, and anointed with appropriate unguents and spices to the accompaniment of the prescribed prayers; the body cavity might be packed with wads of linen. The incision made in the lower abdomen on the left side was sewn up and often covered with a leather or metal plate bearing the image of the *udjat*, the eye of Horus, the powerful amulet of completion and protection. The dehydrated viscera were separated into four groups, wrapped, and placed in four containers, each group protected by one of the four Sons of Horus: Duamutef (stomach), Qebhsenuef (intestines), Hapy (lungs) and Amsety (liver). The containers themselves were identified with, and protected by, four female deities: Neith, Selkis, Nephthys and Isis. Apart from the evidence of the compartmented alabaster chest of Queen Hetepheres, this kind of provision for the embalmed viscera of the deceased does not appear to occur before the early Middle Kingdom. Sets of four jars, placed in wooden chests, have been found with burials from the Twelfth Dynasty. The jars are usually made of Egyptian alabaster (calcite), and are topped with human-shaped heads, sometimes made of painted wood. From the end of the Eighteenth Dynasty the heads were individually

107 Calcite mummy Canopic Jars inscribed for the lady Neskhons. The wooden stoppers are in the forms of Qebhsenuef (falcon), Duamutef (jackal), Hapy (baboon) and Amsety (human). From Thebes. Twenty-first Dynasty. H.37 cm.

shaped to represent more precisely the four Sons of Horus: Duamutef, jackal-headed; Qebhsenuef, falcon-headed; Hapy, baboon-headed; and Amsety, human-headed. These containers are commonly called Canopic Jars, mistakenly so; when first found in modern times, they were connected by scholars with a legend found in classical authors concerning the pilot of Menelaus, who was drowned, buried at Canopus on the Delta coast, and revered locally in the form of a bulbous jar with a human head.

The unsatisfactory results of the regular process of mummification during the New Kingdom led to considerable refinements during the Twenty-first Dynasty, a time when the priesthood in Thebes was made aware of the inadequacies of earlier practices when they supervised the rescue and rewrapping of royal and other mummies of the Eighteenth to Twentieth Dynasties. It seems probable that those who examined the mummies of the very great rulers of these earlier dynasties could see that in their poor condition they scarcely offered the proper possibility for eternal survival, which was the sole purpose of body-preservation. New procedures, therefore, were introduced, the ultimate purpose of which was to produce a more self-contained, well-formed body, which would offer better prospects for the future survival and enjoyment of the individual in the afterlife. Great efforts were made to improve the appearance of the body by packing subcutaneously the dried-out collapsed limbs with various materials, and to plump out the bodily form – linen, fats and even mud were used. Also, the prepared, dehydrated viscera were packaged in the groups found in the jars, and placed in the body cavity, often accompanied by a small image of the appropriate Canopic deity. In spite of this alternative method of dealing with the internal organs, important burials were still provided with sets of Canopic Jars, often handsomely carved; they were dummy jars, placed with a burial simply to satisfy the practice of earlier times.

These elaborations in mummification were not very practical, and were soon discontinued, to be followed by a distinct deterioration in the processes used to prepare the body for burial. In later periods, particularly the Ptolemaic and Roman, an apparently casual attitude was taken towards the actual preparation of the body, with more attention being paid to the way in which it was packaged for burial; the aim seems to have been to end up with a neat attractive mummy, often bandaged with intricate patterns. What lay within was not to be probed. X-rays of late mummies have shown that it was not uncommon to make up a body from parts not all of which belonged to the same person. Clearly the appearance not the reality was what was sought.

At all periods when mummification was practised, the stage that resulted in what may properly be termed a mummy was the wrapping of the wretched dehydrated corpse. Here was the possibility of restoring a kind of dignity to the remains of the deceased. In some burials of the Middle Kingdom huge quantities of linen sheeting were employed to bulk out and protect the virtual skeleton within. In the New Kingdom, linen bandaging was used more sparingly, but within the bandaging might be enclosed protective amulets and jewellery, some of which may have been worn during the lifetime of the deceased. The most instructive and extreme example of this practice was the mummy of King Tutankhamun, within the bandaging of which were placed more than 150 pieces of amuletic and personal jewellery. One of the most important of these inclusions, and found with most mummies, was the heart scarab, which carried an

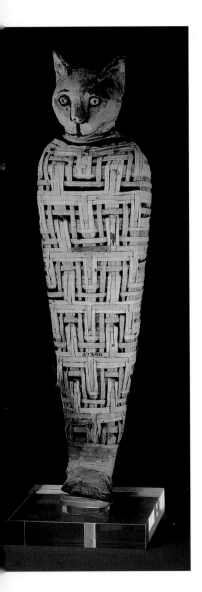

108 Carefully wrapped and bandaged mummy of a cat. The elaborate patterning of the outer wrappings is typical of the Roman Period. H.46 cm.

inscription invoking the scarab to intervene on behalf of the deceased in the judgement of Osiris after death. An unusual and very early example is that of King Sobkemsaef of the Seventeenth Dynasty, now in the British Museum as already mentioned. It seems to have survived the robbing of that king's tomb and the desecration of his mummy, which are described in one of the so-called Tomb Robbery papyri of the late Twentieth and early Twenty-first Dynasties, mentioned in chapter 4.

One may ask: 'Why mummy?' Like so much in the archaeology of ancient civilizations, mistaken ideas and terminologies are absorbed into the scholarly tradition, and are not easily eliminated – indeed elimination is not truly necessary. Such is the case with the term Canopic Jars. The term mummy derives from an Arabic word taken from Persian, meaning a body preserved in bitumen; the word *mummiya* in Arabic means 'bitumen'. The usage seems reasonable in that many mummies look as if they have been preserved in bitumen, or at least a bituminous material. As is so often the case, the usage is erroneous. Bitumen, which was available in the Near East in antiquity, was never employed in mummification; the bituminous appearances of some mummies was due to the blackening of the various unguents and other materials used in the final processes of Egyptian embalming.

An account of mummification cannot neglect mentioning the practice of animal and bird mummification which was common in later times, particularly during the Ptolemaic and Roman Periods. It is possible that the idea of such mummification may have been inspired by the individual embalming of the Apis bull and his mother, which has been mentioned earlier (see chapter 5) in connection with the Ptah cult at Memphis; the practice of these bull burials at Saqqara can be traced back at least to the New Kingdom. The mass embalming of creatures, however, was a late development, and it is difficult to determine how it truly began – what prompted people to indulge in the acquisition of the mummified bodies of creatures representative of a particular cult, and then to deposit them in a cemetery or catacomb associated with that cult. It is perhaps not surprising that cat cemeteries were established at Bubastis, the cult centre of the cat-goddess Bastet, or that baboon and ibis mummies occupied catacombs near Hermopolis, the cult centre of Thoth, whose manifestations were as ibis and baboon. It is not so clear why a considerable variety of bird and animal mummies were deposited in well-established catacombs at Saqqara. The bodies within the wrappings were not well prepared, but they were carefully wrapped so as to produce very well-finished packages, attractive to those who acquired them for presentation in pious reverence to the priests of the cult, who, no doubt, encouraged the practice as a lucrative activity for the maintenance of the cult.

Coffins

Care in the preparation of the body after death required the subsequent attention to the interment of the body in whatever way it had been treated. The kinds of coffin to be seen in all major museum collections date mostly from advanced periods in the dynastic history of the ancient Egyptians. The intention at all times, however, was to provide protection for the body, as the receptacle of the spirit of the deceased, the integrity of which secured lasting possibilities of comfortable survival after death. In predynastic times, and even much later for very humble burials, no coffin was provided. As mentioned earlier in this chapter, the body, mummified, was simply placed in a shallow grave, sometimes in a basketwork tray along with appropriate but few grave goods, and covered with cloth or leather or more basketwork. The grave was filled with sand and might be marked with a small mound. In some superior burials the graves were more carefully dug and the sides provided with a revetment of wickerwork or wood, resulting in a kind of box filling the grave. In Early Dynastic times this revetment was developed into a rectangular coffin which, containing the body of the deceased, could be lowered as a unit into the grave. The coffins used for royalty have not survived, but may be assumed to have been of a similar box-like form, but, as might be expected, better constructed.

During the Old Kingdom, stone sarcophagi were first made for royalty and even for some important nobles and officials. In the case of King Cheops quite a modest undecorated granite chest was provided; it still stands in the burial chamber of the Great Pyramid. A much more striking chest with panelled decoration on the sides was made in basalt for King Mycerinus, who was buried in the smallest of the three main Giza pyramids. Sadly, it was lost at sea while being transported to Britain. Drawings made at the time of its discovery show that it was much bigger than Cheops' simple chest. Some private stone sarcophagi were quite massive; that in the burial chamber of Khentika, a vizier in the time of King Teti of the early Sixth Dynasty (*c.* 2330 BC), is, with its huge lid, 3.15 m long, 1.48 m wide and 2.00 m high (10 × 4 x 6 ft). Such stone chests were aimed at providing extra security for the mummified individual, which was separately placed in a much smaller wooden coffin, simply inscribed and carrying the protective eyes of Horus.

109 Granite sarcophagus from an unidentified private tomb at Giza. The sides have a panelled decoration with 'false doors' at each end to facilitate the egress and access of the deceased after death. Fifth Dynasty. L.2.25 m.

110 Base of the outer coffin of Gua, with a map of the underworld to assist the travel of the deceased after death; part of *The Book of the Two Ways*. From El-Bersha. Twelfth Dynasty. L.2.6 m.

The great wooden coffins mentioned later in this chapter as carrying *The Coffin Texts*, with *The Book of the Two Ways* on the inside bottom, were made from thick planks of cedar wood, brought to Egypt all the way from Syria; they were splendidly made, with precise joints, and held together with pegs. Apart from *The Coffin Texts* they were also often decorated with representations of ritual objects and materials, weapons and tools – items required by the deceased in the afterlife. A full coffin equipment for an important provincial official might consist of one or two further, smaller rectangular coffins nested within the great main coffin. Royal burials of the time were contained in simple, panelled stone sarcophagi. As ever there were exceptions, such as the stone chests provided for the Eleventh Dynasty princesses at Deir el-Bahri, which were decorated on the outsides with scenes showing domestic and ritual activities.

In the preparation of mummies during the Middle Kingdom, as already mentioned above, large quantities of linen sheeting were used to bulk out the form of the desiccated body, and the practice developed of providing a mask made of cartonnage (a kind of papier mâché consisting of layers of linen stiffened with gesso-plaster), moulded to form a helmet fitting over the head, with facial features purporting to represent the deceased. The mask was painted and sometimes gilded. The resulting mummy, a padded body with mask, served as the pattern for the actual coffin which held the mummy; it was itself mummiform, and is now often termed anthropoid. In this shape it became an identification with Osiris, who was commonly represented mummiform. During the Second Intermediate Period, heavy wooden coffins were so shaped, and usually painted or gilded with a feather pattern called *rishi* (Arabic for 'feather'), thought to represent the protective wings of the goddess Isis.

The mummiform coffin became standard during the New Kingdom, made of wood or cartonnage, a good burial often consisting of several coffins fitting within each other, and the mummy itself sometimes protected additionally by a shaped cover, perhaps with an openwork design. The practice in the later New Kingdom was to decorate the coffins with ritual scenes and texts, brightly painted, both inside and outside. Nests of coffins containing the mummies of important people were usually placed in stone sarcophagi, which might themselves be mummiform. The stone sarcophagi of kings were not usually mummiform, the best-known example being that of King Tutankhamun; it is made of quartzite, with a simple flat lid, and contained three mummiform coffins, the outer two of gilded wood and the innermost of solid gold. The head of the mummy within was protected by the great golden mask which has become such a symbol of royalty and royal burial in ancient Egypt. As ever in funerary matters, the possibilities of variation were almost infinite. A few burials of important non-royal individuals were furnished with mummiform inner stone coffins, with carved texts to some extent following the pattern of royal sarcophagi. The chest of the coffin of King Sety I is made of Egyptian alabaster, and finely carved with extensive texts from the regular royal funerary compilations. It can now be seen in a suitably atmospheric setting in the basement of the Sir John Soane Museum in London.

The care taken in the preparation of the mummy in the Twenty-first Dynasty was

111 The Theban Necropolis, burial place for the nobles of the New Kingdom. The modern village of Qurna occupies much of the area, and its inhabitants treat its buried antiquities as part of their heritage.

112 (left) The painted and gilded mummy case of Artemidorus, incorporating the portrait of the deceased painted in coloured wax. The symbolism on the cartonnage is wholly Egyptian. From Hawara. Second century AD. H.1.67 m.

(right) Wooden mummy board from the burial ensemble of an unnamed Theban priestess. It is painted with a remarkable series of religious and amuletic motifs, and a vastly elaborate floral collar. From Thebes. Twenty-first Dynasty. H.1.62 m.

matched in the shaping and decoration of the coffins provided to contain it. The repertoire of ritual scenes and magical components used in the decorations was considerably enlarged, often including funeral processions, the judgement before Osiris, and the passage of the sun-god through the underworld. These decorations were usually moulded in relief on the cartonnage shell, and very finely painted. This decoration in effect took the place of the tomb scenes found in tombs of the earlier New Kingdom, for the burials of this later period were not made in individual tombs with scenes and texts arranged accordingly but in undecorated collective family tombs; such was certainly the case in the Theban Necropolis. The careful mummification practices of the Twenty-first Dynasty were not continued in the later periods of Pharaonic Egypt; frequently very large wooden mummiform coffins were made, usually ponderous, and not always very well constructed. Some of the large stone sarcophagi for important people were also not very carefully made, as if the skills of the stoneworkers had diminished. But not so for the siltstone (schist) chest and lid made for the influential princess and God's Wife of Amun, Ankhnesneferibre, of the Twenty-sixth Dynasty (EA 32, fig. 45). The surface of the lid carries a finely carved representation of the not-very-handsome lady herself, with a somewhat more seductive carving of the sky-goddess Nut on the inside. The coffer and lid are very precisely carved, and inscribed in fine hieroglyphs with texts from *The Book of the Dead*. This coffin is in the British Museum, and so too the great royal sarcophagus of Nectanebo II, the last native Egyptian king; it lacks its lid and was used up to the time of its discovery by the Napoleonic expedition as an ablution bath in a mosque in Alexandria. The texts carved on the inside and outside are taken from *The Book of what is in the Underworld*. When it was found, it was thought to be the sarcophagus of Alexander the Great.

In the Graeco-Roman Period, while the actual mummification process became rather careless, and the majority of wrappings and coffins very indifferently made, some bodies were carefully bandaged with elaborate cross patterns, and sometimes provided with painted portraits or plaster masks. The portraits represent a most striking development of the early centuries AD, and show by style and method of painting the influence of Roman portraiture in the manner described by Pliny the Elder as 'encaustic'. It is thought that these portraits, painted mostly in coloured wax on thin wooden panels, were usually prepared in the lifetime of the subject in readiness for burial, but doubts can be cast on this idea. The majority of surviving examples come from burials in and around the Faiyum, where there were many Graeco-Roman towns; the genre is consequently called Faiyumic. Examples have, however, been found at other sites throughout Egypt. A particularly fine example still in position on its mummiform coffin is that of Artemidorus, for whom a gilded Greek text laments, 'Artemidorus, Farewell!' (EA 21810, fig. 112).

113 Painted stone *shabti* of an unnamed Singer of Amun. It is shown carrying two hoes and two baskets for use in shifting earth. H.25.3 cm.

OPPOSITE

114 Painted wooden *shabti* box of the singer of Amun, Henutmehyt, with some of its contents displayed. On its side Henutmehyt makes an offering to the Canopic deities Qebhsenuef, Hapy and Amsety. From Thebes. Nineteenth Dynasty. H.34.5 cm.

Shabtis and other grave goods

The Osirian kingdom in which all Egyptians (if they qualified) expected to pass eternity was thought to be a land very like Egypt itself – what could be better? There would, however, be snags which might make the afterlife not quite as cosy and privileged as the deceased would expect. Scenes of existence in the afterlife picture the deceased, often accompanied by his wife, cultivating the fields and harvesting the crops. These were the activities proper for an idyllic existence in an idyllic land. Nevertheless, in real life, in ancient Egypt, the pastoral idyll was compromised by the chores that resulted from the annual flood and the inundation of the land for several months every year. When the flood receded in the autumn, a huge operation of land reclamation and rehabilitation took place. This work was organized locally in the nomes of Upper and Lower Egypt, and the labour needed was recruited by a corvée, the forced call-up of men who were required to clear canals, re-establish dykes, confirm the boundaries of properties, and generally tidy up the fields ready for cultivation. In real life some categories in the population were able to obtain exemption from the corvée – for example, priests and scribes, i.e. the clergy and the civil service – and those who could afford to provide a deputy to fulfil the required duties. What about the afterlife? Would things be different there? To overcome the problematic matter of the posthumous corvée the ancient Egyptians took pragmatic steps to make a suitable provision of alternative service. The *shabti* was the result.

The idea behind the *shabti* is made clear by a short invocation found in *The Coffin Texts* of the Middle Kingdom. It calls on the figure to act for the deceased in the underworld if he is subjected to the corvée. The text was more fully developed in the New Kingdom, and was incorporated in chapter 6 of *The Book of the Dead*, a fairly standard version of which reads:

O *shabti*! If N (the name of the deceased) is called, or detailed for any task that has
to be done in the god's land (the underworld); if the unpleasant duty of a man at his
work should be assigned to me, on each time of sowing the fields, of flooding the
banks, and of shifting sand from the east to the west; 'Here I am', you should say.

Some version of this spell was commonly inscribed on the *shabti* figure from the New Kingdom onwards; there were many variants. The earliest *shabtis* were simple wooden mummiform figures with just the name of the deceased inscribed in black ink. During the New Kingdom many fine figures were produced in stone and faience, burials usually being provided with single examples. Royal burials, strangely, in view of the different posthumous expectations of the king, were provided with not just one but multiple numbers of *shabtis*. Tutankhamun's burial, for example, contained 413 figures of many different types and materials, some of large and very beautiful form and offered to the royal burial in homage by important officials. The large number has been analysed as made up of 365 daily *shabtis*, 36 overseer *shabtis* controlling groups of about 10, and then 12 monthly overseers. This may not, however, be a true analysis of the group, for the actual *shabti* figures are too varied to be precisely categorized. Nevertheless, it is the case that from the late New Kingdom important private burials often included 360 daily *shabtis* and 36 overseers.

In order that the *shabti* could successfully perform the necessary tasks, it was usually represented carrying a mattock, a hoe and a basket; it was also in mummy-form to establish the proper relationship with the mummified deceased. The overseer *shabtis*, however, carried whips, and were commonly not mummiform but shown wearing skirts. Sometimes little bronze baskets, hoes and mattocks were provided separately for use by the *shabti*. The word *shabti* is of uncertain meaning and origin; in the New Kingdom the form *shawabty* became common; in later times *ushabti* was used, the word then clearly reinterpreted to mean 'answerer', a suitable designation for the figure that should answer for the deceased in response to the corvée.

The purpose of the *shabti* at the simplest level was to ensure that the dead person's existence in the afterlife was not rudely interrupted from time to time by the requirements of the corvée. Yet, from the evidence provided by scenes in tombs of the New Kingdom, there was some expectation that the deceased would be involved in some manual labour, spending part of his time for eternity in cultivating crops in the Field of Reeds – the idyllic mirror image of the Nile Valley in the underworld. Expectations, however, included a posthumous way of life at least as well equipped and comfortable as that enjoyed on earth. Consequently, the burial equipment should include much of the material possessions needed to support such a life. Not many almost complete burial equipments have been found in controlled excavations, apart from the magnificent cornucopia of Tutankhamun's tomb, and the splendid furnishings of the tomb of Yuia and Tjuiu, parents of Queen Tiye, the principal wife of King Amenhotep III, also in the Valley of the Kings. The virtually intact tombs of some of the workmen of the village community of Deir el-Medina, like those of Kha and Sennedjem, have shown what people of fairly modest means were prepared to take into eternity to provide the comforts enjoyed on earth. The older collections of Egyptian antiquities, benefiting from the profitable activities of modern Egyptian tomb-robbers, contain many examples of the furniture, household equipment, and food-and-drink containers which stocked the burials of people of importance in antiquity. It might be mentioned as a kind of excuse for the work of these illicit labourers that they did not see what they did as robbery but as the harvesting of their heritage from the graves of their distant ancestors. Beds, bed linen, chests full of clothes, chairs, stools – the common contents of ancient Egyptian homes – exist in considerable numbers, and often in excellent condition. Occasionally a piece of furniture may show signs of use in daily life; sometimes a similar piece may be painted and inscribed with offering texts, specifically prepared for inclusion in the burial. Some pieces testify to the intimate relationship between life on earth and life in the hereafter, which characterized the Egyptians' practical attitude to death.

115 Limestone *shabti* of King Ahmose, first king of the Eighteenth Dynasty; the earliest known royal *shabti*. From Thebes. H.30 cm.

Funerary texts

Most people have heard of *The Book of the Dead*, and few collections of Egyptian antiquities lack copies, large or small, of that compilation of texts designed to help the owner accommodate his- or herself to the life after death. More properly its title is *The Book of going-forth by day*; the greater part of most papyrus collections consists of copies ranging in date from the Eighteenth Dynasty to Roman times. As it exists in its various versions, it represents the last substantial stage in the development of funerary texts applicable to non-royal persons. But the tradition of funerary texts exemplified by *The Book of the Dead* can be traced back to compilations which were exclusively royal in their application. It must be presumed that there existed in the early Old Kingdom a body of religious texts which could be recited from papyrus copies in appropriate ceremonies to inform the dead king of the nature of his afterlife and the means by which he could achieve his final destination among the imperishable stars. The destiny was celestial and not subterranean. From the late Fifth Dynasty substantial selections from this body of funerary spells and incantations were carved on the walls of the burial chamber and adjacent rooms in the royal pyramids. Not surprisingly they are known as *Pyramid Texts*, first carved in the pyramid of King Unas (*c.* 2350 BC), and then in the kings' and some queens' pyramids of the Sixth Dynasty. It is quite clear that the individual spells are very various in their content, purposes and antiquity. Some seem quite primitive in their wording and intention, and sit strangely with those which concentrate on the celestial destiny of the king, the latter being, to put it simply, very high minded.

116 Part of *The Pyramid Texts* in the burial chamber of Unas, last king of the Fifth Dynasty. The signs are deeply carved and painted blue. The royal cartouche is clearly visible. Saqqara.

In the tombs of private individuals during the Old Kingdom the funerary texts concentrated on the provision of necessary food, drink and other materials, usually set out in tabular form – a kind of menu – and in expressing the hope that the deceased would travel safely on the road to the West. Osiris develops as the principal funerary deity, and the afterlife is conceived as taking place in his realm, subterranean but to a very great extent like the earthly land, which provides the ideal pattern for eternal existence. *The Pyramid Texts* fell out of use during the First Intermediate Period, and were never again directly used in royal tombs, although parts are to be found in some large but non-royal tombs of the Twenty-fifth and Twenty-sixth Dynasties, a period of archaizing tendencies, when texts, representations and forms of sculpture from earlier times were revived. But from *The Pyramid Texts* in part was developed a new compilation of funerary texts, which were written in cursive hieroglyphs and simple hieratic on the large wooden coffins of important people. The best examples have come from the provincial cemeteries of Middle Egypt – Beni Hasan, Asyut, El-Bersha, Meir – and they are known as *The Coffin Texts*. Again, the spells, which could be consulted magically by the deceased lying in the coffin, were composed with the intention of allowing the dead person to consider the future, which retained some of the solar aspects of *The Pyramid Texts*, but concentrated more on the realm of Osiris in the netherworld. A component of *The Coffin Texts*, often inscribed on the floor of the principal coffin, was *The Book of*

117 Burial chamber of Ramesses VI in the Valley of the Kings. The ceiling is barrel-shaped and painted with celestial beings; the walls are decorated with scenes and texts from the royal mortuary compositions. Twentieth Dynasty.

the Two Ways. It provided helpful indications on how to escape some of the hazards to be encountered on the way to meet Osiris; it included a schematic map to assist the dead voyager (fig. 110).

In the New Kingdom, from the beginning of the Eighteenth Dynasty, new and very considerable bodies of funerary materials were employed in royal tombs, and for non-royal persons. As was the case with *The Pyramid Texts*, the compositions placed on the walls of the great tombs in the Valley of the Kings were organized into a series of helpful 'books' designed to direct the deceased king through the hazards and terrors of the night in the underworld so that he could ultimately be, as it were, reborn with the sun-god at dawn, to join him in the celestial barque in which eternity would be spent. Among these long texts, the most important were: the *Amduat*, i.e. *The Book of what is in the Underworld*; *The Book of Gates*; and *The Book of Caverns*. They were lavishly and wonderfully illustrated in the royal tombs, with highly imaginative scenes depicting many of the disagreeable creatures to be encountered as well as the beneficent genii and minor deities who were devoted to helping the dead king forward in his subterranean journey.

Parts of some of these books were adapted for the use of non-royal individuals, men and women, in the late New Kingdom and subsequently; but the common series of funerary texts for non-royal people was contained in *The Book of the Dead*, already mentioned at the beginning of this section. A full series of spells or chapters amounted to about 200; the great majority of these are found in papyri of the New Kingdom, the remaining 30–40 being added in the Saite Period and later. This later revision is some-times called the Saite Recension, which does not satisfactorily describe the somewhat unstructured nature of the changes. Nevertheless, a more regular sequence of spells was developed in the Late Period, superseding the more casual order which is found in ear-lier examples. The copies prepared for individuals never contained the whole series of spells; it would seem that the size and order of the selection in a particular example depended on what could be afforded by the person from whom it would be required. The best copies, it seems, were specially commissioned in accordance with the wishes of the individual, whose name and title(s) were inserted at the appropriate places in the texts at the time of writing of the main document. In many cases, however, stock copies were prepared to which names and titles were added before they were handed over to the new owner. In the best examples – not always those made for the most important people – the illustrations or vignettes were excellent examples of Egyptian miniature painting. They were pertinent to the texts and sometimes of superior quality to the actual texts. Among the large collection of copies in the British Museum, that prepared for the royal scribe Ani has superb vignettes, but a rather indifferent text (EA 10470). The version made for the steward of the treasurer Nu, on the other hand, has an excel-lent text, but fairly simple vignettes (EA 10477).

Among the sections which were thought to be essential for inclusion in all copies of *The Book of the Dead* were an initial prayer to and invocation of the sun-god Re-Herakhty, and spell 125 which deals with the judgement of the deceased. This latter spell is usually illustrated by a vignette showing the heart of the dead person placed in a balance to be weighed against Ma'at, the goddess of Truth. An examination is made by forty-two assessor gods, each of whom asks a question concerning the behaviour of the dead person during his life; in each case the correct answer is 'No!'. This examination has usually been called the Negative Confession, but a more suitable term, it has been suggested, would be Declaration of Innocence. The answers to the forty-two questions are recorded by the divine scribe Thoth, and the balance is checked by jackal-headed Anubis, the necropolis-god. If the deceased fails the test, the heart will be eaten by the creature 'the Heart-swallower' – part crocodile, part lion and part hippopotamus; if the test is passed, the successful candidate is declared 'true-of-voice', 'justified', and led by Horus into the presence of Osiris.

Although it has been possible for scholars to establish a reasonably standard version of the texts in *The Book of the Dead*, it has not been possible for them to determine how in antiquity the texts were standardized. We may presume that the priestly schools attached to the great cult-temples oversaw matters of this kind, and were perhaps even responsible for the production of many copies of the book. Furthermore, these establishments were probably responsible for the major changes that took place in the organizing and revising of the individual spells from time to time, and even in the different ways in which the texts were presented. It seems that for reasons of ritual purity, religious texts were com-monly written on new papyrus. During much of the New Kingdom a form of modified semi-cursive hieroglyphs was employed for the writing of copies of *The Book of the Dead*, superseded in the later New Kingdom by a very regular form of hieratic, and then in the Saite Period and later usually by a form of very neat, precise hieroglyphs written

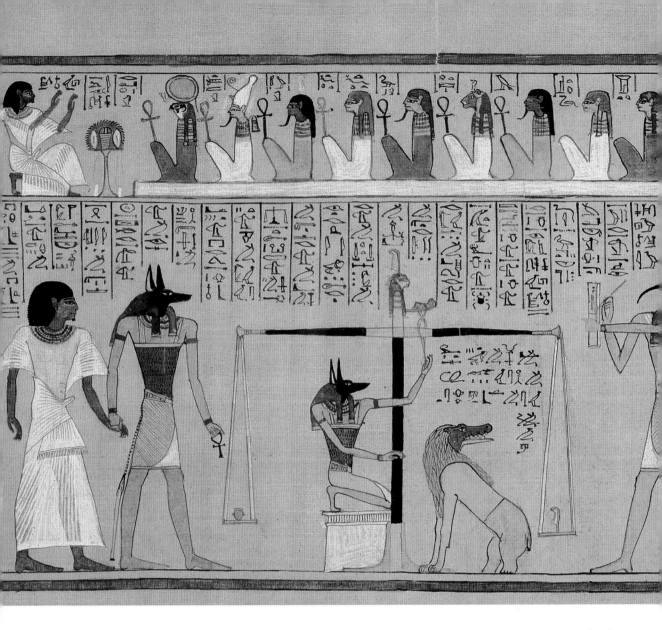

118 The Judgement scene from *The Book of the Dead* of the royal scribe Hunefer. From the left: Hunefer is brought to judgement by Anubis; his heart is weighed against *ma'at*; he is justified and led by Horus 'avenger of his father' before Osiris. Nineteenth Dynasty. H.39.5 cm.

with a fine brush. In the later texts the vignettes were commonly not coloured but handsomely drawn in black ink. One of the most remarkable copies in the British Museum, with drawn vignettes on a large scale, was prepared for the lady Nesitanebtashru, daughter of the High Priest of Amun, Pinudjem I of the Twenty-first Dynasty (*c.* 1050 BC); it is 37m long and 49.5 cm high (121 ft × 19 in) (EA 10554).

Some indication has been given in the preceding pages of the great variety of materials which might be included in an ancient Egyptian tomb. It would be wrong to suggest that there would have been some kind of checklist which might be used by the family of the deceased person to ensure that nothing was left out. Nevertheless, certain items were essential for a proper burial: the mummified corpse in its coffin(s), the Canopic equipment, the *shabti* figure(s) and a copy perhaps of *The Book of the Dead*. What else might be included depended to some extent on the size of the tomb prepared for the

deceased, on what might be available in the form of household goods, and, perhaps more importantly, on the prevailing practice at the time of burial. During the New Kingdom most people of consequence in the Theban area, for example, would expect a well-prepared sepulchre with chapel and separate burial chamber, providing therefore good accommodation for a substantial ancillary equipment. In the Late New Kingdom, individual tombs were not common, and group burials were made, for example of the priests of Amun, in which the barest minimum of essential equipment accompanied the mummy and coffin. Still, from all periods and from all parts of Egypt, the evidence confirms conclusively how important the business of death and burial was to the ancient Egyptians; and in spite of the extravagance which could attend the burial of an important person, what really mattered was that the body should survive in as good a state as possible to enable the dead to continue to enjoy the afterlife – notional as well as actual – for eternity; and also that the deceased's name might continue to live.

Builders and Decorators

119 The three pyramids of Giza on the plateau overlooking the Nile Valley, with Cairo in the background: to the left, Cheops; in the centre, Chephren; to the right, Mycerinus.

If visitors to the Egyptian galleries of a museum first rush to see the mummies, those who travel to Egypt itself are mostly impelled first to see the pyramids. And by 'the pyramids' the majority would think primarily of the group at Giza, which includes the Great Pyramid – the greatest and most impressive of all pyramids both for its external shape and internal features. Further travels in the country would lead to Luxor, where the Luxor and Karnak temples on the east bank of the Nile and the impressive mortuary temples to the west – Deir el-Bahri, the Ramesseum and Medinet Habu, to mention but the most famous – mightily astound by their size, construction and decoration. The chronological range is extraordinary, extending from the Step Pyramid of King Djoser of the Third Dynasty (c. 2650 BC) to the mighty temples of the Ptolemies and the early Roman Emperors at Dendera, Edfu and Philae. And then there are the jewels of artistic achievement: the private mastabas of the Fifth and Sixth Dynasties at Saqqara in particular; the rock-cut tombs of Middle Kingdom dignitaries at Beni Hasan; and the tombs of the New Kingdom nobles and officials in the Theban Necropolis. In some of these the phenomenal artistry of anonymous Egyptian painters may be observed.

Much has already been said in the first chapter of this book about the availability of fine building stones in the hills bordering the Nile Valley, in particular limestone, sandstone and granite. From the early Old Kingdom, ancient Egyptian builders and quarrymen showed exceptional skill in identifying suitable sites from which high-quality stone could be extracted, and they developed techniques for extraction which were unusually effective and economical. They also developed an understanding of the use of different building stones, which allowed them to select the most suitable kinds for particular purposes in the construction of their great buildings. And their great buildings, especially the freestanding tomb structures of pyramids and mastabas, and the monumental temples, were made of stone because they were buildings for eternity. They should outlast their construction by many years, and remain testimonies of the ancient Egyptian beliefs in the afterlife and the working of the great deities.

ABOVE RIGHT

120 Brick-making on the banks of the Nile in Middle Egypt: on the right, the moulded bricks are laid out to dry; on the left, a simple kiln, not part of the ancient brick-making process.

Stone, however, was not necessary for the construction of buildings which were in a sense ephemeral, and certainly not for eternity, in particular domestic structures: the houses of the village-dwellers, the villas of the nobles, the palaces of the royal family. Apart from the incidental use of stone for architectural features in the most important domestic buildings, Nile mud provided the essential material in the form of bricks, regularly and carefully moulded. Mud-brick was in some respects the most characteristic building material in Egypt, not only in antiquity, but even today. Bricks were easily manufactured out of the abundant annual deposits of silt during the inundation, with the addition, if thought necessary, of chopped chaff and similar organic material to produce a more stable, less crumbly product. The ancient techniques of puddling the mud with water to achieve a workable mixture, the shaping of the bricks individually using a wooden rectangular mould and the laying out of the moulded bricks to dry in the sun can still be seen in practice today in the many small brickworks to be found on

121 Two great mud-brick enclosures in the desert at Abydos. Both are now thought to be mortuary structures of Second Dynasty kings. That on the left, the Shunet ez-Zebib, is associated with Khasekhemwy.

the banks of the Nile. The processes can similarly be seen in the wall paintings in the tomb of the vizier Rekhmire in the Theban Necropolis. The one process lacking in antiquity was the baking of the bricks after drying to produce a long-lasting building material impervious to rain and suitable for the construction of tall buildings. There can be no doubt that the ancient Egyptians knew that baked brick had qualities lacking in the unbaked brick, but they chose, no doubt deliberately, not to bake until Roman times. There were various practical reasons for this choice. Firstly, it was quicker and more economical to make simple sun-dried mud-bricks; secondly, buildings of mud-bricks apparently were more comfortable to live in, the unbaked material conducting heat and cold less readily than the baked variety; thirdly, unbaked brick was more environmentally friendly, although the Egyptians would not have thought of it in such modern terms. An old building could easily be levelled, its bricks being partly recovered for reuse, and the remainder pulverized and used as the basis or foundation of a replacement building. It was no particularly wasteful thing to abandon a villa, or even a royal palace, in which bricks of Nile mud formed the principal constituent material.

Before the adoption of stone for the building of tombs and temples in the early Old Kingdom, mud-brick was the constructional material of choice, and was employed to build structures of very considerable size, by any standard of assessment. In the Early Dynastic Period, huge enclosures of mud-brick were built at places like Hierakonpolis and Abydos, structures with walls of such thickness that they survive to this day in relatively good condition. The great tombs of the kings and nobles of the early dynasties were also provided with massive mud-brick superstructures, substantial traces of which can still be seen, especially at North Saqqara. The practice of building the great walls surrounding temple complexes and other protected enclosures in mud-brick persisted down to the late Dynastic Period. Many still survive in remarkable condition surrounding huge temple precincts, as at Karnak (late New Kingdom), Tanis (Twenty-first Dynasty) and Dendera (Ptolemaic-Roman Period); the method of construction in sections, with undulating courses, seems to have been designed to enable the structures to endure earth tremors and other material disasters. Frequently the bricks were stamped with the names of the kings in whose reigns the walls were built, the most remarkable examples of which is the great wall at Tanis. Investigations by Flinders Petrie demonstrated that every brick in this massive wall was stamped with the cartouches of Psusennes I of the Twenty-first Dynasty (c. 1000 BC) in whose reign undoubtedly it was built. Petrie estimated that the wall, when complete, was on average 14 m (45 ft) high, 21 m (70 ft) thick and 1035 m (3400 ft) in length, containing therefore over twenty million stamped bricks. There was plenty of Nile mud in the north-eastern Delta.

While the principal buildings within a temple enclosure were constructed of stone, subsidiary structures were commonly made of mud-brick. Sometimes they are of considerable architectural interest, like the barrel-vaulted store chambers in the enclosure of the Ramesseum, the mortuary temple of Ramesses II. In spite of their relatively flimsy method of construction, these vaults remain virtually intact after almost 3300 years, although they, unlike the temple itself, were not constructed for eternity. It is, sadly, the case that the same state of preservation has not been enjoyed by the domestic buildings of ancient Egypt. In some respects, the best evidence for a town of varied neighbourhoods can be found at El-Amarna, the ancient Akhetaten, the capital city of Akhenaten's Atenist state. The site chosen by the king was virgin; there was ample room in the desert area to the east of the cultivated strip along the river for a large city to be laid out, with spaces for great temples, ancillary religious buildings, royal palaces, official establishments, and residential districts to accommodate important officials and prospective inhabitants of less-elevated status. There were wide roads and plenty of room for expansion. As the city remained occupied for a very short period – scarcely twenty years on a generous estimate – the domestic districts had been little affected by rebuilding, and the plans of many houses have been revealed by careful excavation. Sadly, on abandonment, the whole of Akhetaten was subjected to dismantlement with the removal of almost all reusable materials – stone and wooden elements like door-jambs, lintels, beams and pillars – so that much of the individual character of houses and palaces has been lost. Nevertheless, a better idea of the Egyptian house in the Eighteenth Dynasty can be gained from the excavated areas of Akhetaten than from anywhere else in Egypt.

A great house like that of the vizier Nakht might have as many as thirty rooms, with additional accommodation on the roof – not quite a second storey – reached by a wooden stair. In what was the public part of the house there were reception rooms for visitors; beyond in the private part were rooms for family activities, bedrooms and a rather larger apartment for the house-owner with what would now be called en suite facilities – a bathroom and a lavatory. There is much evidence that the principal rooms were brightly decorated, the rough brick walls being finished with gesso-plaster, mostly painted white but with floral friezes and other gaily painted decoration. Wooden pillars were painted red, and ceiling beams blue. The effect of the decorative schemes in these houses was surely dramatic. The evidence from private houses at Akhetaten is not substantial, but the predilection for highly decorative schemes in domestic settings is better seen in the remains of painted scenes from some of the royal palaces. The freedom of artistic expression, one of the notable characteristics of Amarna art, and a distinct interest in the natural world, yielded wall paintings of remarkable quality. Of particular note are the marsh scenes with interweaving papyrus plants, almost prefiguring certain of the wallpaper designs of William Morris. Birds flit among the twisting stems of papyrus, the floral heads of which bend as if in constant movement. As we shall see later, colourful decoration was not confined to the Amarna Period. All the great temples were brightly

122 Part of a painted pavement from the building called Meruaten at El-Amarna. It shows ducks flying out of a papyrus thicket. H.93 cm.

painted, the vibrant effect of the brilliant pigments providing a wonderful contrast to the drab colours of stone, especially sandstone. Tombs were filled with painted reliefs and mural paintings on plaster. It must be concluded that the insides of homes were, when possible, equally brightly decorated. Externally houses were probably painted simply white, as may be seen in the scene in *The Book of the Dead* of the royal scribe Nakht in the British Museum (EA 10471). Here, Nakht and his wife Tjuiu are shown leaving their house, which is represented in simplified form; the walls are painted white, as are the air vents on the roof designed to catch the breeze; the window grids and doorway are painted a brownish red, which may indicate wood or even painted stone.

A short letter in the British Museum (EA 10102) gives a brief idea of how a house might be built and its construction supervised. The mayor Mentuhotep writes to the scribe Ahmose, who is acting as his agent in the building of a house. After a long formal epistolary greeting, Mentuhotep continues:

In addition: You should have installed the matting and the beams of the storerooms along with the back part of the house, the wall being six cubits high [c. 3 m]. And allow for the doors of the storerooms to be five cubits high [2.6 m], and the doors of the sitting room to be six cubits high. And you should instruct the builder, Amenmose, so that he does it exactly so, and hastens the building of the house. See to it! What a good thing my brother is with you. It is on you that I place my trust.

In addition: Get a shelter made out of some of the matting, and have it given to Benia.

In addition: Have the cost of the house-plot be given to its owner, and make sure he is satisfied. See to it! Take care that when I arrive he doesn't have words with me.

One might think that some of the detailed specifications mentioned in the letter ought 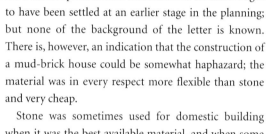 to have been settled at an earlier stage in the planning; but none of the background of the letter is known. There is, however, an indication that the construction of a mud-brick house could be somewhat haphazard; the material was in every respect more flexible than stone and very cheap.

Stone was sometimes used for domestic building when it was the best available material, and when some degree of permanence in habitation could be expected. Such was the case for the workmen's village of Deir el-Medina, where a planned settlement for specialist craftsmen was occupied from the early Eighteenth Dynasty down to the Twenty-first Dynasty, a period of approximately 450 years. Built in a shallow valley in the Theban hills, the village houses were constructed of local limestone and put together from flattish slabs and

123 The main workmen's village at Deir el-Medina. The houses are built close together and constructed of stone.

rubble, the method in some respects resembling the technique of dry-stone walling found in hilly parts of Great Britain. Within this walled settlement space was strictly limited and the houses built close together, with no room for expansion; and so they remained, often occupied by successive generations of the same families. Economy in the use of the available space led to a fairly regular lay-out for many of the houses. From the street a few steps led into a room roughly square, which was used, apparently, both for the reception of visitors and for certain domestic religious acts. Beyond was the largest room in the house, the floor being raised above that of the first room, and the roof, supported by wooden pillars, higher still and made of palm-logs and thatch. From this room a short stair led to a subterranean store chamber, not very large. A smaller room lay beyond the principal room, and a passageway opened on a small unroofed area used for cooking and storage, from which a stone-built stair led up to the roof. These houses were not spacious, yet they succeeded in accommodating quite big families. Sleeping arrangements were not very formal, and many family members would have slept on the roof, especially in hot weather. It is not unlikely that the houses of Deir el-Medina, occupied by workmen of some status, were not as comfortable as the mud-brick dwellings of the peasants who lived in villages raised above the flood-levels in the Nile Valley itself.

In considering building in stone in ancient Egypt, the simple houses of settlements like Deir el-Medina are scarcely worthy of notice in the context of great temples and funerary structures, except in that they point very distinctly to the building priorities of the Egyptians. Stone, as has already been mentioned, was not for domestic building, whether for royalty or for other classes of the population. From very early times the rich resources of stones readily available for exploitation in the barren and rocky region of the Eastern Desert were collected and worked by the inhabitants of the Nile Valley for the production of tools (especially flint, or more precisely chert) and the manufacture of stone vessels. The stones mostly used were hard and difficult to work, but the evidence presented by the many thousands of vessels in hard stones like granite, breccia, greywacke (schist), diorite, quartzite and basalt, shaped very precisely and carefully hollowed out by drilling and grinding, demonstrate a wonderfully developed technique of working stone, and also the possession of excellent discrimination in the selection of materials. It was almost certainly the case that the stones used in the manufacture of these vessels were retrieved from the Eastern Desert as individual boulders, and were not in general quarried from the living rock.

Quarrying, however, became necessary when the building of great stone structures was developed in the early Old Kingdom. Again the ancient craftsmen showed an extraordinary competence in identifying places where the required stone could be extracted with minimum effort and then conveyed with relative ease to the river's edge; from suitably built quays the roughly shaped blocks could then be placed on barges, in itself

124 The gneiss quarry at the Mons Claudianus in the Eastern Desert, mostly worked in Roman times. The stone is greyish and granite-like; an unfinished bath-shaped sarcophagus can be seen.

not an easy process, and transported by water to the construction site. Ideally, it would seem, the direction of transportation from quarry to site was downstream to avoid the necessity of working against the natural flow of the river. From the outset Egyptian stonemasons and architects demonstrated supreme confidence in perceiving the capabilities of stone construction, and its drawbacks. How precisely great buildings were planned and how the order of their construction from plan to completion was organized are wholly unknown, but students of Egyptian architecture have been able to offer some solutions and many suggestions concerning the ancient ways and means. The evidence provided by great structures that remain virtually intact reveals that the ancient Egyptians, to put the case at its simplest, knew what they had to do and how to do it, though there can be little doubt that many toes were crushed and many limbs broken in the building of the Great Pyramid. But not all of the many thousands of men employed at the pyramid site at the height of the construction season would have been

125 Some of the wonderfully preserved mud-brick vaulted store chambers within the great enclosures of the Ramesseum, the mortuary temple of Ramesses II.

skilled craftsmen, or even labourers experienced in the movement of stone; perhaps most were simple farmers, recruited by corvée to work on the great royal monument during the flood when agricultural activities were not possible.

The Step Pyramid of King Djoser of the Third Dynasty displays many signs of architectural innovation, and also good evidence that several modifications were made in the design of the completed monument. What was probably first planned as a rectangular stone mastaba, the natural development following the building of great mud-brick mastabas during the first two dynasties, ended up as a stepped structure with six stages. The bulk of the pyramid consisted of relatively small blocks of locally quarried limestone, the whole finally being faced with fine-quality limestone from the quarries at Tura on the other side of the Nile, in the hills of the Eastern Desert. The limestone of Tura became the stone of choice for superior buildings in the Old Kingdom, and one may wonder at the prescience and discrimination of the early stone surveyors who first identified the deposits of this first-class building material. Furthermore, at this early stage, those who exploited the stone of Tura would not have known how well it would weather over the centuries, its colour changing from brilliant white to an indeterminate greyish pink. One further remarkable innovation in the construction of the Step Pyramid was a subterranean burial chamber constructed entirely out of the pink granite of Aswan, painstakingly worked in the south, and then brought 600 miles, or more, by river to the quays of Memphis; from this point the final journey to Saqqara was a matter of a few miles, much of which was probably by barge along canals. What is abundantly clear in the planning and construction of the Step Pyramid is that there was in Egypt at this early time (*c.* 2650 BC) a clear appreciation of the principal sources of different stones, and a developed knowledge of how they should be worked, and for what purposes they were best used – local limestone for the bulk of construction, fine limestone for facing, and granite for those parts in a structure which needed special strength or protection.

126 A fully restored dummy shrine in the *sed*-festival Court in the Step Pyramid complex at Saqqara. The small engaged columns reproduce plant elements. The doors of these shrines are made in stone, and shown half open. Third Dynasty.

In the intimate subterranean parts of the Step Pyramid, and in those of the enigmatic South Mastaba at the south side of the pyramid enclosure, there were niches with representations of King Djoser engaged in religious ceremonies, very finely carved in low relief; and also panels of blue-glazed faience tiles simulating hangings of woven reed matting. These embellishments, much more religio-magical elements for the use of the king in his afterlife than simple decoration, were not to be seen by the living once the royal burial had been completed. The private nature of much Egyptian tomb decoration, and also the painted reliefs in some of the more remote chambers of the great temples, has always to be kept in mind in judging the work from an artistic as well as a technically skilful point of view, and in considering the training and devotion of the sculptors and painters who executed the work. We shall have frequent reason for admiring the skills of the ancient craftsmen, but shall also occasionally experience a particular wonder at the achievement of those whose craftsmanship becomes fine artistry.

A final consideration here, in the case of the Step Pyramid, involves the extended exploitation of stone, the new material, for construction. In the design and detail of the many subsidiary structures within the pyramid enclosure – the forms of incidental features like engaged columns, roofing and doorways – inspiration came from the simple plant-based elements employed along with mud-brick in the buildings of previous ages. The natural sources for the designs of these structural features continued to provide patterns for Egyptian architecture throughout the Pharaonic Period, mostly restrained and simple in the columns, with palm and lotus or papyrus capitals found down to the New Kingdom, but elaborate and ebullient in the Graeco-Roman temples, particularly at Esna and Philae. At the Step Pyramid also we find the first substantial royal sculpture used in a funerary context. The limestone seated statue of the king found in the chamber adjacent to the pyramid on the north side, life-size and impressive in its relative simplicity, is but the best preserved of several royal statues planned for this pyramid complex; they were the forerunners of the great colossi which became such an important feature of the great temples of later ages.

The great lapidary skills of the builders of the Step Pyramid were, within a very few

127 The so-called Bent Pyramid of Snofru at Dahshur. The angle of inclination was changed when the structure was half completed to reduce its overall height. Some of the fine Tura limestone facing still survives. Fourth Dynasty.

decades, tested to a point almost beyond reason and good judgement in the building of the vast pyramids of King Snofru at Dahshur and by his Fourth Dynasty successors at Giza. Four huge mortuary monuments were built in less than a century; in size they exhausted the potentialities of the form, and undoubtedly the energies and resources of the land of Egypt. The Great Pyramid is, probably rightly, considered the most note-worthy of the four, but in the matter of size alone it did not exactly dwarf the others. Some simple measurements will place Cheops' structure in context: Snofru's Bent Pyramid at Dahshur, base 190 m sq (620 ft sq), height *c.* 104 m (340 ft); Snofru's Northern Pyramid at Dahshur, base 220 m sq (722 ft sq), height *c.* 105 m (345 ft); Cheops' Great Pyramid, base 230 m sq (756 ft sq), height *c.* 146 m (480 ft); Chephren's Giza Pyramid, base 216 m sq (708 ft sq) height *c.* 144 m (470 ft). A final series of mea-surements, for the third of the Giza pyramids, built for Mycerinus, demonstrates how soon a kind of moderation entered into pyramid planning; his structure measured at base 108 m sq (356 ft sq), with an estimated height of 70 m (228 ft). It is not possible to decide what motivated this massive reduction in size, but it is difficult to avoid the con-clusion that a huge expenditure of labour was avoided by this change, and that the strain on the resources of Egypt was therefore decreased. Nevertheless a kind of com-pensation for the reduction in size seems to have prompted an extravagant use of granite in this pyramid, for the construction of the entire burial chamber and, as was the apparent intention, for the casing of the whole pyramid. The lower sixteen courses have granite facings; the blocks, however, are rough and undressed. The upper courses are faced with Tura limestone. A complete pyramid, wholly faced with polished-smooth granite would have presented a remarkable sight, and rendered it in no way insignificant within the Giza group of monuments. It must be supposed that such a scheme was abandoned either because of the death of Mycerinus, or because the extraordinarily laborious process of cutting and dressing the granite blocks was seen to be beyond the capabilities of the available specialist craftsmen to do the work in a reasonable period of time.

The evidence provided by these great stone structures demonstrates quite clearly how excited the architects and builders of the early Old Kingdom must have been at the discovery of the possibilities of building in stone. And, in a sense, in the construction of the Fourth Dynasty pyramids they were testing the limits of what was possible in the new medium. At the same time they were developing techniques and skills in extraction, preparation, moving and raising of great blocks – skills which were to be exploited throughout ancient Egyptian history in the construction of monumental works. The enormity of the works may be suggested by the facts that approximately 2,300,000 blocks of limestone were used in the main structure of the Great Pyramid, with an average weight of two and a half tons (*c.* 3 metric tonnes), and that the 9 granite roofing blocks of the King's Chamber within the pyramid weighed together about 400 tons (406 metric tonnes). The means by which the pyramids were built are still much debated. Egyptian engineers, if that term may be used for the supervisors and gang-masters who oversaw construction, had no special lifting tackle, no wheeled vehicles, no pulleys. It is generally accepted that blocks were moved to the site on sledges, which were dragged laboriously by gangs of men along prepared paths, possibly with the help of rollers. It is also thought likely that a system of brick and stone ramps was used to raise blocks to the level of construction, but there is no unanimity on the way in which the ramps were employed. A further undetermined matter is how the internal passages and chambers were planned, and then built as the pyramid increased in height. The problem of internal construction was not one to be solved in the case of most pyramids, the passages and chambers of which were subterranean. But lofty chambers with corbelled roofs were included in both of the Dahshur pyramids of Snofru, while in the Great Pyramid a remarkable granite burial chamber with five relieving chambers above was approached by a fantastic ascending corridor – the Grand Gallery – 27 m (153 ft) in length and 6 m (28 ft) in height. All the work on these internal parts was executed to a fine degree of precision, their building implying a high level of detailed planning so that they could be incorporated in the pyramid as it was being built around them. It has recently been suggested that internal ramps may have been used in pyramid construction, an interesting idea that has yet to be tested by further investigation. Much, no doubt, could be discovered by dismantling parts of these massive structures, but such a process of invasive exploration is of course wholly out of the question.

Nothing quite on the scale of the largest pyramids was ever attempted in later times. The great temples erected in the New Kingdom and the Graeco-Roman Period were of quite a different order of construction, and were in most cases built over longer periods of time than the few decades required for a single king's mortuary monument. In this respect the surviving mortuary temples of Ramesses II (the Ramesseum) and Ramesses III (at

128 Part of the inner facing of the wall of the Valley Temple of Chephren's pyramid. The granite blocks are carefully fitted together, but not of uniform size or shape.

129 General view of the great Temple of Karnak. In the background can be seen the tops of the columns of the Hypostyle Hall. The obelisks are those of Thutmose I (left) and Hatshepsut (right).

Medinet Habu) are not to be dismissed as trivial structures, and indeed the biggest parts of these temples, the pylons and the pillared courts, involved major constructional techniques of kinds which were different from, but wholly comparable with, those employed in pyramid building. The quarrying and moving of huge quantities of stone, their shaping and erection on the temple sites required the employment of large numbers of skilled workmen and armies of labourers, and the vigilant services of planners and overseers. The Temple of Karnak as it is seen today represents the work of many centuries; the Temple of Luxor was principally a construction of two reigns, of Amenhotep III and Ramesses II. On the other hand, the latter king's mortuary temple, the Ramesseum, was completed within his single reign, certainly a long one. Yet this great complex is thought to have been considerably smaller than the adjacent temple of Amenhotep III, known erroneously as the Memnonium. Ramesses clearly thought so highly of his predecessor's 'cult chapel' that he probably copied its plan for his own mortuary temple; it was once thought erroneously that he may even have dismantled much of it to provide materials for the Ramesseum. The surviving Colossi of Memnon provide the best indication of the size and magnificence of the earlier temple.

The redundant mortuary monuments of long-dead kings were regularly plundered for new monumental constructions, and the great temples of the Delta – at Piramesse,

130 Colossal granite statue identified by inscription as representing Ramesses II, but iconographically undoubtedly a king of the Twelfth Dynasty, possibly Amenemhat II or III. Memphis. H.11.14 m.

131 Carving of Thutmose IV offering incense to Amun, on a pillar fragment of the colonnade of the king retrieved from the filling of the third pylon in the Karnak Temple. The royal sceptre is casually hanging from the crook of the arm.

Bubastis and Tanis – were largely built of stones quarried not from the south of Egypt but from existing structures such as the temples at Memphis and Heliopolis, and embellished with colossi, recycled and renamed for the later monarchs. The convenient northward flow of the Nile allowed such wholesale plunder of stone to be effected without too much difficulty. For the great Graeco-Roman temples in Upper Egypt, however, there were no ancient temples suitably sited upstream which could be dismantled for the new constructions. But the quarries in the region from Esna down to Aswan, particularly those at Gebel es-Silsila, were waiting to be re-exploited, and they were more than capable of supplying any quantity of good building material. It was not necessarily malice that prompted the destruction and reuse of earlier buildings, but prudent economy. Malice may have led to the dismantling of the Aten temples at Karnak erected in the early years of Akhenaten's reign, but it was prudence that led to their reuse as filling for the great pylons built in Horemheb's reign at Karnak, and also to the reuse of much earlier structures like the shrine of Senusret I and the buildings of Hatshepsut and Thutmose III in the filling of the third Karnak pylon, which was begun in the reign of Amenhotep III. There can be little doubt that if all the standing temples of Egypt were to be dismantled carefully, remarkable remains of more ancient structures would be revealed, identified by the surviving texts and representations on previously hidden surfaces of reused blocks. Such intimate examination of standing buildings could, however, only be contemplated if an existing structure suffered partial collapse from, for example, subsidence or earthquake, as has happened at Karnak with some of the pylons.

A notable feature of most Egyptian buildings from the late Old Kingdom right down to Graeco-Roman times is the lavish use of internal and external decoration. The effect is overwhelming in many cases, with texts and scenes seemingly covering every available space; it is as if the Egyptians suffered from *horror vacui*, a distaste for leaving any space on a wall unoccupied. In some great temples, used over many centuries, it is quite clear that no space remained for any significant inscriptional or representational addition. At Karnak, for example, a new portal was erected to accommodate the important texts of Osorkon in the Twenty-second Dynasty. Sometimes an earlier text might even be erased to make space for a later inscription. And we should not forget the practice of usurpation, whereby a king might replace the name of a predecessor with his own. Again it was usually not malice but practicality which determined such acts.

A visit to the magalithic valley temple of Chephren's pyramid at Giza surprises in that no decorations or texts embellish the walls inside or out. It seems almost as if the work is incomplete, as if the building is 'undressed'. Decoration was certainly never intended here. The practice of some partial decoration began with the private mastabas of the Fourth Dynasty, and within a century or two the most wonderful carved and painted reliefs

157

were being made for the mortuary temples of kings and the chapels of nobles and high officials, whose tombs at Giza, Abusir and Saqqara still amaze visitors. Where relief carving could not be provided, simple painting on plaster might be used, although there was nothing simple about the quality of the painting, or the artistry of those special scribes whose skills seem already to be wholly developed in the famous scene of geese from the Fourth Dynasty mastaba of Nefermaat and Itet at Maidum, now in Cairo.

The variety of decoration provided for temples and tombs, for kings and for high officials and nobles, and in some cases even for the rather humble craftsmen, like those who occupied the village at Deir el-Medina, was extremely diverse not only in content but also in quality. 'Decoration' is perhaps not quite the right word to use for the graphic content of temple and tomb scenes. For the most part, what was provided for ritual purposes and for the dwelling-places of the deceased was designed specifically to form part of the functional ensemble embodied in these houses of eternity. A royal tomb of the New Kingdom without its proper complement of texts and representations could scarcely perform its purpose of securing the safe passage of the dead king through the hazards of the underworld so that he might finally join the sun-god in his journey across the heavens. Similarly, the aim of wall embellishments provided for the non-royal tombs from the Old Kingdom through to the New Kingdom, and to some extent in later times, was to secure the adequate provision of offerings for the sustenance of the deceased in his afterlife, and to depict for that afterlife the activities and environment in which the deceased could feel at home.

These categories of 'decoration' by no means exhausted the range of what might be included in temples, the palaces of kings and the villas of the prosperous. Inside the principal halls and chambers of the great cult and mortuary temples, the nature of the inscriptions and representations was almost wholly concerned with the cult and rituals conducted there by the king or his priestly deputy, in communion with, and in honour of, the deity or deities who 'dwelt' within. There

132 Finely outlined in black paint, offerings in the burial chamber of the vizier Mereruka in Saqqara. Such drawings would commonly have been the preliminary stage towards a carving in low relief. Sixth Dynasty.

remained huge areas of vacant walls on the outside of the temple, waiting to receive the graphic representations of warlike acts and foreign conquests, with the vast spaces on pylons devoted to the most grandiose royal deeds, actual or putative. The most memorable and triumphant graphic commemorations are those of the dubious victory of Ramesses II over the Hittites at Qadesh. No matter that the outcome may not have been as decisive as Ramesses and his propagandists claimed, the battle was conclusive for his reputation, and required maximum presentation on temple walls, as at Luxor and the Ramesseum. But an exception had to be made at Abu Simbel where, in the absence of good external surfaces, the Qadesh struggle and other martial activities were portrayed on the walls within the first hall of the temple. In general, no rule was strictly followed: convenience and availability of space in the end determined where a scene or an important inscription might be placed.

The nature of 'house' decoration can only partially be judged from the few surviving examples of painted plaster from the palaces of Amenhotep at Malkata in Western Thebes, and of Akhenaten at El-Amarna, and from a few villas also to be found at El-Amarna. The sad remnants of highly decorative schemes involving plants and wildlife provide tantalizing hints of how dramatic and vibrant were the rooms within which the great of Egypt passed their days in the height of the New Kingdom. Even the floors of some palace rooms were elaborately decorated with painted plaster, and it remains to be determined by what medium these latter paintings were carried out so that they might survive daily wear and tear and the traffic of human feet, even if such feet were sandal-less.

133 A painting by Howard Carter of an ibis perched on a papyrus plant; reproduced from the tomb of Khnumhotep III at Beni Hasan. Twelfth Dynasty.

Of all surviving mural decorations from ancient Egypt, the most varied and enchanting are to be found in private tombs, especially those at Saqqara for the Old Kingdom, at Beni Hasan for the Middle Kingdom, and at Thebes for the New Kingdom. In quantity what has survived is enormous, and offers the very best evidence of the capabilities and artistry of the carvers and painters who produced work for tombs, scarcely ever to be seen by more than a handful of people who might visit a tomb chapel to bring offerings or in pious homage. Yet their training was so thorough and their innate artistic sensibilities so acute that rarely does the entirety of a tomb's decorative scheme fall below the quality of good; often it may be considered very fine; occasionally it is superb by the very highest standards. An examination of Old Kingdom mastaba chapels and the private tombs at Thebes which are cut in the best strata of limestone suggests that the ideal decoration for a tomb should be executed in low relief and painted. The most notable mastaba chapels are constructed of good limestone blocks, capable of receiving very fine and precise low-relief carving. When carving was not possible, when, for example, the native stone was not suitable, the common practice was to apply mud-plaster to achieve level surfaces, facing them with a hard white gesso-plaster upon which paintings in tempera could be applied, using egg or some form of gum as the medium for the pigments, which were mostly composed of mineral colours not subject to fading even in strong sunlight. This last characteristic of Egyptian painting has resulted in the extraordinary preservation of colour on many Egyptian monuments, where the surfaces have not been subjected to adverse element, like windblown sand, wear and general vandalism. It is clear that most great buildings in antiquity in Egypt were ablaze with colour, to a degree that might be thought excessive, even vulgar, today. The massively scaled scenes carved on the outer walls of the great temples were probably painted in a generous but not very careful technique, any quality of subtlety existing in the carving of the reliefs rather than in the painting. This was by no means the case in work on a less grandiose scale.

The most striking examples of painted relief occur in the mastabas of the Fifth and Sixth Dynasties at Saqqara, in some of the royal tombs of the New Kingdom in the Valley of the Kings, and in the Osiris Temple of Sety I at Abydos. In all these cases the colour impressively supplements the fineness of the relief itself, not in a garish manner but as a necessary finish to complete the effect; incidental detail may be added by the final graphic artist. The overall effect on the visitor of, for example, the principal offering room in the mastaba of Ptahhotep, just to the west of the Step Pyramid, or of the representations of King Sety engaged with the gods and in performing sacred activities in the Osiris complex of the Abydos temple is overwhelming; not simply because of the surviving colour, but for the combination of this colour with exquisite carving. Yet the purist might claim that the paint conceals the carving, and to that extent partially obscures the stupendous quality of the sculptor's work. In this temple of Sety, where it is possible to compare excellent examples of painted relief with relief that has lost its colour, it is not unreasonable to conclude that a greater aesthetic satisfaction may be obtained by the modern observer from the unpainted rather than the painted relief. The same effect is apparent in a few of the great low-relief scenes in some of the best nobles tombs in Western Thebes. For example, in the tomb chapel of Ramose, vizier under King Amenhotep III and his successor Amenhotep IV/Akhenaten, one wall carries carved scenes of guests at the funerary banquet. The only colour is a little black paint delineating the eyes and the eyebrows of the participants. The effect is so restrained, and yet so effective. No additional colour obscures the sublime sensitivity of the moulding of the features and the contours of the bodies. There is no evidence that colour was ever added, or, perhaps, even contemplated for these scenes. Another wall of this tomb has scenes showing the burial cortège of Ramose fully painted on a smooth, washed limestone surface. A third wall, to the rear of the entrance to the chapel, bears a further group of scenes in which King Akhenaten and his wife Nefertiti receive foreign emissaries and also present the 'gold of honour' – marks of royal favour – to important dignitaries. Parts of this group are carved in low relief, others are sketched out in black paint, preparatory to carving; there are no traces of further painting. It is known that this important tomb was under construction and decoration when Akhenaten made his decisive move to Akhetaten (El-Amarna); Ramose as vizier was possibly obliged to move with his sovereign, readily or unwillingly, to the new capital. But there is no mention of him in surviving remains at El-Amarna; there is no tomb for him among those prepared for the important officials there. It could therefore have been the case that Ramose did not move north, but either remained in Thebes, or even died before the move. There is no doubt that his tomb was unfinished. We may speculate on whether the fine low-relief scenes

134 Finely carved, unpainted low-relief scene of the ritual purification of Ramose, vizier of King Amenhotep III, in his Theban tomb.

135 Painted limestone relief of soldiers engaged in the expedition to Punt during the reign of Queen Hatshepsut. From her mortuary temple at Deir el-Bahri.

would ultimately have been painted; it would be good to think that those in charge of the preparation of the tomb recognized the chaste beauty of the unpainted reliefs and chose to leave them uncoloured. But caution should ever be exercised in ascribing to an ancient people the judgements and feelings which accord with more modern sentiments.

The various decorative techniques to be seen in a well-planned tomb like that of Ramose illustrate what were the capabilities of the artist/craftsmen who lived to create fine environments for the living and the dead. At the heart of it all lay draughtsmanship. Young Egyptians who by heritage or good fortune were selected to be trained in scribal schools were mostly destined to become civil servants, who composed and wrote official documents, maintained accounts and generally ran the administration of the country. Some student scribes, again by family tradition or evident talent, became 'outline scribes': those who could wield the brush, draw within the conventions of Egyptian art or even show artistic ability beyond the requirements of ordinary competence. And the basis of all their training was draughtsmanship – how to draw a fluid line with sensitivity. In all graphic work in tombs and temples, scenes were first sketched out by the best outline scribes, whose initial drawings formed the model – the blueprint – of what might then be carved in low or sunk relief, or more simply developed as two-dimensional paintings. 'Sketched out' scarcely does justice to the work of these outline scribes, but sadly their initial drawings were fated to be concealed or destroyed by the subsequent stages of work on the production of tomb or temple decoration. In places where examples of the initial drawings have survived, through the incompletion of a monument or by happy chance, the consummate skill of the outline scribe is patently evident.

When a wall was prepared and ready to receive its initial 'cartoon' of representations and texts, it was usually marked out with a grid of squares in red paint. This grid provided the guide for the insertion of figures, of people in particular but other elements also, in accordance with the system of proportions, usually described as the canon, enabling the artist to draw his initial outlines with relative ease and confidence. In cases where the grid and initial drawings have not been eliminated or obscured by later carving or painting, it is often abundantly clear that the well-trained skilled artist scarcely needed the grid. His sweeping brushstrokes, outlining the body of a standing man, for example, are applied to the wall with complete assurance. Nevertheless, the grid was there as a control. Yet other examples occur where corrections have been made, probably by a busybody supervisory outline scribe. Usually, however, the initial drawing displays not only the artist's confidence in his line, but also a remarkable sensitivity. At least that is how it seems to the modern observer, and it would be hoped that the ancient artists and their supervisors would have judged similarly.

In the private tombs of the Old Kingdom, scenes show the activities of daily life, magically endowed to provide the proper environment for the deceased in the afterlife. Frequently the humble workers on the tomb-owner's estate engage in backchat, designed to add verisimilitude to what is shown. In a scene of men butchering oxen in the Saqqara mastaba of Khentika, a vizier of kings Teti and Pepy I of the Sixth Dynasty, comments are thrown back and forth by the men dismembering the dead animals: 'Pull then, my friend, by your life', 'Hold firm, properly', 'Let the blood flow, properly', 'Hold firm, properly', 'I shall do it', 'Pull then!', 'Finish it off then, hurry up!', 'I shall do it to please you'. In providing such remarks, great liveliness is added to a conventional scene of butchery. In the tomb of Paheri at Elkab, of Eighteenth Dynasty date, the funerary banquet scene is enlivened by the comments made by some of the guests as the wine is circulated. A man offers wine to a guest, 'To your soul. Drink to drunkenness. Have a good time. Listen to what your neighbour says. Do not stop talking.' A lady says, 'Give me eighteen cups of wine. I love to get drunk. My inside is like straw.' A servant tries to persuade another lady, 'Drink up! Don't sip at it. I shall not leave you alone.' A further lady rejoins, 'Drink! Don't spoil the fun. Let the cup come to me. We owe it to the prince [the host] to drink.' Such banter no doubt was designed to set the deceased at ease in his posthumous banqueting.

The addition of informal scenes and the inclusion of small vignettes of amusing detail were characteristics of private tomb decoration; they would be wholly out of place in the ritual-bound representations placed in royal tombs. For a non-royal person the tomb was to be the ultimate home for his body, and the inclusion of these 'personal touches' in the decoration of the walls confining his posthumous existence might be considered a form of self-indulgence. We shall never know whether such informalities were inspired by the prospective tomb-owner during the course of planning the decoration or suggested by the decorators themselves, the outline scribes who were to execute the scenes and inscriptions. Artists in general love to caricature, and Egyptian artists were no exception, as is clear from the many casual drawings on ostraca and even more so from the drawings in the so-called satirical papyri (e.g. EA 10016). But good ideas can lose their point if repeated. Many Old Kingdom tombs contain stereotyped chitchat between the workers in the scenes of daily life; but for many tomb-owners these small personal additions to the more formal contents of tomb scenes would be seen as special in each case. Surely no one in the Sixth Dynasty made a survey of these *Reden und Rufen* (chat and backchat), as diligent German scholars have called them, from which selections could be made by the prospective tomb-owner. They were, however, well known to the artists regularly employed on decoration and their supervisors, or whoever organized a tomb's scheme of decoration; presumably suggestions were made to the client, the tomb-owner, for his approval.

One would like to think that the special little scenes, or details within scenes, found in private tombs were quite individual, sometimes even inspired by some event in the life of the tomb-owner. So, in the small chapel of Nefer at Saqqara, a baboon is shown assisting the wine-makers in the extraction of the grape juice. In the double tomb of Niankhkhnum and Khnumhotep, also at Saqqara, a series of market scenes, unusual in itself, is enlivened by amusing detail and lively chatter as might be found in any open market in antiquity and even today. A man restrains a baboon on a lead as it steals fruit from a stall; a market official apprehends a shoplifter, while his monkey sinks its teeth into the thief's leg; a woman, at her wit's end no doubt, snaps at a child, 'Do you want to go home?', while at the same time she barters a bowl of fruit, the salesman saying, 'Hand over what you have brought for very sweet figs'.

In Theban tombs of the New Kingdom, especially the less grand in which the decoration is mostly tempera painting on plaster, the wealth of incidental detail is exceptional, enriching the general themes of fairly standard scenes. Harvest scenes were particularly suitable for individual vignettes, such as the pair of girls squabbling over the gleaning of barley in the tomb of Menna; in the same tomb a girl is shown removing a thorn from the foot of another. In the tomb of Nakht a labourer leaps into the air to help compress the barley in a basket, while another labourer takes a break to drink from a waterskin which is slung in a tree. Such scenes are, moreover, painted with a freedom and élan which could not have been achieved so easily in the low-relief medium common to the most spectacular tombs in the Theban Necropolis.

Indeed, it is in the smaller tombs of Western Thebes that Egyptian painting attains a particularly high level of achievement. The restrictions of the grid, canon and formality of conventional representations are relaxed, even abandoned, in the presentation of everyday scenes which give individuality to each tomb, even when, it must be assumed, the same artists worked in several at the same time. In many cases there seems to permeate the work a real joy in painting, in being able to express a degree of artistic freedom which is so rarely to be detected in standard Egyptian graphic work. A quite special group of paintings, now in the British Museum, comes from a tomb of a 'scribe and counter of grain', named almost certainly Nebamun, who exercised his modest offices in the reign of King Amenhotep III. His tomb decoration was of the very best, and in its surviving fragments exemplifies just how good were the interior decorators of ancient Egypt (see figs 7, 56, 137 and 138).

136 Limestone ostracon with an informal drawing of a baboon eating figs from a bowl on a stand. The drawing in black is heightened with red wash. New Kingdom. H.10.5 cm.

The Nebamun tomb paintings

LEFT 137 Nebamun with his wife and daughter hunt birds in the marshes, attended by a retriever cat; the finest of the fragments from this tomb. H.81 cm.

ABOVE 138 Cattle are brought for inspection by Nebamun. The painter has skilfully differentiated between the cattle by subtle variations of colour and texture. H.58.5 cm.

The painter of these scenes – it is hard to accept that they were executed by a team of artists – was in every respect a master: an expert delineator, deft in drawing a controlled line, but instinctively skilled in departing from the controlled to the free expression of detail; a wizard in the representation of texture in hair and clothes, the fur of animals and the hides of others; a virtuoso in the mixing of colours to produce tone and shades which contrast so strikingly with the bright simple pigments of conventional work. By some chance Nebamun secured, or was assigned by necropolis officialdom, an artist or artists team for his tomb who were exceptionally gifted, and his good fortune resulted in a tomb chapel decorated beyond normal expectations. Was Nebamun himself to some extent responsible for the excellent quality of the result, by discussing with the artist(s) the content and style of what was to be painted? Nebamun was a scribe. Did he have special contacts with good outline scribes? Did he himself have a special interest in painting? Sadly we shall never know.

The Mastery of Crafts

139 Greywacke head of a youth with curly hair; a piece which combines Greek features with Egyptian technique in working hard stones. From Alexandria. First century BC. H.24.5 cm.

Much was said in the last chapter about the ability of ancient Egyptian masons and sculptors to quarry and work stone, including the very hard granite, diorites and quartzite, and also of those craftsmen who worked in fine low relief in temples and tombs, and painted the remarkable tomb scenes which distinguish so many tomb chapels. There was no word for artist in the ancient language, and it should be accepted that those craftsmen who produced fine work were categorized thus, as craftsmen – workmen of special training and often of special talent, whose skills were undoubtedly recognized, but not to the extent that they might be named. However, among the workmen who belonged to the élite gang working on the royal tombs of the New Kingdom, and living in the select community at Deir el-Medina, there were many craftsmen who are known by name but not by their works. So, Pay, an outline scribe, or draughtsman who lived in the reign of Ramesses II, most probably worked on the laying out of the texts and scenes in that king's tomb, possibly along with one or more of his sons who were also draughtsmen. Similarly, the names of many relief carvers are recorded, although again not as the proud producers of identified pieces of work. The term used to describe them is as negative as 'outline scribe'; they were 'chisel wielders', which again emphasizes the craft aspect of their work. It is difficult, however, to consider these men simply as sculptors in stone. The chisel wielders Any and Nakhtamun, for example, who also worked in the reign of Ramesses II, are shown in painted scenes in the tomb of their father Ipuy engaged in making furniture. A chisel could be wielded on wood as well as stone.

In the consideration of crafts and the products of crafts in ancient Egypt, it is salutary to reflect that according to the literary tradition, those who worked in the crafts were not highly regarded. A didactic composition generally known as *The Satire of Trades*, a complete text of which is preserved on a papyrus in the British Museum (EA 10182), does its best to denigrate all activities involving hard manual work in order to extol the virtues of the scribal profession. It is a story we have met before, and one that is singularly one-sided surely because any text on any theme will have been written down and possibly composed by scribes. They took every opportunity to glorify their own calling at the expense of others who were less able to proclaim the virtues of their professions in written texts, but whose activities in the context of ancient Egyptian civilization were equally important. Only by training and tradition could the outline scribe, the draughtsman, be included in the ranks of scribes generally; their work was closely allied with that of the other craftsmen employed in tombs and temples, but they were literate and may even have considered themselves superior to the general run of scribes, the workaday pen-pushers. But within the ranks of the gang which cut and

decorated the royal tombs and lived in Deir el-Medina there is little evidence that the outline scribe occupied any special position or was allowed any special advantages. But the author of *The Satire of Trades* thought differently. For him the scribe was altogether superior; he was from an early age picked out for special duties. Who, for example, had ever seen a sculptor or goldsmith sent as an envoy? A carpenter is worn out by his labour; a jeweller, working on hard stones, is exhausted at the end of the day, with his knees and back aching from being constricted for hours. And what can one say about the potter? He is still to be counted as a human being, but he digs about in the mud like a pig, and his clothes are stiff with clay.

We can with confidence set the views of this jaundiced author to one side, and judge the craftsmen of ancient Egypt by their works. One may hope that in antiquity they recognized the attitude of scribes as sour grapes. Could any scribe engaged in administration and the writing of reports ever enjoy the satisfaction to be derived from the making and completion of a fine object? Among the craftsmen laughed at in the *Satire*, those who worked on stone came in for special treatment. Yet, in fact, the products of these workers were among the greatest achievements of ancient Egyptian culture. We have already mentioned the exploitation of hard stones readily available in the Eastern Desert by the stone-vessel makers of late Predynastic and Early Dynastic times. It was undoubtedly at this early time that Egyptian stone craftsmen showed a fine appreciation of what could be exploited and made into beautiful vessels, and also developed techniques for the working of very hard stones with great precision. There is still uncertainty about how precisely the ancient mason set about shaping a vessel both outside and inside. Rough forms could be obtained by pounding and chipping, the skilled craftsmen having learned, probably at his father's knee, how to strike a block with a tool made from some harder material to obtain a rough form on which he would then have to spend many laborious hours in grinding and polishing. He had ready at hand, in ample quantities, sand, the best possible abrasive for his work. And sand was undoubtedly the principal medium for grinding out the insides of vessels. For this last operation, drills were developed and flint bits used to work and control the sand. Still it remains difficult to understand exactly how such precise work was effected. One must never underestimate the importance of experience and tradition in the execution of difficult procedures. In matters of stone-working, the Egyptian mason, as we have seen, performed marvels of accurate construction in the making of great buildings, and the same accuracy of working was employed in the smaller-scale manufacture of vessels, and even more so in the fashioning of stone sculptures. The latter are considered by many to be the greatest glory of Egyptian creativity in the field of arts and crafts.

Something was said in the last chapter about the provision of colossal sculptures for the great temples of Egypt. The tradition of monumental statuary started in the Middle Kingdom, but the existence of many surviving colossi was to a great extent obfuscated by the fact that nearly all of the surviving examples were taken over by monarchs of the New Kingdom, and again resurped by kings of the Twenty-first and Twenty-second Dynasties. A

140 Large pottery vessel with elaborate painted decoration characteristic of Amarna ware. The mainly floral blue decoration is heightened with red and black. From El-Amarna. H.70 cm.

better understanding of the sculptural characteristics of the different periods and a healthy suspicion of royal cartouches blatantly and deeply carved to emphasize false attributions have led to the identification of a number of Twelfth Dynasty colossi at Memphis and in Tanis and Bubastis in the Delta, which were formerly erroneously attributed to Ramesses II and later kings. Nevertheless, Ramesses II certainly had many original colossal sculptures made of himself, some of which may be judged great, not only because of their size, but for the quality of the pieces as fine works of art. The bust of the king known as the Young or the Younger Memnon, in the British Museum, is an outstanding example of large-scale royal portraiture (EA 19). At its first being noticed in the Ramesseum in the early nineteenth century, it was held to be 'certainly the most beautiful and perfect piece of Egyptian sculpture that can be seen throughout the country'. When it reached the British Museum in 1818 it pleased the Trustees, but they could not accept that it could be exhibited with 'the works of *Fine Art*', that is classical Greek sculpture. It is no longer the case that comparisons need to be made between Egyptian and Greek sculpture, and it is also to be accepted that William Hamilton's assessment of the 'Memnon' would now be thought somewhat extravagant. But this royal representation remains a noble sculpture on the grand scale, and not least for the way in which the ancient craftsmen chose and carved a huge granite block so that a 'flaw' in the texture and colour of the stone could be exploited to present the face and head with a colour subtly different from that of the torso.

This extraordinary appreciation of the possibilities offered by a particular piece of stone seems to have been specially developed in the New Kingdom. A figure about half life-size of the same Ramesses II, now in the Luxor Museum, displays this perspicacity of the ancient sculptor to an astonishing degree. The stone of the figure is granodiorite, generally blackish grey in colour, but the double crown on the head is reddish brown, again due to some change in the nature of the rock itself which, one must assume, was detected in the unshaped block by the sculptor and then exploited. Sometimes, however, a poor choice of stone was made which resulted in difficulties for the sculptor. In the British Museum there is a fine, almost life-size figure of Khaemwese, son of Ramesses II, a notable priestly official of the cult of Ptah in Memphis and briefly crown prince (EA 987). It must have disappointed its sculptor in the course of its making. A block of conglomerate stone akin to quartzite was selected, no doubt superficially of regular texture but with interesting variations in its generally brownish colour. When the carving was well advanced, with the head and most of the body successfully completed, areas of pebbly consistency emerged, especially in the upper part of the torso. These hard intrusive pebbles greatly hampered the craftsman, who found it difficult to produce a satisfactory surface in this region and also was almost defeated in the carving of the inscription on the back pillar; he was even in one place obliged to cut out a part and replace it with an insert. It must have been an extremely vexatious commission to complete, but the sculptor persisted, no doubt concealing the difficult areas with plaster; the result is still a striking representation, worthily expressing the dignity of the princely subject.

With their skills in working hard stones schooled through making vessels, Egyptian sculptors from earliest times never flinched from tackling granites, diorites, quartzites and other very hard materials for private and royal statues. But the majority of statues in the Old Kingdom, and to a lesser extent in the Middle and New Kingdoms, were made from limestone. This stone was relatively easy to work, and it became the favoured material for the manufacture of the pieces required to represent the deceased tomb-owners in the mastaba tombs of the Giza and Saqqara necropolises. All sculpture in ancient Egypt was made for religious or ceremonial reasons, although there is some evidence that images of deceased relatives may have occasionally been placed in honoured positions in private houses. There is no evidence, however, that sculptures as works of arts were collected and used to embellish buildings and gardens in the classical manner. Stereotyped poses were preferred for tomb sculpture and the votive pieces which favoured people were allowed to place in temple precincts to participate in the bounty of the gods. As with the laying out of scenes on a wall to be carved and painted, the canon of proportions governed the making of statues, with the sculptor marking out his block of stone preparatory to carving, with indications of the canon, so that the proportions of the figure should conform with the ideal. It was, of course, important that the representations of a person to be placed in his tomb should in general be conventional; there was no room for originality in the broadest sense. This does not mean that every statue should be of the same kind. Most pieces made to serve as an alternative for the deceased, if the body were destroyed, were in the form of a standing figure in a fairly rigid pose, but there could be many variants. The subject might be shown seated on a simple block seat; he might be accompanied by his wife and even by his children; if he were a scribe he could be shown squatting in the scribal position, holding an open papyrus on his lap; he might be represented holding some article indicative of his position or profession. The earliest private sculpture in the British Museum dates from the Third Dynasty and shows the boatbuilder Ankhwa (EA 171). He is represented sitting on a block seat, wearing a heavy wig and holding in his left hand an adze, tool of his trade, which is slung over his left shoulder. It is carved from granite and is an amazingly powerful sculpture, foursquare and neither elegant nor sensitive in its portrayal of a well-established craftsman. It may lack the grace and appeal of other Old Kingdom private statuary, but it displays the strength of its subject in an uncompromising manner.

The touch of brutal realism found in this statue of Ankhwa is characteristic of much royal sculpture of the Old Kingdom. The seated statue of Djoser, found in the small serdab-chamber just to the north of the Step Pyramid, is a mysterious image of a monarch, severe in appearance, emerging majestically from the stone, almost Rodin-like in conception, to speak anachronistically. The royal sculptures of the Fourth Dynasty, while being equally uncompromising in their display of majesty, are distinctly more accessible and show a mastery of craftsmanship which was scarcely equalled again in later royal sculptures. The diorite seated figure of Chephren with the open-winged falcon of Horus protecting the head is not only originally conceived, but wonderfully realized in execution. Equally, but differently, wonderful in execution is the series of small-size triads from the pyramid complex of Mycerinus, in each of which the king is shown with a nome-deity and a goddess. All the figures are carved to different levels, and the extraordinary sensitivity of the work and the perfect finish of the

141 Granite statuette of a man with his body enveloped in a long cloak; a fine sensitive private sculpture.
From Athribis in the Delta.
Middle Kingdom. H.62 cm.

surfaces are almost miraculous. They are truly frisson-causing pieces. The stone is greenish grey in colour; it used to be called schist, or slate, but now is more precisely identified as greywacke. It is a stone much favoured by the ancient sculptors, having the capability of being turned into most delicate, almost feminine pieces. The head in this material in the British Museum (EA 986, fig. 142) is a good case where identification of sex is uncertain. Although now thought probably to be Thutmose III, it has often been attributed to his aunt Queen Hatshepsut. Different doubts about identification attend another royal head in the same material (EA 97, fig. 46), which shows signs of having had a new nose inserted to improve its appearance, possibly when it was taken from Egypt to Italy in Roman times. It is now thought to represent Nectanebo I of the Thirtieth Dynasty.

The sympathetic use of greywacke was a characteristic of the ancient sculptor's ability to exploit the different qualities of the many stones used for royal and private statuary. For reasons that cannot now be determined, certain stones were particularly favoured at different periods. Limestone, as has already been mentioned, was commonly used in the Old Kingdom for private sculptures, but it was also much used throughout the Pharaonic Period because of its ready availability and relative ease of carving. A harder limestone, sometimes described as indurated, was much used in the Eighteenth Dynasty and particularly during the Amarna Period, useful deposits of the stone being conveniently found close to Akhenaten's capital Akhetaten. Sadly, many of the fine sculptures carved in this last stone were brutally broken up in antiquity and survive only as tantalizingly attractive fragments. During the same period the much harder quartzite was also used, the very varied colours of the stone rendering it particularly appealing in the production of composite statues in which parts of the figures were made of other materials. Quartzite was also exploited to some extent in the late Middle Kingdom and in later periods, although more careful examination than previously and better methods of identification have led to some 'quartzite' pieces being reclassified as sandstone. Such is the case with the life-size seated figure of Sety II in the British Museum (EA 26, fig. 40), which one distinguished art historian commended for having an undamaged nose. Perfect pieces from antiquity are rare, and facial damage often prevents sure identification and also deters non-specialists from a proper appreciation of the quality of sculptures. Much of the damage was probably the result of ancient accident, not malicious attack.

In the later periods of Egyptian dynastic history, a stone which became especially common was basalt, a volcanic rock occurring in outcrops in many places in the Nile Valley. It had been used extensively in the Old Kingdom for the paving of temples, but rarely for sculpture until the Late Period. During this time the placing of votive sculptures of modest size in temple precincts became common, and many thousands of pieces, many of basalt, now populate most of the important collections of Egyptian antiquities; they crowd together on the upper shelves of the wall cases in the Cairo

142 Greywacke head from a royal statue, most probably of Thutmose III; an exceptionally fine portrayal of one of Egypt's greatest monarchs. H.44.5 cm.

171

Museum, and swell the ranks of unseen pieces in the storerooms of other great museums. Basalt is a very hard, greenish-black stone, capable of receiving a highly polished surface, which is often striking but tends to conceal the run-of-the-mill quality of much of the actual work. Nevertheless, the craftsmanship shown in the working of this rather intractable material is nearly always of a very high standard and, in the best examples, of real artistic quality.

What then is one to make of Egyptian sculpture? So far in this chapter it has been considered largely in terms of skill and craftsmanship, with occasional glances at artistic merit. Mention was made earlier of the unwillingness of the British Museum Trustees to recognize the artistic quality of the great bust of Ramesses, the so-called Memnon, when it went on display in 1818. Its arrival in London was, it might be said, unfortunately timed; it came on the heels of the Elgin Marbles and the much admired Towneley Marbles, the latter consisting to a great extent of Roman copies of Greek originals. Classical art was triumphant, and nothing Egyptian could remotely be compared with the marvels of Greece and Rome. There is no doubt that an appreciation of Egyptian sculpture takes time and knowledge to develop. The formal nature of the statuary, designed for temple and tomb use, required a kind of uniformity in types and postures which to the untutored viewer seemed to remain unchanged over many centuries. One could be immensely impressed by the scale of the great colossi; one could marvel at the skills of the ancient stonemason and sculptor, who seemingly thought nothing of tackling a block of the hardest stone. However, one could be put off by the ancient practice of adding texts to the sculptures, even to the extent, apparently, of developing types like the block statue which could be smothered in distracting texts. There were in fact major impediments hindering the proper appreciation of the special qualities of Egyptian sculpture. Craftsmanship, however, must almost be taken for granted. Quite evidently the training of ancient Egyptian sculptors was of a very high standard, their skills undoubtedly to a great extent inherited. An ancient chisel-wielder could be relied on to produce a satisfactory piece of work, but satisfactory pieces of work are not necessarily great works of art. The term masterpiece is so often misapplied to what is essentially just competent; it is used by dealers to impress potential buyers; it is invoked by museum curators to enhance the status of newly acquired pieces, especially if their institutions are Art Museums. The British Museum, happily, has never claimed to be such an institution; it is a museum of history. The Egyptian collections are large and various; they illuminate the history and culture of a great ancient civilization. Almost by chance some of the pieces may be classed as masterpieces, and many more are better than run-of-the-mill. It is surely the case, as with the paintings dealt with in the last chapter, that highly competent work could be regularly expected from properly trained craftsmen; but occasionally a craftsman will be touched by genius and thus capable of producing work of exceptional quality – masterpieces in fact. Some have been mentioned in the course of this book, others may be identified by the acute, well-informed observer. Such are three granodiorite statues of Senusret III of the Twelfth Dynasty, from Deir el-Bahri. They show the king in formal pose, his hands resting on his stiffened kilt. At a superficial level they are well-carved run-of-the-mill royal sculptures. But observe the faces: none is the same as the others; all are strangely

143 Life-size granite figure
of King Senusret III;
a fine example of dramatic,
if not true, portraiture
of the Twelfth Dynasty.
From Deir el-Bahri. H.1.22 m.

idiosyncratic; scholars see true portraiture in them, which is highly debatable; one is particularly striking (EA 686, fig. 143), with drawn features and an expression which has been described as that of someone worn down with the trials of life and office, even world-weary. It is perhaps fanciful to read so much into a face that is represented so unusually – so 'personally' – while yet conforming with the tradition of royal sculpture. It is a face which draws the observer to look again and again; it repays study and contemplation; it may fairly be called a masterpiece.

In considering the subject of Egyptian sculpture, it is relatively simple to move from stone to wood, and to examine the achievements of the 'chisel-wielder' whose medium was the latter. Throughout the millennia of the Dynastic Period, wood was employed for a wide variety of purposes apart from its principal use as a building material. Coffins were made of wood, furniture was made of wood, small cosmetic objects were made of wood, and wood was also used for sculpture. By the very nature of this material, most of what was produced in antiquity is now lost or gravely damaged, damp and fire, and the depredations of termites being the chief culprits. Egypt was not rich in timber, as we learned in the first chapter of this book, and from an early age quantities of good cedar were imported from Levantine forests in Syria and Lebanon. Of the trees indigenous to Egypt, acacia, sycomore-fig and tamarisk could produce usable pieces for small-scale work. For fine cabinet-making, ebony imported from Equatorial Africa could be obtained, but only when the trade routes operated smoothly. Sculptures in wood were made for tomb purposes from the time of the Old Kingdom, and many have been found in tombs in the Memphite Necropolis and in Middle Egypt; guardian statues like those found in the tomb of Tutankhamun were regularly placed in the tombs in the Valley of the Kings, along with many other smaller wooden figures and, of course, much furniture, most of which has not survived.

Compared with stone, wood was infinitely easier to carve, and Egyptian craftsmen – cabinet-makers, joiners and the carvers of statues – were highly skilled at exploiting the material to its best advantage. Properly treated, wood would yield results of sensitivity and flexibility which stone could not match. In the tomb of Hesy-Re at Saqqara were found, in various states of survival, six niche panels of wood carved in fine low relief with figures of the tomb owner and appropriate texts. Hesy-Re was a senior scribe, with medical offices of uncertain nature, and he lived in the early Third Dynasty. The carving of his figures is miraculous in its purity of line, matched by a distinct severity in the carving of the heads. Within the shallow limits of the relief, the carver has successfully indicated the contours and musculature of the bodies. The accompanying hieroglyphs are detailed and beautifully formed. Produced in about 2650 BC, it is hard to find later relief carvings in wood to match the Hesy-Re panels. The wooden shrines which enclosed the

A masterpiece of wood

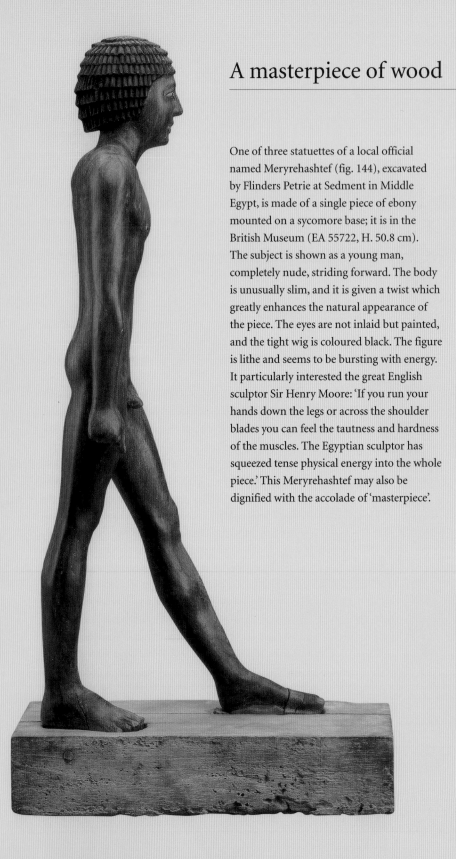

One of three statuettes of a local official
named Meryrehashtef (fig. 144), excavated
by Flinders Petrie at Sedment in Middle
Egypt, is made of a single piece of ebony
mounted on a sycomore base; it is in the
British Museum (EA 55722, H. 50.8 cm).
The subject is shown as a young man,
completely nude, striding forward. The body
is unusually slim, and it is given a twist which
greatly enhances the natural appearance of
the piece. The eyes are not inlaid but painted,
and the tight wig is coloured black. The figure
is lithe and seems to be bursting with energy.
It particularly interested the great English
sculptor Sir Henry Moore: 'If you run your
hands down the legs or across the shoulder
blades you can feel the tautness and hardness
of the muscles. The Egyptian sculptor has
squeezed tense physical energy into the whole
piece.' This Meryrehashtef may also be
dignified with the accolade of 'masterpiece'.

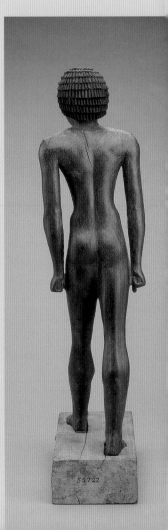

sarcophagus, coffins and body of Tutankhamun are decorated with substantial representations and texts, but they are plastered and gilded and one's critical judgement is dazzled by the expanses of golden surfaces. Hesy-Re's panels in their stark simplicity – unplastered, unpainted, ungilded – need no embellishment to enhance their beauty.

Statues in wood were often rather clumsily made with stick-like limbs and awkward lines; plaster and paint could be used to cover up deficiencies in the carving. But there are many figures which have all the virtues of good stone sculpture, and also a liveliness which can only be accounted for by the greater plasticity of the medium. The famous so-called Sheikh el-Beled from Saqqara, now in the Cairo Museum, is the figure of the priestly official Ka-aper of Fourth–Fifth Dynasty date. It is a first-class example of a sculptor's convincingly capturing the essence of an important official, shown to be not self-important but confident in his position and authority. He is represented as a stout middle-aged man, plump of features, with extraordinarily lifelike inlaid eyes – a particular detail found in many sculptures in stone as well as wood. The figure was probably originally plastered and painted, but all vestiges of colour have been lost, revealing clearly the technique of construction: the arms are made of separate pieces of wood, dowelled to the shoulders and pegged in position; many imperfections in the body reveal the twisted nature of the wood, probably acacia. Nevertheless, the overall impression of power is unaffected, and it is not surprising that the workmen of Auguste Mariette, who discovered it in the nineteenth century, recognized in it their own local village chief, their Sheikh el-Beled.

The quality of the ancient 'chisel wielder's' craft cannot always be so easily appreciated because of the paint or gilding which so commonly obscures the finer details of his work. The numerous statuettes of gilded wood found in the tomb of Tutankhamun may yet be judged because of their evident beauty. Those of the king in ritual acts, as harpooner, as a statue on a leopard, for example, are exceptional in their grace; and even more exceptional are the four figures of the Canopic goddesses which stand around the royal Canopic chest, full of comeliness and the epitome of feminine radi-

145 Wooden figure of a man of high status, showing the sensitive plasticity of late Eighteenth–early Nineteenth Dynasty sculpture, but in the sympathetic medium of wood. H.33 cm.

ance, their shapely forms subtly suggested beneath the pleated garments which so enhance their charming attitudes. The same tomb, however, reveals much more of the art and craft of woodworking in the many pieces of furniture which formed part of the king's funerary equipment.

In the provision of what should be included in the burial of an individual in ancient Egypt, furniture was an important component. If the deceased was to enjoy a comfortable existence in the afterlife, he or she would need a suitable suite of beds, tables, chairs and boxes to furnish the posthumous dwelling. The idea may seem to us fanciful, but for the Egyptian it was important not to miss the comforts of terrestrial living by being neglectful in providing what might be needed hereafter. In tombs of the Old Kingdom, craftsmen are shown preparing items of furniture for the tomb equipment. In the mastaba of Mereruka at Saqqara, among the furniture pictured being brought to the tomb are large chests with carrying poles, an example of which was found in Tutankhamun's tomb. The Tutankhamun chest is simply designed but very carefully made, with a framework of ebony and panels of cedar. Most remarkable are the carrying poles, which can be stowed away beneath the chest when it is not being moved. Such chests were used for storage in houses and in tombs. It would seem that designs and techniques developed in the Old Kingdom and the Middle Kingdom continued to be used in later periods. The cult of novelty was not one which commended itself to a people whose whole attitude to life and to life after death was based on tradition and continuity.

Joinery and carpentry were practised as early as the First Dynasty and most probably in the late Predynastic Period. Tools suitable for woodworking, including saws, chisels and borers, with copper blades and wooden handles, have been found in quantity in Early Dynastic tombs. One tomb at Saqqara, dated to the reign of Djet of the First Dynasty, contained numerous fragments of furniture, including a complete small compartmentalized box measuring $47 \times 21 \times 9$ cm ($18 \times 8 \times 3$ in). No lid was found, and it is possible that there never was one. The construction is simple: the dividers of the compartments are fitted into grooves in the main frame, but the whole is not jointed together, the parts clearly having been held together by thongs threaded through the corners, uniting the sides and the base of the box. It is not an outstanding example of the Egyptian cabinet-makers craft, but it demonstrates an early command of woodworking tools and an understanding of practical techniques. For the best work we must go forward to later dynastic times, from which a great many examples of simple and elaborate furniture have survived, mostly from tombs of the New Kingdom at Thebes. The best and most extravagantly decorated pieces come from Tutankhamun's tomb, such as the great Golden Throne with the inlaid gold back-panel showing the young king and his queen, and the so-called Ecclesiastical Throne, richly decorated with gilding and inlays of semiprecious stones, ivory, and glass arranged in complicated patterns. These two thrones are virtuoso pieces, designed for royalty and displaying a remarkable range of decoration; they were not made for the tomb, but early in the king's reign when he was still called Tutankhaten. One must wonder for what purposes or occasions they were produced, and whether they were ever sat upon by the young monarch.

These thrones incorporate two of the primary designs for seats which were made in great numbers during the New Kingdom. The great Golden Throne elaborates the simple backed seat with arms, examples of which can be seen in museums and tomb scenes. The more common chair has no arms, is rather low and has a seat of woven cord or rushes; it is robustly built with struts supporting the back and cross-members dowelled into the sturdy legs; the joints are very carefully cut, and in good examples seem to be as firm as on the day they left the joiner's workshop. The Ecclesiastical Throne incorporates the design of the folding stool, a particularly useful item of domestic furniture, easily stowed away when not in use and conveniently unbulky for the relatively restricted spaces of most houses. The seats of folding stools were commonly made of some animal hide, or leather; a stool based on the design but not made to be folded, also among the contents of Tutankhamun's tomb, has a fixed seat made of wood inlaid with pieces of ivory, the whole imitating leopard skin.

The shortage of good timber in Egypt led to the practice of concealment of simplicity by superior camouflage. A box, for example, might be made of some ordinary native wood, plain in appearance and not suitable for fine joinery. But such a simple construction could then be transformed by the attachment of veneers of fine wood like ebony; the addition of thin panels of ivory and faience; the fitting of neat feet, again made of ebony or ivory; the application of gold-leaf; and, especially, the provision of elaborate marquetry. One chest from Tutankhamun's tomb, simple in design, has been transformed by applied decoration. The chest is made of acacia or sycomore wood, to which have been applied broad strips of ivory held in place by gilded pins. It is embellished with thin strips of ebony, framing panels of herringbone marquetry consisting of tiny slivers of ivory and ebony, amounting, it is estimated, to more than 45,000 pieces. Sometimes inlaid-ivory panels are engraved with charming scenes including the royal couple, animals and plants. One must marvel not only at the skills of the ancient *ébenistes*, to borrow a term from French fine cabinet-making, but also at the patience they showed in composing, cutting the component pieces of, and fitting such complicated embellishments.

Among the examples of the woodworking craft found in the young king's tomb is one which, while lacking the extravagant decoration found on so many pieces, is in its simple form a triumph of precise joinery, and aesthetically most satisfying. It is a double-sided gaming box, with a drawer to hold the gaming pieces, placed on a stand mounted on a sledge. The box itself is unremarkable except for the fact that its drawer still slides readily in and out. Like so many boxes it is made of some ordinary wood, veneered with ebony; the playing surfaces are marked out with squares of ivory separated by ebony strips. The special feature of the piece is the stand. It is made wholly of ebony, embellished with great restraint. The top, rebated to hold the box, is supported by four lion-legs resting on gilded drums and set on the sledge-shaped base. The legs are splendidly shaped, showing the animal sinews; the claws in the feet are made of ivory, and the braces holding together the legs and the top are neatly gilded. It is an immensely stylish piece, one in which craftsmanship and style are abundantly displayed, and without the distraction of too much applied decoration.

Among the most charming of ancient Egyptian wooden products are the many small cosmetic objects used by both men and women in ritual activities as well as personal

adornment. They are usually ingeniously made, often incorporating inlays of ivory and faience. Most collections contain spoons, beautifully designed and elaborately decorated; many boxes are in the form of animals and humans. Some of the latter are fine examples of small wooden sculptures, and are particularly pleasing. Many small boxes are shaped in the form of birds, especially ducks, and oryxes, antelopes and other related creatures, often shown with bound legs in preparation for sacrifice. Among human representations there are many in the form of a swimming girl pushing before her the cosmetic container, sometimes in the shape of a duck. Outstanding examples of the last can be seen in the Louvre in Paris. Other fine small sculptures show servant girls weighed down with containers for cosmetics. One in Durham depicts such a girl, holding a large vase which rests on her left hip; her body bends to bear the strain of the weight. Another in the British Museum (EA 32767, fig. 146) also shows a naked servant girl, carrying the cosmetic container, a large chest, on her head. The ancient carver has again made a small masterpiece in which the strain endured by the girl is subtly conveyed by the bending of the body and the swelling of the hips.

Small containers for cosmetics and valuable ointments were made in many different materials by ancient Egyptian craftsmen. Extravagantly large and complicated alabaster vessels from the tomb of Tutankhamun represent the extreme manifestation of such objects; they are sometimes thought to represent the epitome of vulgar ostentation, in spite of their outstanding craftsmanship. Much more acceptable to modern taste, and aesthetically pleasing, are the smaller versions, in wood, faience, glass and glazed steatite. A technically and artistically outstanding example in the British Museum is in the form of a fish, probably used for perfume rather than unguent (EA 55193, fig. 147). It is made of polychrome opaque glass, and was excavated at El-Amarna. The piece is a tour de force of the glass-maker's craft. The body of the fish was built up over a sand core, and the bands of decoration applied to the semi-molten body in the form of thin rods of differently coloured glass, then teased in position to achieve the wavy effects which suggest both the scales of the fish and the movement of the water. The final result is wholly fish-like, with gaping mouth (the vessel's entrance), bulging eyes and a general appearance true to the form of the *bulti* of the Nile.

Glass-making in Egypt reached its highest point in the Eighteenth Dynasty, in the reigns of King Amenhotep III and his Amarna successors, but its history, along with that of glazing and faience, go right back to the beginning of the Dynastic Period. The glazing of objects made of certain stones like steatite (soapstone) and serpentine is the earliest manifestation of the vitreous craft in ancient Egypt, but it is impossible

146 Wooden figure of a young servant girl carrying a cosmetic receptacle in the form of a chest on her head. She is shown stooping under its weight, and seems to move forward cautiously. New Kingdom. H.15.5 cm.

to determine whether the primitive glazed beads produced in early Predynastic times – the Badarian Period – were the results at that time of accident or design. It is quite probable that the first glazed objects were made by chance. Steatite objects when heated become harder, and their natural constituents combined with colour applied in liquid form resulted in adventitious glazing, which was soon recognized as an unexpected and attractive improvement in the appearance of the objects concerned. The glazing of steatite and serpentine pieces continued throughout the Pharaonic Period, and was practised particularly for scarabs, small amulets and cosmetic pots.

Faience or Egyptian faience are terms used incorrectly to describe a material which distinguishes the manufacture of attractive small objects, jewellery, amulets and divine figurines from the beginning of the Dynastic Period. A more correct description is glazed quartz frit, but it is now as difficult to object to the use of the word faience as it

147 Opaque glass scent bottle in the form of the *bulti*, a common Nile fish. The base colour is blue, with polychrome decoration applied in the form of molten glass rods. From El-Amarna. L.14.5 cm.

is to the use of 'alabaster' to describe the common calcite used for the manufacture of most stone vessels in Egypt. Egyptian faience is a plastic material which could be modelled or moulded, and which, when heated, became thinly glazed by a process of efflorescence, no doubt seen to be almost magical by the ancient craftsman. The core material was powdered quartz, in the form of sand – very plentiful in Egypt – or ground up quartz pebbles, mixed with an alkaline material, natron or wood-ash, and water. The addition of various colouring agents, of the kinds used to make the pigments employed by artists, provided the possibility of a range of resultant glazes. This plastic material could not in its cold state be moulded or otherwise formed because it was very friable. Some heat needed to be applied to stiffen the mixture, as it were; it could then be shaped and fired to produce a hard material with a glassy surface. Small figurines found in excavations of Early Dynastic sites in Elephantine, Abydos and the Delta show that the simple technology of faience production was practised throughout the country, although the animal and human forms made at this early time were rather crudely moulded and had a very superficial glazing.

The first 'industrial' use of faience was in the manufacture of the small rectangular,

148 Blue-glazed faience model coffin containing a figure of the treasury official Amenmose; a rare example of a votive of this kind. The decoration on the coffin follows that found on stone sarcophagi of the Nineteenth Dynasty. From Thebes. H.29 cm.

convex-shaped tiles used for the decorative panels mounted in the subterranean chambers of the Step Pyramid and of the so-called South Mastaba in the same complex at Saqqara. It is estimated that about 36,000 of these tiles were made, but there is some dispute over whether they were moulded or fashioned by a simple manual process. The project was formidable, and there seems to have been no similar use of tiles in large quantity until the New Kingdom when elaborate, figured, polychrome faience tiles were used to embellish rooms, especially the formal reception halls in royal palaces. In a much smaller way, this decorative employment of coloured faience, as plaques and insets, was very common in furniture and as a material for the components of jewellery. Many composite necklaces have been found in which large numbers of small beads, and elements in the form of flowers, leaves and fruits, were used to make brilliant multicoloured displays. Faience pieces might be used in place of semiprecious stones, as for example in the elaborate decoration on Tutankhamun's Ecclesiastical Throne. But one may wonder whether such jewellery would have formed part of a woman or man's parure in ordinary life because of the great fragility of the material; the tiny terminal loops through which stringing cords passed were particularly vulnerable. But faience jewellery was ideal for funerary purposes, and the fragile components are fine examples of the faience-maker's craft.

Faience amulets were probably of sufficient size to be robust enough for everyday use, even when strung on a necklace or used as pendants. The best amulets, however, were made from appropriate hard and semiprecious stones, but most were made from faience. So too were figures of deities which became very common in the later periods. Most of such figures were moulded, and many moulds have been found in and around the faience workshops – 'factories' as they are often called – which have been excavated at numerous sites throughout Egypt. Objects made in moulds can be repeated, and therefore lack the individuality of hand-shaped pieces. Of the latter, among the most attractive are the hippopotamus figures of Middle Kingdom date, closely associated with the goddess Taweret (Thoueris); squat, rather benign, blue-glazed with marsh plants represented on their bodies, they are some of the most popular of small Egyptian antiquities. Of quite a different order of craftsmanship and beauty is a blue-glazed sphinx inscribed for King Amenhotep III of the Eighteenth Dynasty, now in the Metropolitan Museum of Art, New York. It is not possible to say whether this wonderful small sculpture was moulded or carved; its lines are crisp and flowing, its majesty fully conveyed in spite of its size.

Faience was much used for the manufacture of *shabti*-figures, and many individual pieces were made in the Eighteenth Dynasty; in the Twenty-fifth and Twenty-sixth Dynasties high-quality moulded examples were produced in quantity. At that time, as was pointed out earlier in this book, large numbers of such figures formed part of the burial equipment of important people. From the examination of multiple examples, it is clear that more than one mould was used for the manufacture of a particular person's set, and it may even be possible to detect some handworking of pieces before they were finally fired.

It is very debatable whether the many faience vessels made in the New Kingdom and later were ever used for practical everyday purposes. As has been said above, faience is not a robust material and it seems doubtful whether a faience cup would survive much use. Nevertheless, some of the finest faience objects made in Egypt were the drinking vessels, usually called chalices, made in lotus-form and sometimes decorated with low-relief scenes. A much more sympathetic, though not much more robust, material for drinking vessels was glass. As previously mentioned, glass in the fullest vitreous sense became a major manufactured material during the Eighteenth Dynasty. It has been suggested that Egyptian craftsmen never developed a true glass-making métier, and that the fine products, undoubtedly produced in Egypt, were made from ingots of glass imported from Western Asia. This seems highly unlikely. Egyptian craftsmen may have in many fields learned their skills and techniques initially from foreign sources, but they showed themselves fully competent to pursue procedures, some of which may have been learned from foreign craftsmen, and to develop industrial techniques of considerable complexity. As with faience, many glass-working 'factories' have been identified in Egypt, and there seems little reason to suppose that the many finely shaped, highly decorated vessels, which were prized as luxury objects, were not designed and manufactured in Egypt and by Egyptian craftsmen. They were commonly built up over a sand core, with complicated decoration applied to the semi-molten body by coloured glass rods, which were teased into patterns of chevrons, wavy lines, and even sorts of primitive guilloches. The glass-workers who made them were certainly masters of their craft.

Apart from vessels, like the superb fish bottle from El-Amarna, glass was used for many other purposes: components in jewellery, small divine and amuletic figures, and inlays. In some cases it is evident that glass was employed as a substitute for semi-precious stones, like carnelian and especially lapis lazuli, which was imported from far-distant Afghanistan. It may even have been the case that dark blue glass was preferred to lapis when large quantities of inlay were required and a regularity of colour desirable. Such may have been the case with the great gold mask of Tutankhamun, the striations on the *nemes*-wig of which are inlaid wholly with deep blue opaque glass. All Egyptian glass was opaque until the Roman Period, although it has been claimed that a few small elements in Tutankhamun's jewellery are of clear glass. It is very possible that the Egyptians of the New Kingdom did not want their glass to be clear.

Many elements in Egyptian jewellery were made of faience and glass, often imitating more highly-prized semiprecious stones, as mentioned above. In the design, assembly and technology used in the making of fine pieces, the principal skill lay in the working of metals, particularly gold. In the extraordinary collection of elaborate pieces found on the body of Tutankhamun, and elsewhere in the tomb, it is possible to study the range of techniques used in the manufacture of collars, pendants, armlets, diadems and earrings (more properly ear-pendants in some cases): cloisonné-work of the most intricate kind, involving the soldering of the cloison divisions to back plates, with the inlaying of glass and stone components, individually cut; the products of intricately woven gold chains made of gold wire – the wire not being made by drawing but by cutting and rolling; the application of fine granulation, previously thought to have been best developed by the Etruscans. Some of the glass inlaying is so exact that it has sometimes been identified as true enamelling – the fusion of glass powder within the cloisons – but convincing examples have yet to be identified, the precision of the ancient inlayers rendering enamelling unnecessary. Beyond the technical mastery displayed in these great jewels, there is also a command of design which allowed the incorporation

149 Electrum ornament in the form of a winged scarab, and incorporating the prenomen of King Senusret II of the Twelfth Dynasty. The inlays, set in cloisons, are of carnelian, lapis lazuli, green felspar and blue faience. H.1.8 cm.

150 Painted fragment from the tomb of Sobkhotep showing craftsmen engaged in drilling beads using multiple bow drills, and assembling a large collar. Eighteenth Dynasty. H.66 cm.

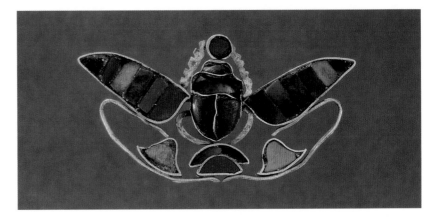

of deeply significant amuletic and divine symbols in eminently satisfactory ensembles. Yet the best judges of ancient Egyptian jewellery find the majority of the Tutankhamun pieces, both in design and technical virtuosity, inferior to the best work of the Middle Kingdom, exemplified by the royal jewellery found at Dahshur and Lahun, and the remarkable suites of pieces made for the three foreign wives of King Thutmose III of the Eighteenth Dynasty, now in the Metropolitan Museum of Art, New York. The delicacy of some of this best work is almost unbelievable when one considers the relatively clumsy tools available to the ancient craftsman. One should also contemplate the good fortune that has allowed such jewels to have survived the wholesale looting of gold – the most sought-after commodity – from the burials of the great and influential people who could afford the best.

Gold technology on the grand scale is nobly exemplified by the great funerary mask of Tutankhamun, made from substantial sheets of gold, beaten and raised to the perfection of an exquisite portrait, chaste and wholly satisfying aesthetically. Gold in the form of leaf, beaten out to a thinness

151 Necklace or girdle
consisting of cowrie shells,
beard pendants and fish,
all of electrum, and of beads
of semiprecious stones,
carnelian, amethyst, lapis
lazuli, felspar, and of
electrum. From Thebes.
Middle Kingdom. L.46.3 cm.

that matches the modern product, was commonly used to embellish funerary objects, furniture and wooden statues, covered with a layer of gesso-plaster as a base for gilding. But for the best work, thicker gold foil was certainly preferred, although technologically speaking it was more difficult to apply than leaf, and, it must be said, less successful than leaf in its final effect. Foil was more substantial, more opulent, and more 'flashy' than leaf. It was much used in funerary equipment, the earliest good examples of which were found in the deposit of Queen Hetepheres, mother of Cheops of the Fourth Dynasty. However, its most extravagant use is on the great shrines of Tutankhamun. For most of antiquity there was rarely a shortage of gold in Egypt. Mines in the Eastern Desert and Nubia yielded what seemed to be adequate quantities for current use, the general 'stock' no doubt regularly supplemented by the recycling of gold obtained by the periodic robbing of tombs. It is not impossible that the huge amount of the metal isolated in Tutankhamun's tomb might have had a serious effect on its availability in the years immediately following the burial, and the frustrated attempts to rob the tomb's contents. Silver, on the other hand, was not available from native mines in anything like the same quantity as gold, and much of what was needed was imported from Western Asia in the form of ingots and scrap jewellery. In Egypt

152 Cartonnage mask for the mummy of a lady named Satdjehuty. The gold leaf decoration is wonderfully executed, and technically a tour de force. Early Eighteenth Dynasty. H.33 cm.

silver was commonly valued more highly than gold because of its rarity. But gold was the metal of choice, and Egypt was renowned in antiquity for its richness in gold.

As in the case of glass technology, some authorities have claimed that most advanced metal-working in Egypt was based on techniques developed in Western Asia. There is little doubt that bronze as a distinct alloy was discovered outside Egypt, and that the technologies of iron-smelting and working were practised by the Hittites and other peoples many centuries before they became common in Egypt at the very end of the Dynastic Period. Copper, the main ingredient of bronze, was mined in Egypt and was used and exploited for the manufacture of tools and vessels from at least the Early Dynastic period. Copper, however, was not an ideal metal for practical uses because of its brittle nature and its inadequacy for casting due to its poor fluidity.

The earliest tools and vessels were not cast, but cold-worked with hammering, a process which itself was liable to increase the brittleness of the resulting object, a serious drawback in the manufacture of tools and weapons. At an early stage, but possibly not before the early Old Kingdom, metal-workers discovered that the addition of arsenic improved the quality of the product, allowing it to flow better, and hence to be cast with greater success than previously. An outstanding example of copper-working from this early time is a life-size figure made of sheets of beaten copper, originally applied to a wooden form, representing King Pepy I of the Sixth Dynasty, and found at Hierakonpolis, the ancient Upper Egyptian capital. It has recently been cleaned and conserved in the Cairo Museum, and can now be better appreciated as a magnificent success for the craft of the early metal-workers of Egypt. It is conceivable that parts of this statue were cast and not just beaten.

Copper with an arsenic addition is sometimes erroneously called arsenical bronze. True bronze, however, is an alloy of tin and copper, and most Egyptian true bronze contains about 10 per cent of tin. The resulting alloy is less brittle, much harder, capable of receiving a tough edge in the case of tools and weapons, and in its molten state flows well and is ideal for casting. Museum collections of Egyptian antiquities are full of bronze statuettes, mostly of gods but also including kings and other important persons. Production of such figures began during the Middle Kingdom in a modest way, continued to increase in the New Kingdom, and proliferated in the Late Period. The statuette of Thutmose IV in the British Museum (EA 64564, fig. 156) is a fine example in which the technique of attaching limbs to the body by dowels is clear; it is apparently the earliest surviving figure of this kind. Later castings are generally superior in quality, and some

153 Bronze mirror with a highly polished disc. The handle has a formalized papyrus shape, and the disc is flanked by falcon figures. Middle Kingdom. H.24 cm.

are exceptionally large, made up of several pieces, separately cast. In this respect the metal craftsmen of the Late New Kingdom achieved results of a size and quality unparalleled in earlier and later times. Two exceptional pieces, one from Upper Egypt and the other from the Delta, demonstrate the spread of metal-working skills throughout Egypt. The one from Thebes represents Karomama, God's Adorer of Amun, a priestess of Twenty-second Dynasty date, now in the Louvre; the other from the north depicts the lady Takushit, of almost the same date, now in Athens. Both are finely cast, with exquisite detail in gold and silver inlaid into their long garments. These pieces were hollow-cast: modelled cores were coated in wax, then enclosed within a mould, from which by heat the wax was withdrawn and replaced with molten bronze; the core was then removed, and the piece finished in detail by cold-working. This technique was much used for larger figures, and is well represented by the splendid cat figures made in honour of the goddess Bastet. A particularly splendid example in the British Museum (EA 64391, fig. 81) is known as the Gayer-Anderson cat, after its donor.

The majority of the figures of deities and of animals representing deities made in the last centuries of the Pharaonic Period and the Graeco-Roman Period were solid cast. Most are ordinary and competent, but undistinguished. There are exceptions, some of the best castings being inscribed personally with dedications to particular deities in the expectation of divine benefits. Some have some gold inlay, displaying in a modest way the fine decorative techniques found on the best earlier figures. Among the wealth of objects surviving from antiquity it is not surprising that large numbers of ordinary products predominate. Technology, if not craftsmanship, made it too easy to cast bronzes on a large scale; the same was the case with faience figures. A few examples can be highly estimated; a mass of examples can only be judged quantitatively.

The craftsmen of ancient Egypt excelled in most fields in which technique, artistry and general competence prevailed. Of all the materials with which they worked, stone in all its rich variety was the premier medium, with products ranging from beautifully shaped vessels to noble sculptures. But in all the practical crafts, fine products were made, distinguishing the work of the ancient craftsmen and characterizing the culture that they represented. It is not our purpose here to discriminate between arts and crafts; the Egyptians certainly did not recognize a difference. High standards generate high achievement; where such is the case, masterpieces will be made from time to time. So it happened in ancient Egypt.

List of Dynasties

(Overlapping dates usually indicate co-regencies. All dates given are approximate.)

FIRST DYNASTY

*c.*3100–2890 BC

DEN

Narmer

Aha

Djer

Djet

Den

Anedjib

Semerkhet

Qaa

SECOND DYNASTY

*c.*2890–2686 BC

Hotepsekhemwy

Raneb

Nynetjer

Peribsen

Khasekhem (Khasekhemwy)

THIRD DYNASTY

*c.*2686–2613 BC

Sanakht

Netjerkhet (Djoser)

Sekhemkhet

Huni

FOURTH DYNASTY

*c.*2613–2494 BC

Snofru

Khufu (Cheops)

Radjedef

Khafre (Chephren)

Menkaure (Mycerinus)

Shepseskaf

FIFTH DYNASTY

*c.*2494–2345 BC

Userkaf

Sahure

Neferirkare Kakai

Shepseskare Isi

Raneferef

Niuserre

Menkauhor Akauhor

Djedkare Isesi

Unas

SIXTH DYNASTY

*c.*2345–2181 BC

Teti

Userkare

Meryre (Pepy I)

Merenre

Neferkare (Pepy II)

SEVENTH/EIGHTH DYNASTIES

*c.*2181–2125 BC

NINTH/TENTH DYNASTIES

*c.*2160–2025 BC

Meryibre Khety

Wahkare Khety

Merykare

ELEVENTH DYNASTY

*c.*2125–1985 BC

Mentuhotep I ⎫
Sehertawy Intef I ⎪ Rulers
Wahankh Intef ⎬ of Thebes
Nakhtnebtepnefer Intef ⎭

Nebhepetre Mentuhotep
2055–2004 BC ⎫
Sankhkare Mentuhotep ⎪ Kings
2004–1992 BC ⎬ of Egypt
Nebtawyre Mentuhotep ⎪
1992–1985 BC ⎭

TWELFTH DYNASTY

*c.*1985–1795 BC

Sehetepibre Amenemhat
1985–1955 BC

Kheperkare Senusret I
1965–1920 BC

Nubkaure Amenemhat II
1922–1878 BC

Khakheperre Senusret II
1880–1874 BC

Khakaure Senusret III
1874–1855 BC

Nimaatre Amenemhat III
1854–1808 BC

Maakherure Amenemhat IV
1808–1799 BC

Sobkkare Sobkneferu
1799–1795 BC

AMENEMHAT III

THIRTEENTH DYNASTY

*c.*1795–*c.*1650 BC

Sekhemre-Sewadjtawy Sobekhotep

Khaneferre Sobkhotep

Khasekhemre Neferhotep

FOURTEENTH DYNASTY

*c.*1750–*c.*1650 BC

FIFTEENTH DYNASTY

(Hyksos)

*c.*1650–1550 BC

Seuserenre Khyan

Aauserre Apepi

SIXTEENTH DYNASTY

*c.*1650–*c.*1550 BC

SEVENTEENTH DYNASTY

*c.*1650–1550 BC

Nubkheperre Intef

Seqenenre Taa

Wadjkheperre Kamose

EIGHTEENTH DYNASTY

*c.*1550–1295 BC

Nebpehtyre Ahmose I
1550–1525 BC

Djeserkare Amenhotep I
1525–1504 BC

Aakheperkare Thutmose I
1504–1492 BC

Aakheperenre Thutmose II
1492–1479 BC

Maatkare Hatshepsut
1479–1457 BC

THUTMOSE III

Menkheperre Thutmose III
1479–1425 BC

Aakheperure Amenhotep II
1427–1400 BC

Menkheperure Thutmose IV
1400–1390 BC

Nebmaatre Amenhotep III
1390–1352 BC

Neferkheperure Amenhotep IV
(Akhenaten)
1352–1336 BC

AMENHOTEP III

Neferneferuaten
1338–1336 BC

Nebkheperure Tutankhamun
1336–1327 BC

Kheperkheperure Ay
1327–1323 BC

Djeserkheperure Horemheb
1323–1295 BC

SETY II

NINETEENTH DYNASTY

*c.*1295–1186 BC

Menpehtyre Ramesses I
1295–1294 BC

Menmaatre Sety I
1294–1279 BC

Usermaatre Ramesses II
1279–1213 BC

Baenre Merenptah
1213–1203 BC

Menmire Amenmessu
1203–1200 BC

Userkheperure Sety II
1200–1194 BC

Siptah
1194–1188 BC

Tausret
1188–1186 BC

RAMESSES III

TWENTIETH DYNASTY

*c.*1186–1069 BC

Userkhaure Setnakht
1186–1184 BC

Usermaatre-meryamun, Ramesses III
1184–1153 BC

Ramesses IV
1153–1147 BC

Ramesses V
1147–1143 BC

Ramesses VI
1143–1136 BC

Ramesses VII
1136–1129 BC

Ramesses VIII
1129–1126 BC

Ramesses IX
1126–1108 BC

Ramesses X
1108–1099 BC

Ramesses XI
1099–1069 BC

TWENTY-FIRST DYNASTY

*c.*1069–945 BC

Hedjkheperre Nesbanebdjed
(Smendes) *c.*1069–1043 BC

Aakheperre Pasebakhaenniut
(Psusennes) I *c.*1039–991 BC

Amenemope
*c.*993–984 BC

Siamun
*c.*978–959 BC

Pasebakhaenniut (Psusennes) II
*c.*959–945 BC

PIMAY

TWENTY-SECOND DYNASTY

*c.*945–715 BC

Hedjkheperre Sheshonq I
*c.*945–924 BC

Sekhemkheperre Osorkon I
*c.*924–889 BC

Takelot I
*c.*889–874 BC

Usermaatre Osorkon II
*c.*874–850 BC

Hedjkheperre Takelot II
*c.*850–825 BC

Usermaatre Sheshonq III
*c.*825–773 BC

Usermaatre Pimay
*c.*773–767 BC

Aakheperre Sheshonq V
*c.*767–730 BC

TWENTY-THIRD DYNASTY

*c.*818–715 BC

Usermaatre Pedibast I
*c.*818–793 BC

Usermaatre Osorkon III
*c.*777–749 BC

TWENTY-FOURTH DYNASTY

*c.*727–715 BC

Tefnakht Bakenrenef (Bocchoris)

TWENTY-FIFTH DYNASTY

(Nubian or Kushite)

*c.*747–656 BC

Py (Piankhi)
*c.*747–716 BC

Neferkare Shabako
*c.*716–702 BC

Djedkaure Shabitko
*c.*702–690 BC

Khunefertemre Taharqo
690–664 BC

Bakare Tantamani
664–656 BC

TWENTY-SIXTH DYNASTY

(Saite)

664–525 BC

Wahibre Psammetichus I
664–610 BC

Wehemibre Necho II
610–595 BC

Neferibre Psammetichus II
595–589 BC

Haaibre Wahibre (Apries)
589–570 BC

Khnemibre Ahmose II (Amasis)
570–526 BC

Ankhkaenre Psammetichus III
526–525 BC

NECTANEBO I

TWENTY-SEVENTH DYNASTY

(Persian Kings)

525–404 BC

Cambyses
525–522 BC

Darius I
522–486 BC

Xerxes
486–465 BC

Artaxerxes I
465–424 BC

Darius II
424–405 BC

Artaxerxes II
405–359 BC

TWENTY-EIGHTH DYNASTY

404–399 BC

Amyrtaeus
404–399 BC

TWENTY-NINTH DYNASTY

399–380 BC

Nefaarud (Nepherites) I
399–393 BC

Khnemmaatre Hakor (Achoris)
393–380 BC

THIRTIETH DYNASTY

380–343 BC

Kheperkare Nakhtnebef
(Nectanebo I)
380–362 BC

Djedhor (Teos)
362–360 BC

Snedjemibre Nakhtorheb
(Nectanebo II)
360–343 BC

PERSIAN KINGS

343–332 BC

Artaxerxes III Ochus
343–338 BC

Arses
338–336 BC

Darius III
336–332 BC

MACEDONIAN KINGS

332–305 BC

Alexander the Great
332–323 BC

Philip Arrhidaeus
323–317 BC

Alexander IV
317–305 BC

THE PTOLEMIES

305–30 BC

Ptolemy I Soter I
305–282 BC

Ptolemy II Philadelphus
284–246 BC

Ptolemy III Euergetes I
246–222 BC

Ptolemy IV Philopator
222–205 BC

Ptolemy V Epiphanes
205–180 BC

Ptolemy VI Philometor
180–145 BC

Ptolemy VII Neos Philopator
145 BC

Ptolemy VIII Euergetes II
170–116 BC

Ptolemy IX Soter II (Lathyros)
116–107 BC

Ptolemy X Alexander I
107–88 BC

Ptolemy IX Soter II (restored)
88–80 BC

Ptolemy XI Alexander II
80 BC

Ptolemy XII Neos Dionysos (Auletes)
80–51 BC

Cleopatra VII Philopator
51–30 BC

CLEOPATRA VII

Names of the Principal Kings of Egypt (including the Roman Emperors)

During the Early Dynastic Period, the chief name (Horus-name) of the king was written in a rectangular frame called a *serekh*. The bottom part of the frame contained a design of panelling, and the whole was surmounted by a figure of a falcon – the god Horus. In the case of Peribsen of the Second Dynasty, the Seth-animal replaced the falcon, while the *serekh* of Khasekhemwy was surmounted by both falcon and Seth-animal. A second name sometimes accompanied the Horus-name, or was used independently; it was introduced by one or both of the two titles ⟨glyph⟩ 'King of Upper and Lower Egypt' and ⟨glyph⟩ 'The Two Ladies'.

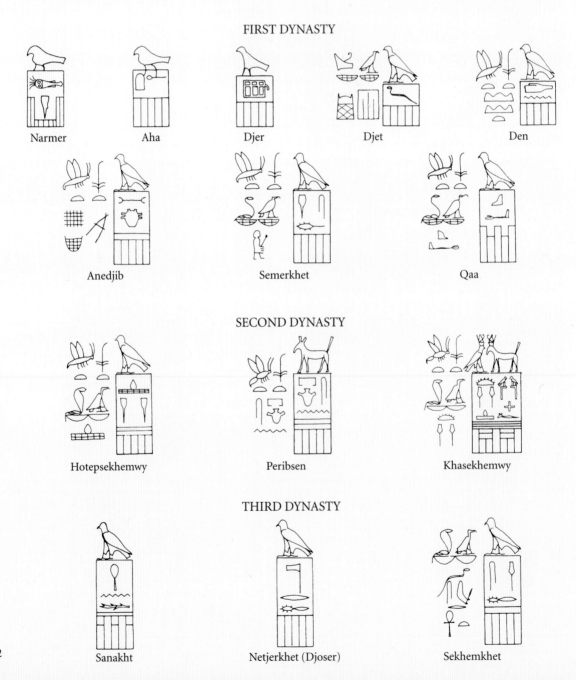

FIRST DYNASTY

Narmer   Aha   Djer   Djet   Den

Anedjib   Semerkhet   Qaa

SECOND DYNASTY

Hotepsekhemwy   Peribsen   Khasekhemwy

THIRD DYNASTY

Sanakht   Netjerkhet (Djoser)   Sekhemkhet

From the Old Kingdom the Egyptian king normally possessed five names: the Horus-name, the 'Two Ladies'-name, the Golden Horus-name (of uncertain origin), the prenomen (preceded by the title 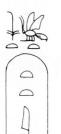 , translated usually 'King of Upper and Lower Egypt') and the nomen (preceded by the title 'Son of Re'). The nomen was first used by kings of the Fifth Dynasty who were specially devoted to the worship of Re. Prenomens and nomens were regularly enclosed within ovals called cartouches, which depict loops of rope with tied ends. By having his name so enclosed, the king possibly wishes to convey pictorially that he was ruler of all 'that which is encircled by the sun'. From the late Eighteenth Dynasty onwards additional epithets were regularly introduced into the cartouches. In later times when the claim to the throne of all Egypt was disputed kings sometimes avoided the 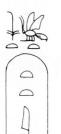 –title and used ⹁𓏏, 'the perfect god'. The names within cartouches are those by which a king is normally identified.

FOURTH DYNASTY

Snofru

Cheops (Khufu)

Chephren (Khafre)

Mycerinus (Menkaure)

Shepseskaf

FIFTH DYNASTY

Userkaf

Sahure

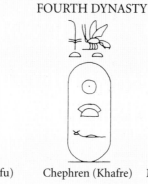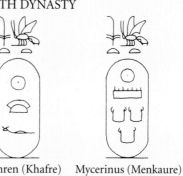
Niuserre Ini

Unas

SIXTH DYNASTY

Teti

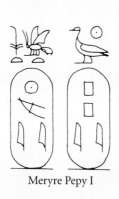
Meryre Pepy I

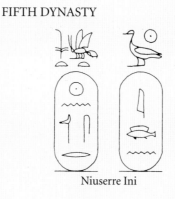
Merenre

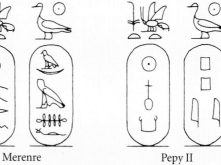
Pepy II

193

ELEVENTH DYNASTY

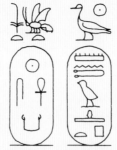

Nebhepetre Mentuhotep

Sankhkare Mentuhotep

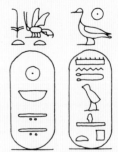

Nebtawyre Mentuhotep

TWELFTH DYNASTY

Amenemhat I

Senusret I

Amenemhat II

Senusret II

Senusret III

Amenemhat III

Amenemhat IV

THIRTEENTH DYNASTY

Sekhemre-Sewadjtawy
Sobkhotep

Khaneferre Neferhotep

FIFTEENTH DYNASTY
(Hyksos)

Seuserenre Khyan

Aauserre Apepi

SEVENTEENTH DYNASTY

Nubkheperre Intef

Seqenenre Taa

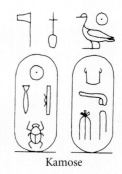

Kamose

EIGHTEENTH DYNASTY

Ahmose I

Amenhotep I

Thutmose I

Thutmose II

Hatshepsut

Thutmose III

Amenhotep II

Thutmose IV

Amenhotep III

Akhenaten

Tutankhamun

Horenheb

195

NINETEENTH DYNASTY

Ramesses I

Sety I

Ramesses II

Merenptah

TWENTIETH DYNASTY

Ramesses III

Ramesses IV

Ramesses IX

TWENTY-FIRST DYNASTY

Nesbanebdjed (Smendes)

Psusennes I

TWENTY-SECOND DYNASTY

Sheshonq I

Osorkon II

TWENTY-FIFTH DYNASTY

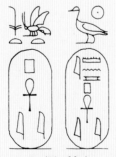

Py (Piankhy)

Shabaka

Taharqo

TWENTY-SIXTH DYNASTY

Psammetichus I

Necho II

Psammetichus II

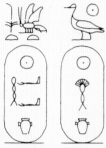

Wahibre (Apries)

Ahmose (Amasis) II

Psammetichus III

TWENTY-SEVENTH DYNASTY

Cambyses

Darius

Xerxes

Artaxerxes

TWENTY-NINTH DYNASTY

Achoris

Nectanebo I

THIRTIETH DYNASTY

Nectanebo II

MACEDONIAN KINGS

Alexander the Great

Philip Arrhidaeus

PTOLEMAIC DYNASTY

Ptolemy I Soter

Ptolemy II Philadelphus

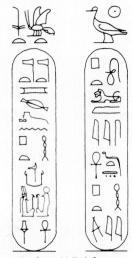

Ptolemy V Epiphanes

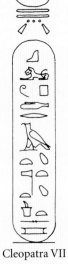

Cleopatra VII

ROMAN EMPERORS

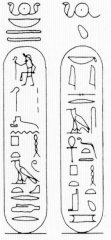

Augustus

Tiberius

Trajan

Diocletian

Museums with Egyptian Collections

The most important museum of Egyptian antiquities is the Egyptian Museum, Cairo, which houses the results of 150 years of excavation throughout Egypt. In Egypt there are also important collections in Alexandria (the Graeco-Roman Museum), Aswan (the Nubian Museum), and especially Luxor (the Luxor Museum) which shows many outstanding pieces from the Luxor area.

GREAT BRITAIN: The British Museum contains large collections in all categories of antiquities. Important collections also in Cambridge (Fitzwilliam Museum), London (Petrie Museum, University College London), Manchester (the Manchester Museum) and Oxford (Ashmolean Museum). Useful collections in Bristol (Bristol Museums and Art Gallery), Birmingham (Museum and Art Gallery), Bolton (Museum and Art Gallery), Durham (Oriental Museum), Edinburgh (National Museums of Scotland), Glasgow (Art Gallery and Museum, Burrell Collection, Hunterian Museum), Liverpool (Liverpool Museum), Swansea (Egypt Centre, University of Wales, Swansea).

UNITED STATES OF AMERICA: The most representative collections are in Boston (Museum of Fine Arts), New York (Metropolitan Museum of Art, Brooklyn Museum of Art), Philadelphia (University Museum). Good collections also in Ann Arbor (Kelsey Museum), Baltimore (Walters Art Museum), Berkeley (Phoebe Apperson Hearst Museum), Chicago (Oriental Institute Museum, Field Museum), Cleveland (Museum of Art), Detroit (Institute of Arts), Pittsburgh (Carnegie Museum of Natural History), Richmond (Virginia Museum of Fine Arts), St Louis (Art Museum), Toledo (Museum of Art), Washington (Freer Gallery, the Smithsonian Institution).

AUSTRALIA: Small but useful collections in Adelaide (South-Australian Museum), Melbourne (National Gallery of Victoria), Sydney (Nicholson Museum of Antiquities).

AUSTRIA: Important collection in Vienna (Kunsthistorisches Museum).

BELGIUM: Good general collection in Brussels (Musées royaux d'Art et d'Histoire).

CANADA: Good representative collection in Toronto (Royal Ontario Museum); a largely archaeological collection in Montreal (Redpath Museum, McGill University).

DENMARK: Two good collections in Copenhagen (Nationalsmuseet, Ny Carlsberg Glyptotek).

FRANCE: The outstanding collection in Paris (Musée du Louvre). Many provincial cities contain useful collections, particularly Avignon (Musée Calvert), Lille (Institut de Papyrologie et d'Égyptologie), Lyons (Musée des Beaux-arts), Marseilles (Musée d'Archéologie), Strasbourg (Institut d'Égyptologie).

GERMANY: The great Berlin collection, divided after the Second World War, is now reunited as the Ägyptisches Museum und Papyrussammlung, but displayed in two places, on the Museum Island and in Charlottenburg. Important collections also in Hanover (Kestner-Museum), Hildesheim (Roemer-Pelizaeus-Museum), and Munich (Staatliches Museum Ägyptischer Kunst). Good collections in Dresden (Albertinum), Hamburg (Museum für Kunst and Gewerbe), Leipzig (Ägyptisches Museum), and Tübingen (Ägyptologisches Institut der Universität).

ITALY: Outstanding collection of papyri and funerary material in Turin (Museo egizio). Important collections in Bologna (Museo civico), Florence (Museo archeologico); interesting collections in Naples (Museo nazionale), Palermo (Museo nazionale), Rome (Museo Barracco, Museo Capitolino, and Museo Gregoriano egizio in Vatican City), and Venice (Museo archeologico del Palazzo Reale di Venezia).

NETHERLANDS: The Collection in Leiden (Rijksmuseum van Oudheden) is one of the oldest and most representative in Europe. Smaller but interesting collection in Amsterdam (Allard Pierson Museum).

POLAND: A good general collection in Warsaw (Muzeum Narodwe) containing remarkable wall paintings from churches in Sudan. A small but useful collection in Krakow (Archaeological Museum).

RUSSIA: Two very important collections in Moscow (State Pushkin Museum of Fine Arts) and St Petersburg (Hermitage Museum).

SPAIN: Useful general collection in Madrid (Museo Arqueológico Nacional); a growing collection in Barcelona (Museu Egipci de Barcelona).

SUDAN: The National Museum in Khartoum contains a rich assemblage of material from Egyptian, Kushite and Meroïtic sites.

SWEDEN: The most representative collection is in Stockholm (Medelhavsmuseet). A good collection also in Uppsala (Victoriamuseum).

SWITZERLAND: The best general collection is in Geneva (Musées d'Art et d'Histoire). A smaller general collection in Basel (Antikenmuseum Basel und Sammlung Ludwig).

Chapter Bibliographies

CHAPTER 1

One of the best general books about Egypt, the country, as the background for Egyptian culture is H. Kees, *Ancient Egypt. A Cultural Topography*. A fine archaeologically focused study by B. Kemp, *Ancient Egypt. Anatomy of a civilization*, considers the bases of life in ancient Egypt from a material rather than a textual standpoint. On the Nile, an excellent account can be found in W. Butzer, *Early hydraulic civilization in Egypt*. The classic work on the material resources of the country is A. Lucas, *Ancient Egyptian Materials and Industries*. It has not been wholly superseded by P. T. Nicholson and I. Shaw (eds), *Ancient Egyptian Materials and Technology*, which contains, however, much up-to-date information from specialized material studies and recent excavations. Useful accounts of quarrying and stone working are to be found in Somers Clarke and R. Engelbach, *Ancient Egyptian Masonry*, and D. Arnold, *Building in Egypt*.

CHAPTER 2

Egyptian history is an unrewarding subject in that the evidence is patchy and discontinuous. For a good comprehensible outline of the sources, see A. H. Gardiner, *Egypt of the Pharaohs*, which includes a consideration of the Manetho dynasties list with the identification of kings named on monuments. Gardiner's study of the Turin list, *The royal canon of Turin*, remains fundamental, but now needs reconsideration. For a general survey of the whole range of Egyptian history, *Egypt of the Pharaohs* is textually based; *A History of ancient Egypt*, by Nicolas Grimal, is also comprehensive and includes much evidence drawn from excavations. On Predynastic and Early Dynastic Egypt M. Hoffman's *Egypt before the Pharaohs*

provides a reliable account, backed by results from his own excavations. Good specialized studies of the successive periods of Egyptian history remain to be written, but some older volumes retain much of value: D. Redford, *History and chronology of the Eighteenth Dynasty*; C. Aldred, *Akhenaten, King of Egypt*; K. A. Kitchen, *The Third Intermediate Period in Egypt (1100–650 BC)*. For the Ptolemies and Romans, see A. Bowman, *Egypt after the Pharaohs*.

CHAPTER 3

The standard work on the Egyptian language remains A. H. Gardiner, *Egyptian Grammar*, but first published almost eighty years ago. New approaches to the study of Egyptian have generated many books, of which, for general purposes, A. Loprieno's *Ancient Egyptian. A linguistic introduction* presents a very balanced account. On scribes and writing, J. Černý, *Paper and books in ancient Egypt* still offers valuable material details derived from a lifetime of work on papyri and ostraca; also the appropriate sections in P. Nicholson and I. Shaw (eds), *Ancient Egyptian Materials and Technology*; T. G. H. James, *Pharaoh's People*; M. L. Bierbrier (ed.), *Papyrus. Structure and Usage*. On hieroglyphic texts, R. A. Caminos and H. G. Fischer, *Ancient Egyptian epigraphy and palaeography* deals with matters of recording texts. On literacy and the workmen's village, there is a good general account in M. L. Bierbrier, *The Tomb-builders of the Pharaohs*. For the use of archival documents and the inscription of Mose, see Gaballa A. Gaballa, *The Memphite Tomb Chapel of Mose*. Decipherment and the Rosetta Stone have most recently been discussed in R. Parkinson, *Cracking Codes*, and R. Solé and D. Valbelle, *The Rosetta Stone. The Story of the decoding of hieroglyphics*.

CHAPTER 4

Private and public documentation are mostly dealt with in specialist studies. Many are used as historical sources in A. H. Gardiner, *Egypt of the Pharaohs* and N. Grimal, *A History of ancient Egypt*. A very representative selection of biographical and historical texts is included in M. Lichtheim, *Ancient Egyptian Literature*; letters are well translated in E. Wente, *Letters from Ancient Egypt*. The Hekanakhte letters may be consulted in T. G. H. James, *The Hekanakhte Papers and other Early Middle Kingdom Documents*, and more recently, James Allen, *The Heqanakht Papyri*. The primary translation of the tomb-robbery papyri is T. E. Peet, *The Great Tomb-robberies of the Twentieth Egyptian Dynasty*; the account of the robbery of the tomb of King Sobkemsaef in the Leopold-Amherst Papyrus may be found in *Journal of Egyptian Archaeology*, vol. 22. The inscriptions of Ankhtifi at Moalla are touched on in the histories of Gardiner and Grimal, mentioned above; a new archaeological investigation of the tomb may in due course result in a full study of the texts. The Qadesh texts of Ramesses II's famous 'victory' are fully considered in A. H. Gardiner, *The Kadesh inscriptions of Ramesses II*. On the surviving documentation from Deir el-Medina, see M. L. Bierbrier, *The Tomb-builders of the Pharaohs*.

CHAPTER 5

The religious beliefs of the ancient Egyptians have been a source of fascination since antiquity, and much has been written about them, often esoterically based, often sentimentalized. In modern times scholars have tried to penetrate the ancient beliefs by careful studies based on the ancient religious texts. A good general account can be found in

S. Morenz, *Egyptian Religion*, and in the appropriate sections of J. Assmann, *The Mind of Egypt*. The gods in their multiplicity are well treated in G. Hart, *A Dictionary of Egyptian Gods and Goddesses*, and *Egyptian Myths*. The most thoughtful discussion of plurality and the idea of divinity is presented in E. Hornung, *The Conception of God in Ancient Egypt*. Views on Atenism and Egyptian monotheism vary widely and generate much controversy. The so-called heresy is discussed sensibly in the volumes of Morenz, Assmann and Hornung mentioned above; more particularly, see C. Aldred, *Akhenaten, King of Egypt*, D. Redford, *Akhenaten, the heretic king*, and the relevant chapter in J. Assmann, *Moses the Egyptian*. Translations of the Amarna hymns and other New Kingdom religious texts are included in M. Lichtheim, *Ancient Egyptian Literature*, vol. 2.

CHAPTER 6

The important compilations of funerary texts from the Old, Middle and New Kingdoms have all been carefully translated by R. O. Faulkner in *The Ancient Egyptian Pyramid Texts*, *The Egyptian Coffin Texts* and *The Ancient Egyptian Book of the Dead*. The elaborate and confusing texts found in the royal tombs of the New Kingdom are discussed in context in E. Hornung, *The Valley of the Kings*. All these texts in the tomb of Ramesses VI are translated in A. Piankoff, *The tomb of Ramesses VI*. Piankoff also translates the versions found in the tomb of Tutankhamun in *The Shrines of Tut-ankh-amon*. On the paraphernalia of death and burial, there remains much of interest and value in E. A. W. Budge, *The Mummy*. The general archaeology of the topic is well covered in

A. J. Spencer, *Death in Ancient Egypt*; and J. H. Taylor gives a brief but authoritative account of one important category of object in *Egyptian coffins*. C. A. R. Andrews, *Egyptian Mummies* provides a good conspectus of the eternally fascinating subject of embalmed bodies. Many of the topics and categories of texts and objects discussed in this chapter are very well treated in E. Hornung and B. Bryan (eds), *The Quest for Immortality*.

CHAPTER 7

The standard work on Egyptian building techniques has for many years been Somers Clarke and R. Engelbach, *Ancient Egyptian Masonry. The Building craft*. It has now been largely superseded by D. Arnold, *Building in Egypt. Pharaonic stone masonry*, and P. Nicholson and I. Shaw (eds), *Ancient Egyptian materials and Technology*. I. E. S. Edwards, *The Pyramids of Egypt* remains a reliable guide to these remarkable monuments, although some of its technical discussions are rather outmoded. *The Art and Architecture of Ancient Egypt* by W. Stephenson Smith, in its revised form by W. K. Simpson, provides a useful introduction to the subject; more up-to-date is G. Robins, *The Art of Ancient Egypt*, which includes a discussion of the canon. A useful reference volume on Egyptian building in general is D. Arnold, *The Encyclopaedia of Ancient Egyptian Architecture*; and for brick building, A. J. Spencer, *Brick Architecture in Ancient Egypt*. A classic, but difficult study of the underlying theory of Egyptian artistic practices is H. Schäfer, *Principles of Egyptian Art*. On painting in particular, see W.V. Davies (ed.), *Colour and Painting in Ancient Egypt*, and T. G. H. James, *Egyptian Painting*; and on art, C. Aldred, *Egyptian Art*.

CHAPTER 8

The sources of the materials used by Egyptian craftsmen, and many of the techniques used by them are described in A. Lucas, *Ancient Egyptian Materials and Industries*, and P. Nicholson and I. Shaw (eds), *Ancient Egyptian Materials and Technology*. On sculpture, a seminal work is W. Stevenson Smith, *Egyptian sculpture and painting in the Old Kingdom*. See also, C. Aldred, *Egyptian Art*, T. G. H. James and W. V. Davies, *Egyptian Sculpture*, and E. Russmann, *Egyptian Sculpture: Cairo and Luxor*. The crucial study of late sculpture is B. V. Bothmer, *Egyptian Sculpture of the Late Period*. For Egyptian furniture, the most comprehensive study is G. Killen, *Ancient Egyptian Furniture*, 2 vols; H. S. Baker in *Furniture in the Ancient World* takes a more aesthetic approach to the subject. Glass and glazed ware are studied in E. Riefstahl, *Ancient Egyptian Glass and glazes in The Brooklyn Museum*, and especially, J. Cooney, *Catalogue of Egyptian Antiquities in the British Museum*, IV. *Glass*; jewellery in C. Aldred, *Jewels of the Pharaohs*, and A. Wilkinson, *Ancient Egyptian Jewellery*. For metal-working, including gold and bronze, see the section by J. Ogden in the Nicholson and Shaw volume mentioned above.

General Bibliography

C. Aldred, *Akhenaten, King of Egypt*. London, 1988.

C. Aldred, *Egyptian Art*. London, 1980.

C. Aldred, *Jewels of the Pharaohs*. London, 1971.

J. P. Allen, *The Heqanakht Papyri*. New York, 2002.

C. A. R. Andrews, *Egyptian Mummies*. London, 1984.

D. Arnold, *Building in Egypt. Pharaonic Stone Masonry*. New York, 1991.

D. Arnold, *The Encyclopaedia of Ancient Egyptian architecture*. London, 2003.

J. Assmann, *The Mind of Egypt*. Cambridge, Mass. and London, 2002.

J. Assmann, *Moses the Egyptian*. Cambridge, Mass. and London, 1997.

J. Baines and J. Malek, *Atlas of Ancient Egypt*. London, 1979.

H. S. Baker, *Furniture in the Ancient World*. London, 1966.

M. L. Bierbrier (ed.), *Papyrus. Structure and usage*. London, 1986.

M. L. Bierbrier, *The Tomb-builders of the Pharaohs*. London 1982.

B. V. Bothmer, *Egyptian Sculpture of the Late Period, 700B.C. to A.D. 100*. Brooklyn, 1961.

A. K. Bowman, *Egypt after the Pharaohs*. London, 1986.

E. A. W. Budge, *The Mummy*, 2nd edn, London, 1925.

W. Butzer, *Early Hydraulic civilization in Egypt*. Chicago and London, 1976.

R. A. Caminos and H. G. Fischer, *Ancient Egyptian epigraphy and palaeography*. New York, 1976.

J. Capart, A. H. Gardiner and B. van de Walle, 'New light on the Ramesside tomb-robberies', in *Journal of Egyptian Archaeology* vol. 22. London, 1936.

J. Černý, *Paper and Books in ancient Egypt*. London, 1953.

S. Clarke and R. Engelbach, *Ancient Egyptian masonry. The building craft*. Oxford, 1930.

J. D. Cooney, *Catalogue of Egyptian Antiquities in the British Museum*. IV. *Glass*. London, 1976.

W. V. Davies (ed.), *Colour and Painting in Ancient Egypt*. London, 2001.

W. V. Davies and R. Friedman, *Egypt*. London, 1998.

A. B. Edwards, *A Thousand Miles up the Nile*. London, 1887.

I. E. S. Edwards, *The Pyramids of Egypt*. Rev. edn, London, 1985.

R. O. Faulkner, *The Ancient Egyptian Book of the Dead*. London, 1985.

R. O. Faulkner, *The Ancient Egyptian Pyramid Texts*. 2 vols. Oxford, 1969.

R. O. Faulkner, *The Egyptian Coffin Texts*. 3 vols. Warminster, 1973-8.

G. A. Gaballa, *The Memphite tomb-chapel of Mose*. Warminster, 1977.

A. H. Gardiner, *Egypt of the Pharaohs*. Oxford, 1961.

A. H. Gardiner, *Egyptian Grammar*. 3rd edn, Oxford, 1957.

A. H. Gardiner, *The Kadesh inscriptions of Ramesses II*. Oxford, 1960.

A. H. Gardiner, *The royal canon of Turin*. Oxford, 1959.

N. Grimal, *A History of ancient Egypt*. Oxford, 1992.

G. Hart, *A Dictionary of Egyptian gods and goddesses*. London, 1986.

G. Hart, *Egyptian Myths*. London, 1990.

M. Hoffman, *Egypt before the Pharaohs*. London, 1979.

E. Hornung, *Conceptions of god in ancient Egypt*. London, 1983.

E. Hornung, *The Valley of the Kings*. New York, 1990.

E. Hornung and B. Bryan, *The Quest for immortality. Treasures of Ancient Egypt*. Washington, 2002.

T. G. H. James, *Ancient Egypt. The Land and its legacy*. London, 1988.

T. G. H. James, *Egyptian Painting and drawing in the British Museum*. London, 1984.

T. G. H. James, *The Hekanakhte Papers and other early Middle Kingdom Documents*. New York, 1962.

T. G. H. James, *The Mastaba of Khentika called Ikhekhi*. London, 1953.

T. G. H. James, *Pharaoh's People. Scenes from life in imperial Egypt*. London, 1984.

T. G. H. James and W. V. Davies, *Egyptian sculpture*. London, 1983.

H. Kees, *Ancient Egypt. A Cultural topography*. London, 1961.

B. J. Kemp, *Ancient Egypt. Anatomy of a Civilization*. Cambridge, 1989.

G. Killen, *Ancient Egyptian Furniture*. 2 vols. Warminster, 1980, 1994.

K. A. Kitchen, *Pharaoh triumphant. The Life and times of Ramesses II*. Warminster, 1982.

K. A. Kitchen, *The Third Intermediate Period in Egypt (1100–650 B.C.)*. Warminster, 1986.

M. Lichtheim, *Ancient Egyptian Literature*. 3 vols. Berkeley, 1973-80.

A. Loprieno, *Ancient Egyptian. A Linguistic introduction*. Cambridge, 1995.

A. Lucas, *Ancient Egyptian Materials and industries*. 4th edn, London, 1962.

Manetho, *Aegyptiaca*. Loeb Classical Library. London, 1940.

S. Morenz, *Egyptian Religion*. London, 1983.

W. J. Murnane, *The Penguin Guide to Ancient Egypt*. Harmondsworth, 1983.

P. T. Nicholson and I. Shaw (eds), *Ancient Egyptian Materials and Technology*. Cambridge, 2000.

R. B. Parkinson, *Cracking Codes*. London, 1999.

R. B. Parkinson, *The Tale of Sinuhe and other ancient Egyptian poems, 1940-1640 BC*. Oxford, 1998.

R. B. Parkinson, *Voices from ancient Egypt*. London, 1991.

R. B. Parkinson and S. Quirke, *Papyrus*. London. 1995.

T. E. Peet, *The Great tomb-robberies of the Twentieth Egyptian Dynasty*. Oxford, 1930.

Sources of Illustrations

A. Piankoff and N. Rambova, *The Shrines of Tut-ankh-Amon*. New York, 1955.

A. Piankoff and N. Rambova, *The Tomb of Ramesses VI*. New York, 1954.

S. Quirke, *Ancient Egyptian Religion*. London, 1992.

S. Quirke and A. J. Spencer (eds), *The British Museum Book of Ancient Egypt*. London, 1992.

D. B. Redford, *Akhenaten, the heretic king*. Princeton, 1984.

D. B. Redford, *History and chronology of the Eighteenth Dynasty*. Toronto, 1967.

E. Riefstahl, *Ancient Egyptian Glass and Glazes in The Brooklyn Museum*. Brooklyn, 1968.

G. Robins, *The Art of Ancient Egypt*. London, 1997

E. Russmann, *Egyptian sculpture: Cairo and Luxor*. London, 1991.

H. Schäfer, *Principles of Egyptian Art*. Oxford, 1974.

W. K. Simpson, R. O. Faulkner and E. Wente, *The Literature of Ancient Egypt*. London, 1972.

R. Solé and D. Valbelle, *The Rosetta Stone. The Story of decoding the hieroglyphs*. London, 2001.

A. J. Spencer, *Brick Architecture in ancient Egypt*. Warminster, 1979.

A. J. Spencer, *Death in ancient Egypt*. London, 1982.

J. H. Taylor, *Egyptian Coffins*. Aylesbury, 1989.

D. A. Welsby, *The Kingdom of Kush. The Napatan and Meroitic Empires*. London, 1996.

E. Wente, *Letters from ancient Egypt*. Atlanta, 1990.

A. Wilkinson, *Ancient Egyptian jewellery*. London, 1971.

Index